MACHINE PERCEPTION

MACHINE PERCEPTION

RAMAKANT NEVATIA

Departments of Electrical Engineering and Computer Science
University of Southern California

Prentice-Hall, Inc.,

Englewood Cliffs, New Jersey 07632

Library of Congress Cataloging in Publication Data

Nevatia, Ramakant.
   Machine perception.

   Bibliography: p.
   Includes index.
   1. Pattern recognition systems. I. Title.
TK7882.P3N48 1982   001.53'4   82-9136
ISBN 0-13-541904-2   AACR2

Editorial/production supervisor: Nancy Milnamow
Cover design: Ray Lundgren
Manufacturing buyer: Joyce Levatino

© 1982 by Prentice-Hall, Inc., Englewood Cliffs, N.J. 07632

All rights reserved. No part of this book
may be reproduced in any form or
by any means without permission in writing
from the publisher.

Printed in the United States of America

10 9 8 7 6 5 4 3 2 1

ISBN 0-13-541904-2

Prentice-Hall International, Inc., *London*
Prentice-Hall of Australia Pty. Limited, *Sydney*
Prentice-Hall Canada Inc., *Toronto*
Prentice-Hall of India Private Limited, *New Delhi*
Prentice-Hall of Japan, Inc., *Tokyo*
Prentice-Hall of Southeast Asia Pte. Ltd., *Singapore*
Whitehall Books Limited, *Wellington, New Zealand*

CONTENTS

1. INTRODUCTION	1
1.1 SOME EXAMPLES AND PROBLEMS	2
1.2 AN OVERVIEW AND HISTORY	5
1.3 RELATIONSHIP TO PSYCHOLOGY	9
1.4 PLAN OF THE BOOK	9
2. PATTERN CLASSIFICATION METHODS	12
2.1 DIGITAL REPRESENTATION OF AN IMAGE	12
2.1.1 Connectivity in Digital Images	13
2.2 TEMPLATE MATCHING	15
2.3 PATTERN CLASSIFICATION IN FEATURE SPACE	16
2.4 PERCEPTRONS	18
2.5 SYNTACTICAL APPROACHES	21
2.6 SUMMARY	22

3. SIMPLE POLYHEDRAL SCENES 24

3.1 PERCEPTION OF SIMPLE POLYHEDRAL SOLIDS — 24
   3.1.1 Extraction of Line Drawings — 26
   3.1.2 Model Matching — 28
3.2 MODEL TRANSFORMATIONS — 30
   3.2.1 Perspective Transformations — 31
   3.2.2 Homogeneous Coordinates — 32
   3.2.3 Geometrical Transformations — 34
3.3 FITTING OF MODELS — 37
   3.3.1 Camera Calibration — 39
3.4 SUMMARY — 40

4. COMPLEX SCENES OF POLYHEDRA 41

4.1 SEGMENTATION OF POLYHEDRAL SCENES — 41
4.2 CLASSIFICATION OF LINES — 45
   4.2.1 Inclusion of Shadows — 49
4.3 GEOMETRICAL CONSTRAINTS FOR POSSIBLE OBJECTS — 51
   4.3.1 Gradient Spaces and Dual Graphs — 52
4.4 DESCRIPTIONS OF OBJECT ASSEMBLIES — 55
   4.4.1 Computation of Descriptions — 56
   4.4.2 Learning of Structural Descriptions — 58
4.5 SUMMARY — 59

5. SHAPE ANALYSIS AND RECOGNITION 61

5.1 REPRESENTATION OF COMPLEX SHAPES — 62
5.2 LINE DESCRIPTIONS — 63
   5.2.1 Storage of Lines — 63
   5.2.2 Line Approximations — 65
   5.2.3 Analytical Line Shape Measures — 66
5.3 AREA DESCRIPTIONS — 67
   5.3.1 Simple Shape Measures — 67

5.3.2 Analytical Measures	69
5.3.3 A Medial Axis Transform	70
5.4 DESCRIPTIONS OF 3-D OBJECTS	72
5.4.1 Generalized Cones	73
5.4.2 Computation of Generalized Cones	75
5.5 RECOGNITION OF OBJECTS	80
5.5.1 Graph Matching	80
5.5.2 Relaxation Labeling	82
5.5.3 Multilevel Matching	85
5.6 SUMMARY	86

6. PERCEPTION OF BRIGHTNESS AND COLOR — 90

6.1 BRIGHTNESS AND COLOR	91
6.1.1 The Human Eye	92
6.1.2 Local Measurements	92
6.2 LATERAL INHIBITION AND LIGHTNESS COMPUTATION	95
6.3 SUMMARY	98

7. EDGE AND CURVE DETECTION — 100

7.1 EDGE DETECTION	101
7.1.1 Edge Enhancement and Differentiation	101
7.1.2 Edge Fitting	103
7.1.3 Edge Detection by Template Matching	105
7.1.4 Statistical Edge Detectors	111
7.1.5 Choice of Thresholds	111
7.2 RESULTS OF EDGE DETECTION	112
7.3 LINE AND CURVE DETECTION	116
7.3.1 Hough Transform	116
7.3.2 Graph-Theoretic Techniques	118
7.3.3 Method of Projections	119
7.4 CONTOUR FILLING AND FEEDBACK	120
7.5 COLOR EDGES	123
7.6 SUMMARY	124

8. REGION SEGMENTATION AND TEXTURE ANALYSIS — 128

- 8.1 REGION SEGMENTATION — 129
  - 8.1.1 Thresholding and Recursive Segmentation — 129
  - 8.1.2 Region Growing — 136
  - 8.1.3 Semantically Guided Region Growing — 137
  - 8.1.4 Tracing Region Boundaries — 138
- 8.2 EDGE VERSUS REGION SEGMENTATION — 139
- 8.3 TEXTURE ANALYSIS — 141
  - 8.3.1 Statistical Texture Measures — 144
  - 8.3.2 Structural Texture Descriptions — 149
  - 8.3.3 Comparison of Texture Features — 151
  - 8.3.4 Texture Segmentation — 152
- 8.4 SUMMARY — 153

9. DEPTH MEASUREMENT AND ANALYSIS — 158

- 9.1 STEREO AND MOTION — 159
  - 9.1.1 Correspondence Search — 161
  - 9.1.2 Global Correspondences — 163
  - 9.1.3 Motion Detection and Analysis — 165
- 9.2 ACTIVE RANGING — 167
  - 9.2.1 Triangulation Ranging — 167
  - 9.2.2 LIDAR Ranging — 170
- 9.3 SEGMENTATION USING RANGE — 170
  - 9.3.1 Boundary Detection — 171
  - 9.3.2 Detection of Planes and Surfaces — 172
- 9.4 SHAPE FROM SHADING — 173
  - 9.4.1 Reflectance Maps — 174
- 9.5 TEXTURE GRADIENTS — 177
- 9.6 CONTOUR ANALYSIS — 181
- 9.7 SUMMARY — 183

10. SYSTEMS AND APPLICATIONS — 187

- 10.1 GENERAL SYSTEMS — 188
- 10.2 KNOWLEDGE BASED SYSTEMS — 189

10.3 APPLICATIONS 193
   10.3.1 Industrial Applications 194
   10.3.2 Photo Interpretation and Change Detection 195
   10.3.3 Guidance, Navigation, and Scene Registration 196
   10.3.4 Medical Applications 197
   10.3.5 Hardware Requirements 198
10.4 SUMMARY AND FUTURE 199

Index 203

PREFACE

The field of machine perception concerns the building of machines that sense and interpret their environments. This book is about visual perception. Potential applications for such systems include tasks such as automation of industrial processes of inspection and assembly, automated medical x-ray diagnosis, vehicle guidance and automatic photo-interpretation. Beginning from the analysis of simple polyhedral scenes in the early 1960s, the field has progressed to the point where useful analysis of complex natural and industrial scenes is possible and many practical prototype and commercial systems are available. Because of its immense potential applications, interest in this field has been growing rapidly.

This book is based on my experience in teaching graduate courses in the field at USC for several years. Similar but less detailed material has also been presented at one-week "short courses" intended for industry professionals. This book assumes no previous knowledge of the field and aims to provide a comprehensive knowledge of its methods. It is intended for use as a text for a one-semester graduate or senior-level course and also as a guide for the practicing professional.

Research literature in the field has multiplied but is scattered over many journals, conference proceedings, and research reports. While the active researchers seem to share much the same knowledge of previous work, a newcomer to the field has a difficult job in sorting out the vast literature. This book is aimed at easing this task by providing basic concepts, details of the major approaches, and a guide to the literature.

The field of visual perception is still maturing. Some aspects of the problems are fairly well understood and have a well developed theory which is described in detail in the text. For other problems, however, comprehensive techniques do not exist, and the literature consists of a large number of methods of limited utility. In such cases I have grouped the techniques by their common themes and described the basic concepts. Varying amounts of detail are given for the specific techniques, based on my judgment of their generality and importance. I have tried to provide fairly complete references. To simplify the logistics of acquiring the pictures, I have provided examples from my own work or those of my students and colleagues, where applicable; similar examples could have been taken from others' work.

This book does not discuss computer programs in detail, but one must be familiar with digital computer programming in order to fully appreciate the difficulties of mechanizing the described processes. The mathematical content of the text is small, and for an overview the mathematical parts can be skipped. However, for a detailed understanding of certain topics, knowledge of a variety of mathematical tools would be helpful. These tools include calculus, analytical geometry, matrix theory and linear algebra, numerical analysis and graph theory. Knowledge of freshman-level physics may also help.

The facilities of the University of Southern California have been essential to the production of this book. Many of the examples were generated using the University's excellent laboratory and photographic facilities, A book in an active research field can hardly be written outside an active research environment. I am grateful for the support of the Defense Advanced Research Projects Agency (DARPA) of the Department of Defense for their support of my work at USC under their Image Understanding Program for many years (under contract numbers F33615-76-C-1203 and F33615-80-C-1080). The DARPA Image Understanding program was initiated by Lt. Col. David Carlstrom and later managed by Lt. Col. Lawrence E. Druffel and Cmdr. Ronald Ohlander.

Valuable comments on the drafts of the text were provided by Drs. Ruzena Bazcsy, Keith Price, and Barry Soroka and by many students at USC, especially David King. Permission of the various authors and publishers for use of their illustrations is gratefully acknowledged (credits are given in the text where used). The manuscript for this book was produced using SCRIBE text formatting system with a Graphics Systems Incorporated photocompositon device. Keith Uncapher made available the use of USC Information Science Institute's Xerox Penguin printer for "debugging" the early versions. Hilda Marti revised many drafts with her excellent typing and formatted the text. The illustrations were drafted by Doyle Howland, and Ray Schmidt took the photographs.

Ramakant Nevatia
Los Angeles, California

1

INTRODUCTION

Machine perception is a field of endeavor attempting to enable man-made machines to perceive their environment by sensory means as humans and animals do. Biological systems sense their environments by a variety of sources such as sight, sound, touch and smell. The process of perception involves making useful models of the environment from a confusing mass of sensory input data.

Visual data are the most complex and most useful sensory input for humans. Visual machine perception is concerned with the machine interpretation of similar visual data. There are many similarities in the ways in which different sensory data are perceived; in this book we will treat visual perception only.

Machines that perceive their environments and perform required tasks have an obvious usefulness for diverse application areas such as industrial assembly and inspection, planetary space exploration, automated medical x-ray screening, monitoring of earth resources by remote sensors, and a variety of military applications. They could assist in many tasks that are routine, tedious and even dangerous for humans to perform but are difficult or impossible to automate without some perceptual ability.

Most industrial assembly tasks, including seemingly simple tasks such as mounting of wheels on an automobile, normally require use of vision (however, blind people do learn to perform some of these tasks effectively by using touch). In hostile environments, such as outer space and undersea, or in the handling of hazardous materials, the use of machines may be essential. For many of these applications, machines need to be autonomous. As an example, for a vehicle to explore the surface of the planet Mars, the long delay in signal transmissions to earth (8 to 30 minutes round trip) virtually rules out human control from earth (by using "tele-operator" systems). Advantages of earthbound self-guided vehicles are also clear for transportation as well as military purposes.

Another important application area is the interpretation of images taken from aircraft or satellites for the monitoring of earth resources, weather patterns, and military surveillance. These tasks are tedious for humans to perform, and the manual interpretation process is a major bottleneck in the total processing system. Also, owing to the high volume of data, on board processing is highly desirable.

The above examples suggest some of the ambitious goals of the field of visual machine perception. Machine perception is a part of the larger field of *artificial intelligence*, which aims at building machines that behave intelligently, in perceptual and other domains. Visual imagery plays a prominent role in human intelligence for diverse tasks, and it is believed that understanding of machine perception will aid in the development of other forms of machine intelligence as well.

1.1 SOME EXAMPLES AND PROBLEMS

Visual perception is so immediate and effortless for us that the noninitiated imagine little difficulty in automating this process. Isn't the process of recognizing an object in an image merely a matter of finding a particular pattern of light intensity seen previously? A little thought, however, reveals numerous traps and complexities. A few simple examples will expose the basic problems.

First, consider the problem of recognizing isolated characters of the English alphabet. A character may be recognized by comparing it to those in the alphabet and choosing the "closest" one. This method will work if the characters are always of the same size and occur in the same orientation and the images contain little noise. But what of changes in scale and orientation, as shown in Fig. 1-1? To meet such situations we may postulate "shape" of a character, say "A," as consisting of two equal length line segments meeting at a point and at an angle of between 20 and 60 degrees, joined by a horizontal bar close to halfway between them. Assuming that such *descriptions* can be extracted from an image, the problems of change in scale and orientation seem to be in hand.

However, the characters in Fig. 1-2 are also likely to be perceived

Figure 1-1: Character "A" in different sizes and orientations

by humans as the letter "A," even though the reader may not have seen these forms before and they do not fit the above description of "A." Clearly, the *representation* of the pattern of the letter "A" is a rather complex and important issue.

Figure 1-2: Different ways of drawing the same character

The words shown in Fig. 1-3 are easily perceived to be "THE CAT." However, the letter representing "H" is printed in the same manner as that representing "A." It is clear that context and our expectations mediate such perception.

TAE CAT

Figure 1-3: An example to illustrate context dependency in character recognition

Now, consider the more complex example shown in Fig. 1-4. There is likely to be little disagreement that the figure is a drawing representing a cube or a box. However, the figure is inherently ambiguous. In the extreme, the figure is just a pattern of lines forming connected parallelograms in a plane. Even if a three-dimensional interpretation is required, there is no direct evidence that the "hidden" part of the surface is that of a cube. The choice of a suitable representation is even more important now.

Figure 1-5 shows a line drawing of one box-shaped object behind

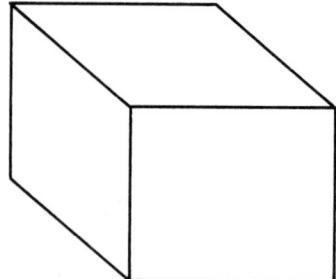

Figure 1-4: Line drawing of a cube

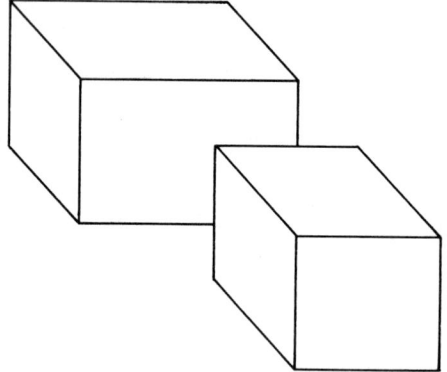

Figure 1-5: Line drawing of two objects

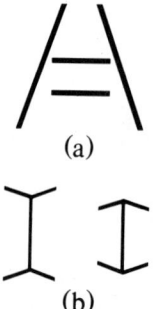

(a)

(b)

Figure 1-6: Two illusions

another. We conclude that the figure contains two objects, even though the lines defining them are connected. The distant object does not seem to be ambiguous even though not all of the "front" surface is visible.

These examples point out the difficulties caused by perception of a three-dimensional world through its two-dimensional projections on an imaging device. Most acute is the occlusion of objects by one another or self-occlusion of parts of their own surfaces. Such occlusion is common among scenes viewed at close range.

Human perception of figures, though remarkably accurate, is hardly perfect. Figures 1-6 (a) and (b) show examples of lines of equal length which are perceived unevenly. These "illusions" can be explained as being due to three-dimensional interpretations of the two-dimensional patterns.

Images of practical interest and of our everyday experience are rather complex. Figure 1-7 shows an image of some industrial parts; Fig. 1-8 shows a typical chest x-ray; Fig. 1-9 shows an aerial outdoor image (of the San Francisco area). In all three examples the major features, such as the parts in the industrial scene, the ribs in the x-ray, and the bay, roads, urban and suburban areas, and hills in the aerial image, are likely to be perceived immediately and with high confidence, even if the reader is unfamiliar with some of the objects in the scene or with the geography of the location of the aerial image. To analyze pictures of such complexity, we need to extract subtle and complex pieces of information from the pictures and efficiently utilize our store of knowledge about the structures and constraints on the objects in our perceptual world.

1.2 AN OVERVIEW AND HISTORY

Two major approaches to pattern perception have evolved: (1) those of mathematical pattern recognition and (2) the descriptive techniques of scene analysis. The first concentrates on the problem of assigning a pattern, not necessarily visual, to one of the known classes of patterns, based on some measurements, known as features, computed from the pattern. Studies in this approach have concentrated on classification methods and their generality rather than on defining useful features.

Scene analysis methods attempt to describe a pattern in terms of simpler primitives extracted from the input, and recognition is by matching of their descriptions. The emphasis is on the choice of the primitives and their descriptions. Utilization of known constraints in the image formation process is encouraged. The techniques developed

Figure 1-7: Picture of some industrial parts (from Perkins [1])

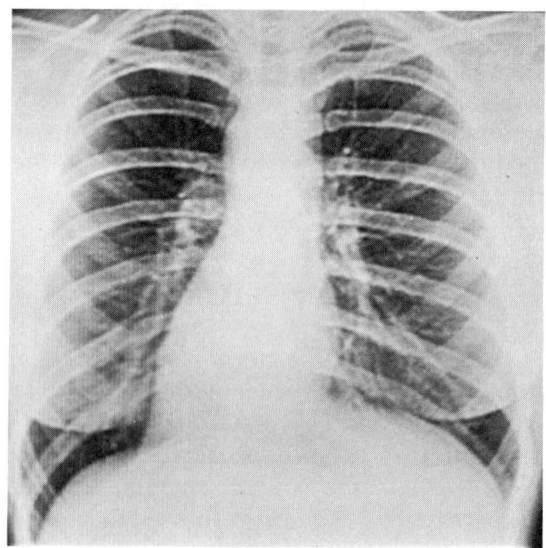

Figure 1-8: A chest x-ray

Figure 1-9: An image of the San Francisco area

often tend to follow those thought to be used by humans, though this is not an essential goal. This book is about these descriptive techniques; pattern recognition techniques are discussed only briefly for comparison (in Chapter 2).

The field of three-dimensional scene analysis originated, in the early 1960s with the pioneering work of L. G. Roberts [2]. He considered the problem of recognizing simple 3-D polyhedral objects from a single view. His system extracted a line drawing and its description from a digitized TV image of a scene. Objects were recognized by matching against computed projections of known objects. In computation of such projections, Roberts also originated the field of three-dimensional computer graphics. His system handled objects with a limited amount of occlusion.

For the next several years, for presumed reasons of simplicity, attention remained focused on scenes consisting of polyhedral objects. The central problem was recognized to be that of *segmentation*—that is, determining which lines and surfaces belonged to a single object. This domain is now well understood, and techniques exist to segment complex scenes of polyhedra, *if* complete and perfect line drawings are available.

In experiments with real images of polyhedra, it was realized that perfect line drawings were rarely extracted; consequently, some techniques that work with incorrect or missing data were developed. It was also realized that a partial analysis of line drawings may provide the essential context for extracting other weaker lines. Visual processing was now thought to proceed at many levels of abstraction, with results of higher level processing sometimes guiding the processing at lower levels in a feedback arrangement. The term *heterarchy*, as contrasted with *hierarchy*, has been applied to such a scheme.

Building on the experience with the so-called *blocks world*, further research has explored many divergent paths. A few attempts were made to extend the techniques of the blocks world to scenes of more general objects, including curved objects. For polyhedra, topological properties of lines and vertices often suffice for their recognition. More powerful descriptions of shape, necessary for curved objects, were developed. Experience with complex, natural outdoor and indoor scenes indicated that the contextual relationships of different objects to each other are extremely useful, if not essential, in their analysis.

Another line of research has been to build special purpose systems for particular applications, taking advantage of the a priori knowledge of the limited environment to simplify the processings. Proper organization and utilization of such knowledge are the key issues for such systems. A wide variety of application areas have been investigated such as industrial automation, biomedical image processing, and interpretation of aerial images. Some typical scenes are shown in Figs. 1-7, 1-8, and 1-9.

Concurrent with the work on *scene analysis* has been work on *image analysis.* Image analysis is concerned with techniques for extracting descriptions from images that are necessary for higher-level scene-analysis methods. The image analysis techniques include computation of perceived brightness and color, partial or complete recovery of three-dimensional data in the scene, location of discontinuities corresponding to objects in the scene, and characterization of the properties of uniform regions in the image.

The capabilities of machines to see are far less than human capabilities, the fantasies of the science fiction writers notwithstanding, and many fundamental issues of processing and representation are unresolved. However, the known techniques are adequate for building machines with limited, but useful, abilities to see for applications to real problems. Experimental and production machines exist to inspect

INTRODUCTION

printed circuit boards for defects and to orient integrated circuit chips for lead bonding, and many machines perform interesting assembly tasks in laboratory environments. A prototype of a Mars rover that functions in a highly simplified environment has been built. Use of image-based surveillance for earth resource monitoring and guidance for military vehicles is growing.

1.3 RELATIONSHIP TO PSYCHOLOGY

The problems of machine perception are analogous to those of human perception that have been studied for a long time by psychologists. A student of either field will benefit from studying the literature of the other. The known results of psychologica l research as well as insights gained by introspection have guided much of the research in machine perception, even though the motivation is not necessarily to simulate human perception. Rather, human (animal) perception is viewed as the only known example of a perceiving system.

The psychological research is not advanced to the extent of providing many concrete models that can be directly programmed for a machine. More is known about the early processing of signals at or near the eye than in in the cortex of the brain. Digital computers provide a rigorous way to test the predictions of psychological theories, and research in machine perception should suggest further psychology experiments. In the near term, the major benefit to machine perception may come from the wealth of experimental data about human visual perception, and its limitations, that is available in the psychology literature.

No attempt is made in this book to relate machine perception techniques in a formal way with psychological models, but analogies with human perception are cited informally. Introductory material about human visual perception may be found in [3-6].

1.4 PLAN OF THE BOOK

The organization of the book follows the overview in Section 1.2. The ordering of material is neither chronological nor hierarchical in levels of processing. Pattern classification techniques are discussed only briefly in Chapter 2, mostly for purposes of comparison; several textbooks are available on this subject [7-9].

The higher level scene analysis techniques for scenes of polyhedral objects are presented in Chapters 3 and 4, followed by a discussion of techniques for nonpolyhedral objects in Chapter 5. Lower-level image analysis techniques are presented in Chapters 6 through 9, which discuss the perception of brightness, color, and depth as well as low-level segmentation techniques. The high-level scene analysis techniques are presented first to give the reader a view of the goals and the desired results of the lower level image analysis. Complete systems and application areas are described in Chapter 10.

Each chapter of the book contains a bibliography of historically important papers and representative papers of the major approaches. More complete and current references may be found in [10].

This book excludes discussion of a field commonly known as *image processing,* which is concerned with the processing of images to produce new images *for human viewing.* Typical applications are enhancement or restoration of degraded images and bandwidth reduction for image transmission. These subjects are covered in several textbooks [11-15]. (Some of these books also contain material overlapping the subject of this book.) To draw a distinction from image processing, the term *image understanding* is also used synomously with visual machine perception.

REFERENCES

[1] W. A. Perkins, "A Model-Based Vision System for Industrial Parts," General Motors Research Laboratories Report GMR-2410, 1977.

[2] L. G. Roberts, "Machine Perception of Three-Dimensional Solids," in *Optical and Electro-Optical Information Processing,* J. T. Tippett, et al. (eds.), MIT Press, Cambridge, Mass., 1963, pp. 159-197.

[3] R. L. Gregory, *The Intelligent Eye,* McGraw-Hill Paperbacks, New York, 1970.

[4] P. H. Lindsey and D. A. Norman, *Human Information Processing,* Academic Press, New York, 1972.

[5] T. N. Cornsweet, *Visual Perception,* Academic Press, New York, 1970.

[6] I. Rock, *Introduction to Perception,* Macmillan, New York, 1975.

[7] R. O. Duda and P. E. Hart, *Pattern Classification and Scene Analysis,* John Wiley & Sons, New York, 1973.

[8] K. Fukunaga, *Introduction to Statistical Pattern Recognition,* Academic Press, New York, 1972.

[9] H. C. Andrews, *Introduction to Mathematical Techniques in Pattern Recognition,* John Wiley & Sons, New York, 1972.

[10] A. Rosenfeld, "Picture Processing," published annually in *Computer Graphics and Image Processing,* since 1975.

[11] W. K. Pratt, *Digital Image Processing*, John Wiley & Sons, New York, 1978.
[12] A. Rosenfeld and A. C. Kak, *Digital Picture Processing*, Academic Press, New York, 1976.
[13] K. R. Castleman, *Image Processing*, Prentice-Hall, Englewood Cliffs, N.J., 1979.
[14] E. L. Hall, *Computer Image Processing and Recognition*, Academic Press, New York, 1979.
[15] R. C. Gonzales and P. A. Wintz, *Digital Image Processing*, Addison-Wesley, Reading, Mass., 1977.

2

PATTERN CLASSIFICATION METHODS

The classical techniques of pattern recognition are concerned with assigning a given pattern to one of the known, finite classes. These techniques are surveyed briefly in this chapter and their possible applications and limitations examined. The problem of perception extends beyond that of classification; often it is necessary to generate descriptions of a new pattern and analyze its similarities and differences with other known patterns.

Before discussing different approaches, we need to study the digital representation of an image.

2.1 DIGITAL REPRESENTATION OF AN IMAGE

An image may be thought of as a function giving the light intensity at each point over a planar region. For operations by a digital computer, we need to sample this function at discrete intervals and quantize the intensity into discrete levels. The points at which the image is sampled are known as *picture elements*, commonly abbreviated as *pixels*. The intensity at each pixel is represented by an integer, say 0 for black and 255 for white, and is determined from the continuous image by averaging over a small neighborhood around the pixel location. It is common to use a square sampling grid with pixels equally spaced along the two sides of the grid.

The distance between grid points obviously affects the accuracy with which the original image is represented, and it determines the fine detail that can be resolved. (Of course, the resolution depends on the imaging system as well.) For most images of interest—those that have a bound on their spatial frequency—a certain sampling distance is sufficient to reproduce the image perfectly according to the well-known Shannon-Whittaker theorem in communication theory [1] (assuming no quantization of intensity levels). In the remainder of the book we will assume the input to be a digital image with a given resolution.

2.1.1 Connectivity in Digital Images

The geometry and topology of a digital plane differ from those of a continuous domain in many important aspects. While horizontal and vertical lines are easily represented on a square grid, straight lines at many other angles can only be approximated by a staircaselike pattern (see Fig. 2-1).

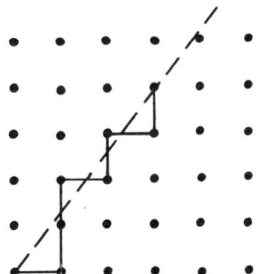

Figure 2-1: Digital approximation of a line

The connectivity of patterns in a discrete representation is more complex than for the continuous case. To determine connectivity, we need to define the notion of adjacency of two points in a digitized plane. In Fig. 2-2, either four pixels, *A* through *D*, or all eight pixels, *A* through *H*, may be considered adjacent to the center pixel. The two adjacencies are known as 4-adjacency and 8-adjacency, respectively. A set of points forms a 4 (or 8) connected figure if there is a path between any two points through 4 (or 8) adjacent points.

These definitions of connectedness can yield counterintuitive results in some cases. In Fig. 2-3, the set of points with value 1 is 8-connected, but so are their "interior" and "exterior" backgrounds. On the other hand, this set of points is not 4-connected, but neither are interior and exterior backgrounds, and we have an unconnected curve

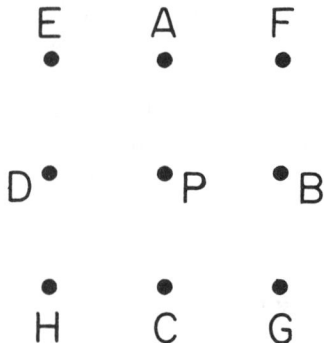

Figure 2-2: Neighbors of a pixel P

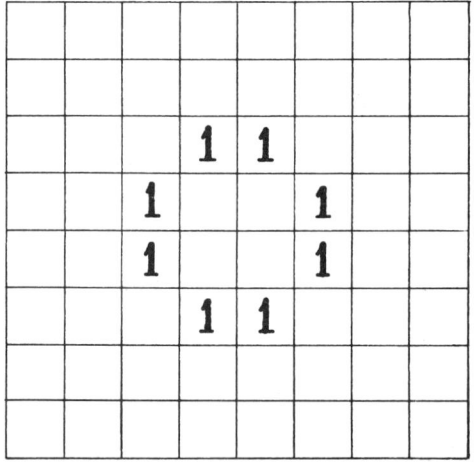

Figure 2-3: Connectivity in digital plane

separating two regions in a plane.

If a hexagonal grid is used, instead of a square one, this anomaly disappears. In a hexagonal grid, a point at the center of a hexagon is considered to be connected to the six pixels at the corners of the hexagon; see Fig. 2-4. However, hexagonal grids have not proved popular, perhaps because of the complexity of the digitization (details of the use of hexagonal grids may be found in [2]). It is interesting to note that triangular grids are the only other symmetric and isotropic grid that can be used to span a plane. A detailed treatment of digital topology may be found in [3].

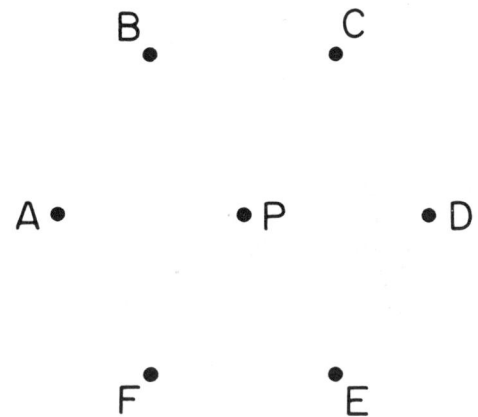

Figure 2-4: A point P and its hexagonal neighbors

2.2 TEMPLATE MATCHING

The most immediate method of classifying a pattern is to compare it with stored models of known patterns and choose the best match. In template matching, this comparison is performed directly on images. Templates consist of images of known patterns, one from each class. Each template is moved over a new image to find the best match. Let $F(i, j)$ represent the image and $A(i, j)$ represent the template. For a translation of the template by (x, y) a measure of the match between the image and the template is given by

$$E(x, y) = \sum_i \sum_j [F(i, j) - A(i - x, j - y)]^2 \qquad (2\text{-}1)$$

where the summation is over the overlapping regions of the image and the translated template. Matches at different values of (x, y) are computed to search for a minimum value of E. The template giving the lowest error, E, is taken to be the best classification for the input pattern. Two simpler measures of match are the sum of absolute differences and the sum of the maxima of the absolute differences, instead of the sum of the squares of differences in Eq. (2-1) above.

Above measures require the patterns to be matched to have the same intensity values. A measure known as normalized cross-correlation is insensitive to the absolute intensity and also to the contrast and is defined by

$$\sigma(x, y) = \frac{\sum\sum\{F(i, j) \cdot A(i - x, j - y)\}}{\sqrt{\sum\sum F^2(i, j)} \cdot \sqrt{\sum\sum A^2(i - x, j - y)}} \qquad (2\text{-}2)$$

with all summations over the same range as in Eq. (2-1) above. σ achieves a maximum value of 1 for an exact match.

As defined above, template matching achieves pattern classification invariant to translation, but not to rotation, scale (size), or perspective changes. Template matching with different scales and orientations is computationally expensive. To account for variations within a class, the template may be stretched and deformed to fit a pattern with a measure related to the amount of deformation [4]. Limited changes in perspective may be accommodated by using a number of templates with different perspective views.

It is sometimes useful to represent a template as consisting of smaller subtemplates with specified spatial relationships. Matching of subtemplates can then be independent of each other, and a further measure of the spatial relationships in the input pattern is used to evaluate the whole match. In one approach, the subtemplates were considered to be attached by springs, and extension or compression of these springs was used as a measure of a global match [5]. This technique allows different weights to be assigned to different spatial relationships and allows some flexibility within a pattern class. However, the basic limitations of sensitivity to changes in scale and perspective remain.

In summary, template-matching techniques are useful for applications where the number of classes and the variability within a class are small. A prime example of successful application is for recognition of printed, fixed-font alphabetic characters in commercially available optical character reader (OCR) devices.

2.3 PATTERN CLASSIFICATION IN FEATURE SPACE

An alternative to template matching, which proceeds at the image level, is to abstract some measurements or features from the pattern and classify it based on these measurements. This paradigm is illustrated schematically in Fig. 2-5 and allows the separation of the recognition problem into two more or less independent parts.

The measured features may be considered to span an n-dimensional feature space, and different regions of this space correspond to different pattern classes. A hypothetical example for two features is shown in Fig. 2-6. The power of this paradigm is strongly

PATTERN CLASSIFICATION METHODS

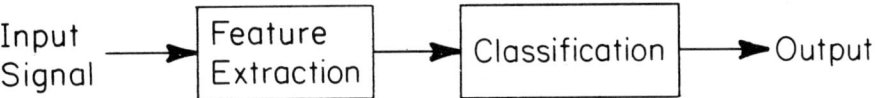

Figure 2-5: Block diagram for pattern-classification approach

dependent on the availability of features that are invariant to the expected changes in the input patterns. The choice of features is problem dependent. However, the classification methods can be independent of the problem domain and need not be restricted to pictorial inputs.

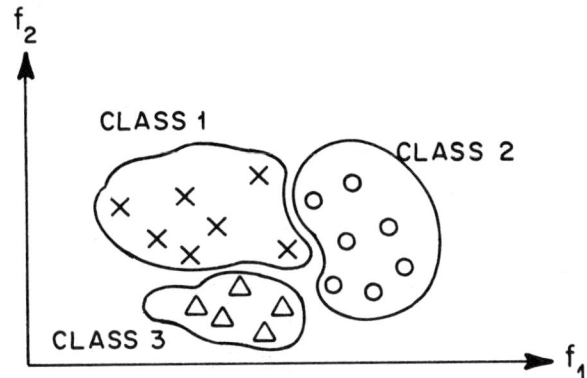

Figure 2-6: Three classes separated in feature space f_1-f_2

Elegant theories have been developed for classification that minimize the probability of false classification based on known (or assumed) a priori probabilities of occurrence of certain patterns and conditional probabilities of their occurrence given a feature vector. A simple technique is to assign a given point in feature space to the same class as that of its nearest (closest) neighbor in this space. This simple method has an error rate no worse than twice that of an optimal method. A major concern of the pattern-classification methods is with the simplicity of the classification rule, and a particular favorite is classification by dividing the feature space into linearly separable regions—that is, by hyperplanes in the feature space (straight lines in a plane). These classification methods are not described in detail here; several comprehensive textbooks on the subject exist [6-8]. A particular pattern classification machine, the perceptron, is discussed in some detail below.

2.4 PERCEPTRONS

A frequently suggested and attractive organization for pattern classification is that the analysis of an input pattern must proceed in stages. At each stage, computations are performed on local areas only, and global relations are derived from combinations of the local computations, in a presumed analogy with the human visual system. A specific scheme is as shown in Fig. 2-7. In the figure ϕ_i's are arbitrarily complex functions limited to operating on a local neighborhood and Ω is a decision function based on the results of computations of various ϕ_i's (the neighborhoods of ϕ_i's may overlap).

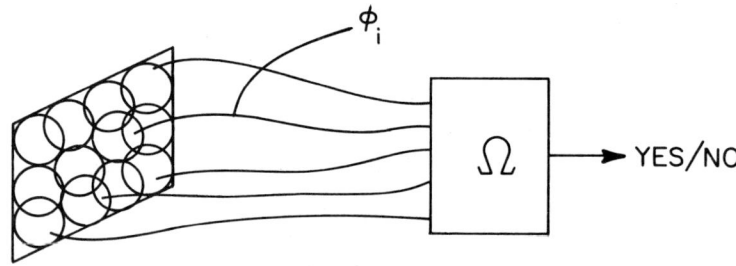

Figure 2-7: A perceptron

To be more specific, let each ϕ_i be a predicate function (that is, with a value of one or zero). Let the decision function, Ω, have value one (yes, true) if a weighted sum of the inputs, ϕ_i, exceeds a certain threshold and zero (no, false), otherwise. That is,

$$\Omega = 1, \text{ if } \sum_i \alpha_i \phi_i > \tau$$

$$= 0, \text{ otherwise}$$

A machine using such a decision function is called a *perceptron* and was proposed by Rosenblatt [9]. The thresholding element was believed to be similar to the simpler models of neurons in animal brains. It has been further suggested that such machines are capable of "learning," by adjustments of the weights in accordance with the output of the machine in response to known input patterns.

As a simple example, consider the problem of recognizing whether the input pattern is a rectangle of any size located at an arbitrary position, with one of the axes bein horizontal (see Fig. 2-8). Let us define four predicate functions $\phi_1(i, j)$, $\phi_2(i, j)$, $\phi_3(i, j)$, and

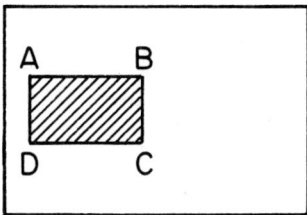

Figure 2-8: A rectangle in an image

$\phi_4(i, j)$, each using three pixels in the input pattern. For these functions to be true, pixel (i, j) must have a value of 1 and neighbors must have values as specified below:

$\phi_1(i, j)$ requires the south and east neighbors—that is, pixels $(i+1, j)$ and $(i, j+1)$—to have value 0,
$\phi_2(i, j)$ requires south and west neighbors to be 0,
$\phi_3(i, j)$ requires north and west neighbors to be 0, and
$\phi_4(i, j)$ requires north and east neighbors to be 0.

These functions essentially detect the presence of a certain type of corner in the input pattern. In Fig. 2-8, ϕ_1 has value 1 at corner A, ϕ_2 at corner B, ϕ_3 at corner C, and ϕ_4 at corner D. The presence of the desired rectangle is indicated if and only if

$$\sum \phi_1 + \sum \phi_2 + \sum \phi_3 + \sum \phi_4 \leq 4 \qquad (2\text{-}3)$$

(verification for the general case is left to the reader).

For many years it was believed that perceptrons were general classifiers capable of learning to discriminate between arbitrary sets of patterns by proper choice of α_i's (and perhaps ϕ_i's), and much effort was devoted to discovering efficient learning algorithms [10]. However, Minsky and Papert, in a classic book [11], demonstrated that the discrimination ability of these machines is extremely limited.

Before results on the power of perceptrons can be established, some restrictions must be placed on the feature detecting functions, the ϕ_i's. We allow the functions to be arbitrarily complex predicate functions, but restrict the range of inputs in the following two ways:

1. Each ϕ_i is allowed to operate in a neighborhood enclosed within a circle of a certain diameter. Machines with this restriction will be called *diameter limited* perceptrons.
2. Each ϕ_i may use at most only a limited number of points, say k,

selected from anywhere in the input pattern. Machines with this restriction will be called *order limited* (of order *k*) perceptrons.

Clearly, if the order or the diameter of a perceptron is allowed to be large enough to include all points in the input pattern, discrimination between any two patterns is possible (as each ϕ_i is arbitrarily complex). Such machines will be said to be *not* of finite diameter (or order). The interesting results are about the capabilities of finite order or finite diameter perceptrons. Some of the principal results of Minsky and Papert's work are stated below.

1. Finite-order and finite-diameter perceptrons can be devised to discriminate rectangles from other figures. Circles can be discriminated by order-limited perceptrons (of order four) but not by diameter-limited perceptrons. However, figures embedded in other figures cannot be so discriminated by *any* finite-order or finite-diameter perceptrons. For example, such machines cannot be devised to correctly answer that a rectangle is contained in Fig. 2-9(a) or (b).
2. If invariance to *any* group of transformations is desired, patterns must be discriminable by area alone.
3. If invariance to *any* topological transformation is desired, the patterns must be discriminable by their Euler number (number of connected components - number of holes).
4. A perceptron of order three can discriminate between convex and concave patterns.
5. A finite-order or finite-diameter perceptron cannot be constructed to discriminate between connected or disconnected patterns, such as in Fig. 2-10, where one of the patterns is connected, the other is not. (In this example, the connectedness property is difficult to perceive for humans as well, but the perceptrons also fail for simpler examples.)

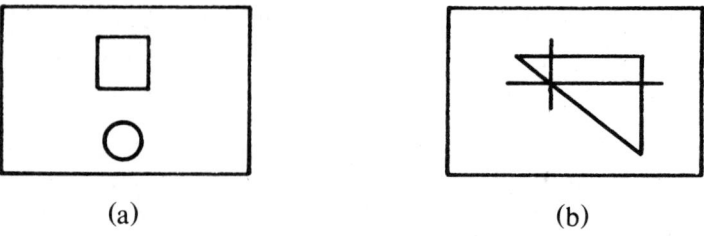

Figure 2-9: The rectangle as a component in two patterns

The above results are largely negative and somewhat surprising in that simple global properties such as connectedness cannot be inferred

PATTERN CLASSIFICATION METHODS

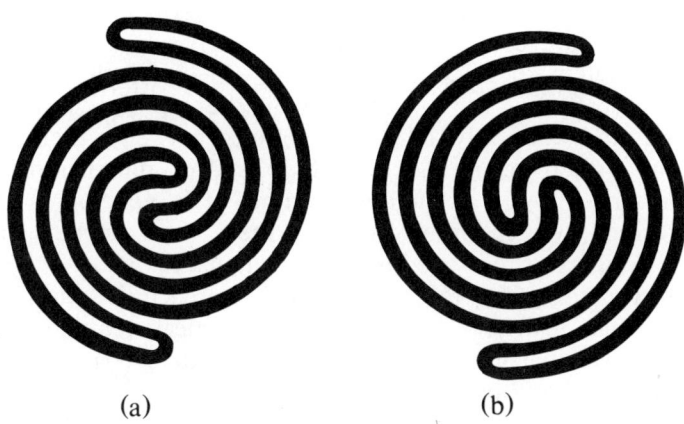

(a)   (b)

Figure 2-10: An unconnected and a connected figure

from local properties by a perceptron. Multilevel perceptrons, utilizing more than one level of composition of local features, have also been proposed. However, no important experimental results or theoretical analyses of such machines have been reported. (Results of preliminary analysis for machines slightly more general than those analyzed by Minsky and Papert also seem to be negative [12].)

2.5 SYNTACTICAL APPROACHES

In the pattern-classification approaches of the previous two sections, the measured features were interpreted to span a feature space and *relations* between features were not considered. An alternative approach is to divide a pattern into primitive subpatterns and use the relations between subpatterns (or their features). For example, it is convenient to represent a triangle as three straight lines (primitives) connected at their end points. Such approaches are said to use *syntactical* or *structural* relations of a pattern.

Syntactical approaches were first applied to the *parsing* of sentences in programming and natural languages. These sentences may be viewed as one-dimensional patterns with words as subpatterns. For programming languages, the allowed relations of adjacency or concatenation of words of certain classes are defined by formal rules, known as *formal grammars*. However, attempts to find similar rules for natural language sentences have not been very successful, and it is widely recognized that the rules of grammar are dependent also on the meaning or the *semantics* of the words, and not just on their positions in the sentence.

Use of formal grammars to specify patterns in two and three dimensions is more complex, as the relationships between subpatterns are not completely specified by adjacency. In one early approach, the primitive subpatterns were restricted to be vectors with a given orientation, and the only allowed relations between them were by attachments at their beginnings or ends [13]. Two-dimensional patterns were represented by a predefined central "axis" vector. Rules for patterns formed by combining vectors in these ways can be specified by grammars similar to those used for string languages.

Unfortunately, the term syntactical approach is often used for techniques that restrict the range of syntactical relations to those specified by a formal grammar; a more appropriate term for the latter would be *grammatical* pattern recognition. If the class of patterns of interest can be specified by a formal grammar, many powerful techniques of formal language parsing become applicable. This has been achieved with some success for restricted applications; some examples are character recognition [14], bubble chamber particle trace analysis [13], and chromosome analysis [15]. However, the search for grammars describing large classes of natural patterns has not yet been very successful.

Grammatical pattern recognition is not discussed in the remainder of this book; a thorough treatment may be found in [16]. However, nongrammatical structural relationships between parts of patterns are a key method used in the techniques described in this book. We will use the term "structural" rather than "syntactical" in the hope of avoiding confusion with the grammatical methods.

2.6 SUMMARY

This chapter has provided a brief overview of mathematical pattern recognition (also called *classical* or *statistical* pattern recognition) techniques. Although the proposed paradigms are of great generality, their applications to pictorial pattern recognition have been limited, owing to difficulties of defining suitable features (or grammars). The view taken in this book is that such techniques may play a useful role in some parts of a complete system, but they do not provide all the capabilities required for machine perception, particularly for three-dimensional scenes.

The descriptive approach is developed in the remainder of the book. A good understanding of many issues can be obtained by studying first the simpler problems of perception of polyhedral scenes.

REFERENCES

[1] J. W. Goodman, *Introduction to Fourier Optics*, McGraw Hill, New York, 1968.

[2] M. J. E. Golay, "Hexagonal Parallel Pattern Transformations," *IEEE Transactions on Electronic Computers*, C-18, August 1969, pp. 733-740.

[3] A. Rosenfeld and A. C. Kak, *Digital Picture Processing*, Academic Press, New York, 1976.

[4] B. Widrow, "The Rubber-Mask Technique, I and II," *Pattern Recognition*, Vol. 5, 1973, pp. 175-211.

[5] M. A. Fischler and R. A. Elschlager, "The Representation and Matching of Pictorial Structures," *IEEE Transactions on Computers*, Vol. C-22, No. 1, January 1973, pp. 67-92.

[6] R. O. Duda and P. E. Hart, *Pattern Classification and Scene Analysis*, John Wiley & Sons, New York, 1973.

[7] K. Fukunaga, *Introduction to Statistical Pattern Recognition*, Academic Press, New York, 1972.

[8] H. C. Andrews, *Introduction to Mathematical Techniques in Pattern Recognition*, John Wiley & Sons, New York, 1972.

[9] F. Rosenblatt, *Principles of Neurodynamics: Perceptrons and the Theory of Brain Mechanisms*, Spartan Books, Washington D.C., 1962.

[10] N. J. Nilsson, *Learning Machines: Foundations of Trainable Pattern Classifying Systems*, McGraw-Hill, New York, 1965.

[11] M. Minsky and S. Papert, *Perceptrons, An Introduction to Computational Geometry*, MIT Press, Cambridge, Mass., 1969.

[12] H. Abelson, "Computational Geometry of Linear Threshold Functions," MIT Artificial Intelligence Laboratory Memo 376, July 1976.

[13] A. C. Shaw, "A Formal Picture Description Scheme as a Basis for Picture Processing Systems," *Information and Control*, Vol. 14, 1969, pp. 9-52.

[14] R. Narasimhan, "Syntax-directed Interpretation of Classes of Pictures," *Communications of the ACM*, Vol. 9, 1966, pp. 166-173.

[15] R. S. Ledley, "High Speed Automatic Analysis of Bio-Medical Pictures," *Science*, Vol. 146, 1964, pp. 216-223.

[16] K. S. Fu, *Syntactical Methods in Pattern Recognition*, Academic Press, New York, 1974.

3

SIMPLE POLYHEDRAL SCENES

The pattern classification techniques described in the previous chapter have been applied primarily to the recognition of images of two-dimensional objects. The world of our everyday perception is, of course, three-dimensional. Perceiving a three-dimensional scene from a single point of view, which gives a two-dimensional image, adds some new and unique difficulties. Interpretation of these two-dimensional images is inherently ambiguous; the same image can be formed by an infinite number of three-dimensional scenes. Also, the image formed by a particular object changes with the viewing angle; this is also known as perspective change. Above all, in scenes with multiple objects, parts of otherwise visible surfaces of some objects may be occluded by others. A perceptual system needs to separate the objects in the image and recognize them from the partial information.

3.1 PERCEPTION OF SIMPLE POLYHEDRAL SOLIDS

The study of machine perception of three-dimensional objects was launched by the classic work of L. G. Roberts [1]. In his work, and much of the early work in three-dimensional scene analysis, the scenes were restricted to consist of polyhedral solids with homogeneous surfaces against uniform backgrounds. Such scenes can be adequately characterized by the intersection lines of the objects. His work contains many concepts that extend beyond the simple scenes considered, and a detailed study of these methods is appropriate.

Consider an image of a simple cube, painted uniformly white against a dark background. We may consider recognition of the cube by the methods described in Chapter 2. As the observed picture changes with the viewing angle, simple geometrical properties are not invariant. A template-matching process could, in principle, be used. We would need to store (or generate) templates for each known object from different viewing angles and different viewing distances. Matching with such a large set of templates is clearly prohibitive in computational cost and still does not account for changes in the lighting conditions.

Instead of operating on the picture directly, it may be simpler to extract a line drawing from the picture, corresponding to the intersection of the planar surfaces of the three-dimensional object, and to attempt recognition from the line drawing. There is evidence that boundaries suffice for many perceptual tasks in human perception [2]. Certainly, for polyhedral objects, the boundaries directly determine the visible faces. Ideally, the boundaries shown in Fig. 3-1 would be extracted from the image of a cube and are adequate to distinguish it from objects with boundaries shown in Fig. 3-2, for example. (Of course, since the projection of three-dimensional scenes is inherently ambiguous, the distinction between the objects is limited.)

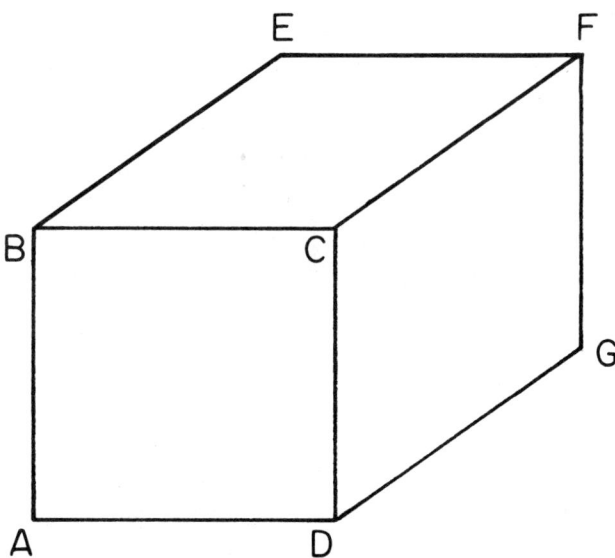

Figure 3-1: Outline of a cube

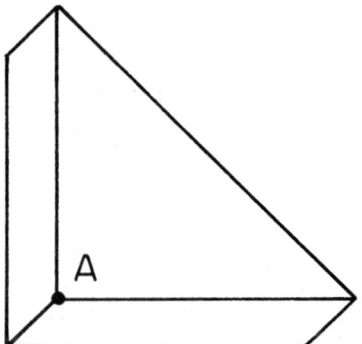

Figure 3-2: Outline of a wedge

3.1.1 Extraction of Line Drawings

Extraction of lines that correspond to object edges is based on the assumption that the light intensity is constant or smoothly varying over the image of an object face and jumps discontinuously at the intersection with the image of another face. This assumption is valid if the object surfaces are smooth, homogeneous, and opaque and the lighting is uniform and arranged to eliminate shadows. It is also assumed that the object surfaces do not have mirrorlike reflections.

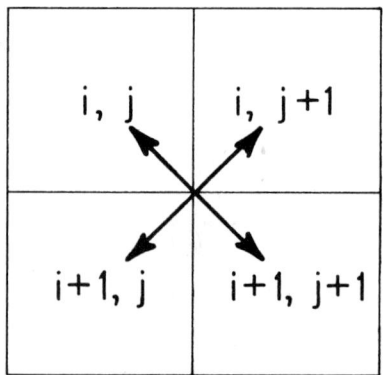

Figure 3-3: Roberts' gradient operator

In a continuous image plane, points at which the intensity changes discontinuously are easily identified to be those where the gradient of the intensity function is infinite (or larger than a threshold). An approximation for this gradient for a digital picture is given by

SIMPLE POLYHEDRAL SCENES

$R(i, j) \simeq \nabla g(i, j)$

$$= \sqrt{\{g(i + 1, j + 1) - g(i, j)\}^2 + \{g(i, j + 1) - g(i + 1, j)\}^2} \qquad (3\text{-}1)$$

where $g(i, j)$ is the image intensity at pixel (i, j) (see Fig. 3-3). Absolute values may be used instead of squared values in Eq. (3-1) above. Also the direction of the gradient is given by the angle α, where

$$\alpha = -\frac{\pi}{4} + \tan^{-1}\left[\frac{g(i, j + 1) - g(i + 1, j)}{g(i + 1, j + 1) - g(i, j)}\right] \qquad (3\text{-}2)$$

The above definition of gradient is due to Roberts [1], and this operator is often called Roberts' cross-operator. An *edge* is said to be present at pixel (i, j) if $R(i, j) > \tau$, where τ is a chosen threshold. If pictures were noise-free, τ could be chosen to be 0. In the presence of noise, τ is chosen by a trade-off between obtaining all desired edges and picking too many noise edges. Figure 3-4(a) shows the image of a complex block and Fig. 3-4(b) the edges detected in it by using the above-described method. (The threshold was chosen interactively for best subjective performance.) In this example, the block is carefully painted and has smooth surfaces. Any markings on the surface or the texture of the material would, of course, also show in these cases.

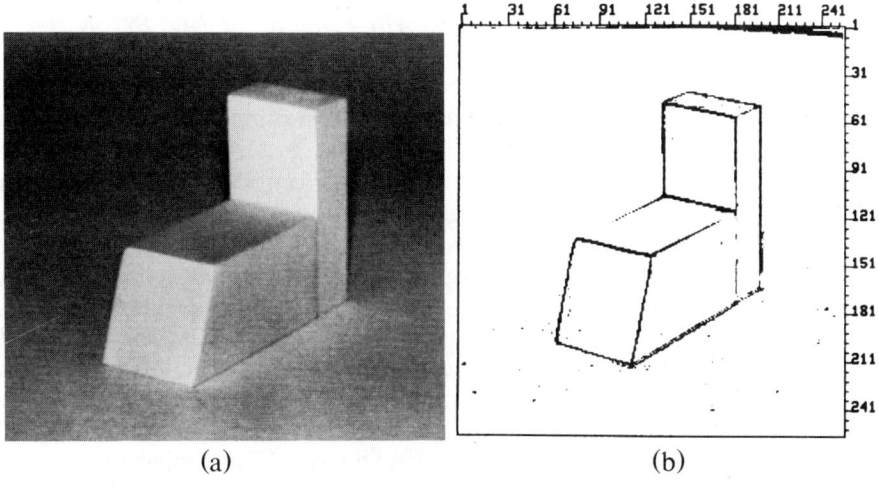

(a)   (b)

Figure 3-4: (a) An image and (b) edges detected in it

The next step is to connect the computed edge points in straight lines and determine the vertices from their intersections. Each edge is specified by a position as well as a direction (normal to that of the gradient at the point) and should be connected only in a line in that direction. Spurious noise points can be removed by eliminating short line segments. Gaps in lines caused by missing edges are bridged by extension up to predetermined lengths. Roberts was able to obtain "perfect" line drawing as in Fig. 3-1, for a limited class of scenes. However, such line detection has proven to be difficult for real scenes. More sophisticated techniques of determining object boundaries are given in Chapter 7. For the remainder of this chapter, it is assumed that perfect boundaries are available for further processing.

3.1.2 Model Matching

Once a line drawing is obtained, recognition can be achieved by determining which of the models can generate, under some permissible transformation, a line drawing that is most similar. The two line drawings must match *topologically* (or structurally)—that is, in the number of lines and vertices and their interconnections. The distances between vertices should also be as predicted by the model transformation.

For a topological match between two line drawings, it is useful to extract *polygons* in them. Further, the polygons corresponding to an object face should be distinguished from others, if possible (for example, in Fig. 3-1, only polygons *ABCD*, *BEFC*, and *CFGD* are desired and not *ABEFGD*, *ABEFCD*, *ABCFGD*, or *BCDGFE*). A clever algorithm to separate interior and exterior polygons was developed by Roberts. As an example, consider starting from an arbitrarily chosen line in a chosen direction, say from *A* to *B* along line *AB*. When vertex *B* is reached, we choose the line making the largest exterior clockwise angle with *AB* (that is, *BC*). If this procedure is repeated, polygon *ABCD* will be traced. Starting along *AB* in the other direction from *B* to *A*, and repeating the same steps, polygon *ADGFEB* is traced. However, this time the traversal of the polygon is in a counterclockwise direction (this can be determined from the scan of the exterior angles of the traversed polygons, $+2\pi$ for counterclockwise and -2π for clockwise traversal). If the above procedure is applied until each line has been traversed in both directions, the interior polygons will be traced in one direction and the outer ones in the other.

For a polygon to possibly correspond to an object face, the number of sides and the number of convex and concave angles of this polygon must be the same as for some polygon in at least one of the models. Such polygons will be called *approved* polygons (partially occluded faces are not approved polygons).

The topological match proceeds by first looking for a vertex completely surrounded by approved polygons (vertex C in Fig. 3-1 is such a vertex). If such a vertex exists, it is characterized by the number of sides of the surrounding polygons and is matched with a model vertex with the same characteristics. Matching of the vertices then leads to the matching of the polygons around them and the other vertices of these polygons.

In a partially occluded object, no vertices of the above types may exist, as would be the case if vertex A were hidden in Fig. 3-1. In this case, the topological match uses a line surrounded by approved polygons (such as line CF for the cube example) to obtain matching lines and then matching polygons and vertices. In case of further occlusion, the desired line may also not exist; in this case, a single approved polygon is used. Failing this also, any vertex with three (or more) lines is used for matching. (A more formal approach to such structural matching is given in [3].)

Once a topological match with a model is found, a geometric transformation for the best geometric match with that model is computed. Suppose that

$V_p = \{v_{1p}, v_{2p}, ..., v_{np}\}$ are the vertices in the picture,

$V_m = \{v_{1m}, v_{2m}, ..., v_{nm}\}$ are the matching model vertices and,

$V'_p = \{v'_{1p}, v'_{2p}, ..., v'_{np}\}$ are the predicted vertices, under a transformation $\mathbf{T}_m$.

We wish to choose $\mathbf{T}_m$ to minimize E_m, which is defined as

$$E_m = \sum_{i=1}^{n} \|v_{ip} - v'_{ip}\| \qquad (3\text{-}3)$$

(Details of a transformation and minimization are given in Section 3.2 below.)

The model producing the minimum matching error is chosen, consistent with one more requirement. The picture positions for the unmatched model vertices must *not* fall outside the picture line drawing—that is, they must be predicted to be hidden. This is verification by picture synthesis.

If the scene contains more than one object, the above procedure will find one object at a time. Once an object has been recognized, the lines corresponding to it are removed and the remainder of the scene processed repeatedly as before. Complex objects formed by composing simpler objects are analyzed similarly. A sequence of such processing is shown in Fig. 3-5. This method is effective only if parts of each object sufficient for recognition are visible. (Analysis of complex, occluding scenes is discussed in the next chapter.)

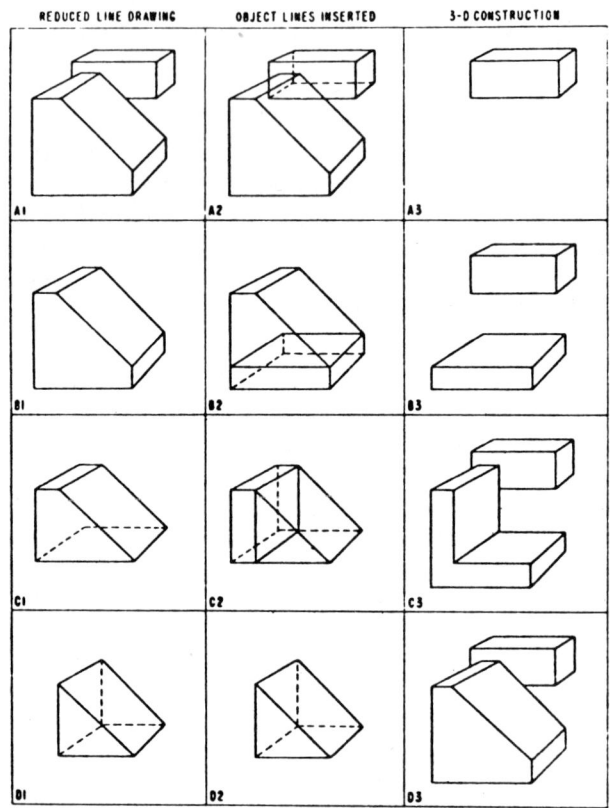

Figure 3-5: Successive analysis of a complex object
(from Roberts [1])

3.2 MODEL TRANSFORMATIONS

A component of object recognition is to verify that a hypothesized model produces an image similar to the observed image, under some permissible transformation. We will consider the transformations of scaling, translation, rotation, and image formation—that is, the perspective transformation.

3.2.1 Perspective Transformations

A typical camera consists of a lens and a plane on which the image is formed. For the purpose of geometrical optics (that is, ignoring diffraction effects), an ideal camera can be modeled as a "pin-hole" camera. Such an ideal imaging system is shown in Fig. 3-6 and consists of a lens center C and an image plane I, a distance f from C. f is known as the focal length of the imaging system. The image of a given point P is formed on the image plane I at point P' determined by the intersection of the ray connecting C and P with the plane I. In Fig. 3-6 the ideal image plane is shown to be in *front* of the lens center; in normal camera systems the physical image plane is *behind* the lens center, and the image is inverted. We assume that for algebraic simplicity the inverted image has been corrected to correspond to the geometry shown. The image using a TV camera, as seen on a TV monitor, corresponds to the image plane being in the front.

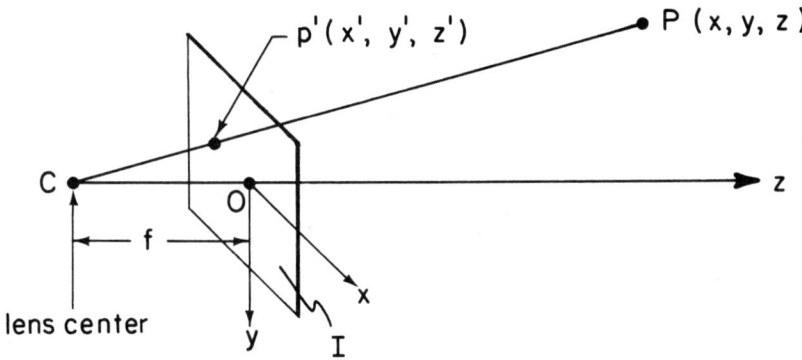

Figure 3-6: An ideal imaging system

Let a Cartesian coordinate system be chosen with the z axis normal to the image plane. Let the origin be on the image plane along the principal ray, which is the line from the lens center perpendicular to the image plane. Then the image $P'(x', y', z')$ of an object point P at location (x, y, z) is given by

$$x' = \frac{fx}{f + z} \qquad (3\text{-}4)$$

$$y' = \frac{fy}{f + z} \qquad (3\text{-}5)$$

$$z' = 0 \qquad (3\text{-}6)$$

The above transformation from (x, y, z) to (x', y', z') is known as a perspective transformation. Note that the transformation is not invertible; that is, given a picture point (x', y', z'), we cannot completely specify the corresponding object point but can only constrain it to lie along a certain straight line.

3.2.2 Homogeneous Coordinates

The perspective transformation involves a division and is thus nonlinear. However, it can be linearized by use of homogeneous coordinates represented in a matrix form. Homogeneous coordinates of a point are defined by appending an extra component to the coordinate vector of the point and are related to the ordinary coordinates as follows. If (x_h, y_h, z_h, w_h) are the homogeneous coordinates of a point P with normal coordinates (x, y, z), then

$$x = \frac{x_h}{w_h} \tag{3-7}$$

$$y = \frac{y_h}{w_h} \tag{3-8}$$

$$z = \frac{z_h}{w_h} \tag{3-9}$$

The choice of w_h is arbitrary and thus the homogeneous coordinates of a point are not unique. Now consider the following matrix transformation

$$\begin{bmatrix} x'_h \\ y'_h \\ z'_h \\ w'_h \end{bmatrix} = \begin{bmatrix} 1 & 0 & 0 & 0 \\ 0 & 1 & 0 & 0 \\ 0 & 0 & 0 & 0 \\ 0 & 0 & \frac{1}{f} & 1 \end{bmatrix} \begin{bmatrix} x_h \\ y_h \\ z_h \\ w_h \end{bmatrix} \tag{3-10}$$

Let the 4-by-4 matrix in the equation above be called **P**. This equation expands to

SIMPLE POLYHEDRAL SCENES

$$x'_h = x_h \tag{3-11}$$

$$y'_h = y_h \tag{3-12}$$

$$z'_h = 0 \tag{3-13}$$

$$w'_h = \frac{z_h}{f} + w_h \tag{3-14}$$

Dividing Eqs. (3-11), (3-12), and (3-13) by w'_h and rearranging them, we get

$$x' = \frac{x'_h}{w'_h} = \frac{fx}{f+z} \tag{3-15}$$

$$y' = \frac{y'_h}{w'_h} = \frac{fy}{f+z} \tag{3-16}$$

$$z' = 0 \tag{3-17}$$

These are identical with the transformation defined earlier [Eqs. (3-4), (3-5), and (3-6)]. Thus we have defined a linear transformation **P**, operating on homogeneous coordinates of a point and its image, that is equivalent to a perspective transformation.

The transformation defined above does not preserve any information about the distance along the z axis of an object point P. It is sometimes useful to augment the matrix **P** to be

$$\mathbf{P} = \begin{bmatrix} 1 & 0 & 0 & 0 \\ 0 & 1 & 0 & 0 \\ 0 & 0 & 1 & 0 \\ 0 & 0 & \frac{1}{f} & 1 \end{bmatrix} \qquad (3\text{-}18)$$

to give

$$z' = \frac{fz}{f+z} \qquad (3\text{-}19)$$

The value of z' no longer corresponds to the actual image point. However, the image point is known to be at $z' = 0$, and the additional information contained in Eq. (3-19) above is useful for shading and hidden line elimination in computer graphics.

3.2.3 Geometrical Transformations

The perspective transformation given above applies when the object and the image points are specified in a coordinate system aligned with the camera. It may be more convenient to express the objects in an independent coordinate system, sometimes called a *world* coordinate system. In this case, the object coordinates must be first transformed to a system aligned with the camera, before the perspective transformation can be applied. The two systems can be aligned by a translation and sequential rotation about the three coordinate axes. The three rotation angles are sometimes referred to as *pan*, *tilt*, and *swing* (or *roll*). (Usually, pan refers to rotation of the principal ray in a horizontal plane tilt to its rotation in a vertical plane, and swing to a rotation of the image plane; see Fig. 3-7.)

Rotation. Any rotation of a model can be decomposed into three consecutive rotations about the three coordinate axes. Let us consider a rotation of axes about the z axis by an angle θ, as shown in Fig. 3-8. The direction of the rotation is from the x axis to the y axis. The coordinates of the point (x, y, z) in the rotated coordinate system are given by

SIMPLE POLYHEDRAL SCENES

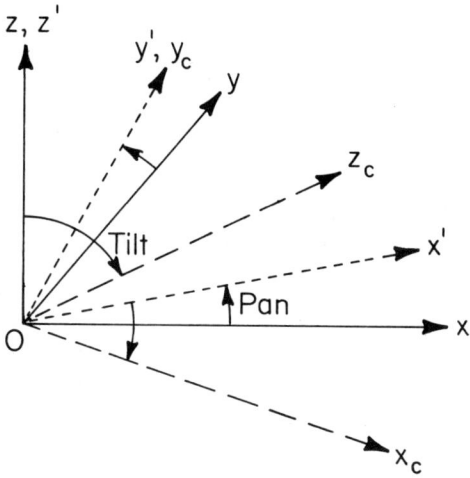

Figure 3-7: An example to illustrate pan and tilt angles

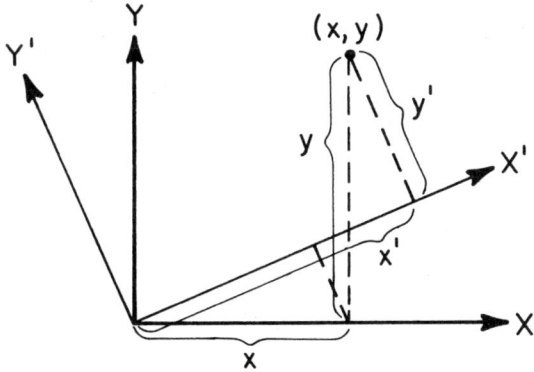

Figure 3-8: Rotation of coordinates about the z axis

$$x' = x \cos \theta + y \sin \theta \qquad (3\text{-}20)$$
$$y' = -x \sin \theta + y \cos \theta \qquad (3\text{-}21)$$
$$z' = z \qquad (3\text{-}22)$$

The above transformation can be represented as the following matrix (for non-homogeneous coordinates):

$$\begin{bmatrix} \cos\theta & \sin\theta & 0 \\ -\sin\theta & \cos\theta & 0 \\ 0 & 0 & 1 \end{bmatrix} \quad (3\text{-}23)$$

Similarly, rotation by angles ϕ and ψ about the x and y axes (in the directions of y to z, and z to x) are given by the following two matrices, respectively:

$$\begin{bmatrix} 1 & 0 & 0 \\ 0 & \cos\phi & \sin\phi \\ 0 & -\sin\phi & \cos\phi \end{bmatrix} \quad (3\text{-}24)$$

and

$$\begin{bmatrix} \cos\psi & 0 & -\sin\psi \\ 0 & 1 & 0 \\ \sin\psi & 0 & \cos\psi \end{bmatrix} \quad (3\text{-}25)$$

Transformation about more than one axis is obtained by a multiplication of the above matrices. The general form of this matrix for homogeneous coordinates is

$$R = \begin{bmatrix} & & & 0 \\ & [R'] & & 0 \\ & & & 0 \\ 0 & 0 & 0 & 1 \end{bmatrix} \quad (3\text{-}26)$$

where $[R']$ is a 3-by-3 matrix, corresponding to rotational transformation in nonhomogeneous coordinates.

Translation. Translation of axes by (x_0, y_0, z_0) is represented by the matrix **T** where

SIMPLE POLYHEDRAL SCENES

$$\mathbf{T} = \begin{bmatrix} 1 & 0 & 0 & -x_0 \\ 0 & 1 & 0 & -y_0 \\ 0 & 0 & 1 & -z_0 \\ 0 & 0 & 0 & 1 \end{bmatrix} \qquad (3\text{-}27)$$

Scaling. Scaling of the model by amount $|s|$ is given by the matrix **S**, where

$$\mathbf{S} = \begin{bmatrix} 1 & 0 & 0 & 0 \\ 0 & 1 & 0 & 0 \\ 0 & 0 & 1 & 0 \\ 0 & 0 & 0 & \frac{1}{s} \end{bmatrix} \qquad (3\text{-}28)$$

Note that different scalings along the three axes may be represented by nonunit terms in the diagonal of matrix **S**.

Any composite transformation of the object to a picture is now represented by a product of the matrices of different transformations. Owing to use of the homogeneous coordinates, it is possible to include the transformations subsequent to the picture formation, such as scaling and rotation in a printing process, into a single matrix transformation. Such a transformation is often called a *camera model*.

3.3 FITTING OF MODELS

We seek to choose a model, m, such that the predicted image of the model under some transformation $\mathbf{T}_m$ is most similar to the observed image. $\mathbf{T}_m$ is chosen to minimize the error E_m between a set of picture points V_p, and the predicted image points V'_p from a set of model points V_m as defined in Section 3.1.2 earlier [see Eq. (3-3)]. Fortunately, this optimal transformation $\mathbf{T}_m$ can be determined analytically.

Let a model point, v_{im}, be represented in homogeneous coordinates by a column vector $(x_{im}, y_{im}, z_{im}, w_{im})'$ and an image point v_{ip} by a vector $(x_{ip}, y_{ip}, w_{ip})'$. Note that the two vectors use different coordinate systems, the model points are given in a world coordinate system, chosen for convenience of measuring model coordinates, and the image points are given in a coordinate system with the x and y axes in the image plane. Let $\mathbf{V}_m$ be a 4-by-n matrix whose n columns are the coordinates of the n model points in the set V_m, and let V_p be a similar 3-by-n matrix corresponding to the picture points in the set V_p. Let matrix H(3-by-4) represent the transformation of model points to picture points. If error E_m could be reduced to zero, we would have

$$HV_m = V_p D \qquad (3\text{-}29)$$

where D is a diagonal, n-by-3 matrix. (This matrix is necessary because the scaling of each point in the homogeneous coordinates may be different.) Note that we have twelve unknowns in the H matrix and n unknowns in the D matrix, one for each point. At least six points are necessary for a nondegenerate solution of Eq. (3-29). Without proof, we present the optimal solution. (This solution ignores the interdependence of the elements of matrix H and is also known as the *pseudo-inverse* solution). Let

$$Q = V_p^T V_p \qquad (3\text{-}30)$$

$$A = V_m^T (V_m V_m^T)^{-1} V_m - I \qquad (3\text{-}31)$$

where I is an identity matrix. Define a matrix S such that $s_{ij} = a_{ij} q_{ji}$. Then D is determined by the solution of the linear equation given by

$$SD = 0 \qquad (3\text{-}32)$$

and

$$H = V_p D V_m^T (V_m V_m^T)^{-1} \qquad (3\text{-}33)$$

After the transformation T_m has been determined, the images of the non-matched model vertices are predicted. These vertices should be nonvisible, and their images should not fall outside the object outline, else the model is an unacceptable match.

The match computed by Eq. (3-32) will be ambiguous with respect to the scale factor. A larger model farther away from the camera produces the same image (ignoring absolute brightness levels). If the distance to the object is known, the size can be computed and vice versa. In simple situations, the distance may be computed by assuming that an object rests on a known plane or on another object. More complex depth-measurement schemes are described in Chapter 9.

The illusions of Figs. 1-6(a) and (b) can now be explained, if we assume that the human system tries to interpret line drawings as representing three-dimensional scenes when possible. In Fig. 1-6(a), the two converging lines may be interpreted as two parallel lines in 3-D viewed with a perspective projection. Then the two horizontal bars must be at different distances from the viewer, and since their lengths in the image are the same, the top bar must be longer in 3-D. In Fig. 1-6(b), the left figure may be interpreted as representing an inside corner of a room, and the right figure as the outside corner. Again, differences in the interpreted distance explain the difference in observed lengths. Note that 3-D interpretation provides only one explanation of these illusions; other explanations can be found in the psychology literature.

3.3.1 Camera Calibration

The transform relating the coordinates of the objects in a certain world coordinate system to the image coordinates, such as the one represented by the matrix **H** above, is also known as the *camera model* or the *camera transform*. For many applications, the camera is fixed relative to a world coordinate frame, and it is useful to measure or calibrate the parameters of the camera transform. The parameters relating the image and the world coordinate systems such as pan, tilt, and swing may be difficult to measure directly. An alternative is to observe a known 3-D object in a known position and orientation and measure points in the image corresponding to known points on the object. The transform can then be computed as in Eq. (3-33) above.

However, this solution may be inaccurate, as the twelve elements of **H** are assumed to be independent. In fact, the matrix **H** is completely determined by the three angles, pan, tilt and swing, and the location of the lens center (three coordinates), assuming that the focal length and the scaling of the image are known. More accurate estimates of **H** can be obtained by using standard, though computationally expensive, nonlinear optimization techniques for minimizing E_m defined in Eq. (3-28). Also, if nonlinear techniques are used, three points are sufficient for determining the parameters of **H** rather than the six needed for the linear solution of Eq. (3-33). Another important consideration is to ignore the effects of isolated points that are in gross error and can have a large effect if the least-mean-square criterion is used. Some non-linear calibration techniques may be found in [4-6].

For some applications, the camera is mounted such that its position may be changed—for example, along a horizontal plane with the camera looking down—or the camera orientation (pan, tilt, or swing) changed to observe different parts of the scene or track an object. In such cases, it is convenient to parameterize the camera transform by the measurable camera position and orientation parameter. One such technique is described in [4].

3.4 SUMMARY

Analysis of simple scenes of polyhedra with limited occlusion was described in this chapter. These techniques are strongly limited by requiring a priori models of the specific objects that may be present in the scene. In the next chapter we discuss the analysis of occluding scenes without the knowledge of such models.

REFERENCES

[1] L. G. Roberts, "Machine Perception of Three-Dimensional Solids," in *Optical and Electro-Optical Information Processing*, J. T. Tippett et al. (eds.), MIT Press, Cambridge, Mass., 1968, pp. 159-197.
[2] F. Attneave, "Some Informational Aspects of Visual Perception," *Psychology Review*, Vol. 61, 1954, pp. 183-193.
[3] E. Freuder, "Structural Isomorphism of Picture Graphs," in *Pattern Recognition & Artificial Intelligence*, C. H. Chen (ed.), Academic Press, New York, 1976, pp. 248-256.
[4] I. Sobel, "On Calibrating Computer Controlled Cameras for Perceiving 3-D Scenes," *Artificial Intelligence*, Vol. 5, No. 2, 1974.
[5] D. B. Gennery, "Modelling the Environment of an Exploring Vehicle by Means of Stereo Vision," Stanford Artificial Intelligence Laboratory Memo AIM-339 (Ph.D. thesis), June 1980.
[6] M. A. Fischler and R. C. Bolles, "Random Samples Consensus: A Paradigm for Model Filtering with Applications to Image Analysis and Automated Cartography," *Communications of the ACM*, Vol. 24, No. 6, June 1981, pp. 381-396.

4

COMPLEX SCENES OF POLYHEDRA

The scene analysis techniques of the last chapter, though general in principle, are likely to be computationally inefficient as the scenes get more complex. As the number of models grows and large parts of objects are occluded by others, recognition by matching with specific models becomes increasingly more difficult and expensive. A major simplification occurs if the lines, vertices, and faces belonging to different objects can be separated. Such *segmentation* is the major subject of this chapter. After parts of complete objects have been segmented, complex objects or structures can be described by relationships of these parts. Structural descriptions are covered in the later parts of this chapter.

4.1 SEGMENTATION OF POLYHEDRAL SCENES

Consider the picture shown in Fig. 4-1 (the polygonal regions have been numbered for convenience). Most human observers would agree that it consists of one rectangular block occluding another. Here, we will be interested in techniques for separating the two objects, without the knowledge of specific objects in the scene (they are only constrained to be polyhedral). A simple technique that establishes relationships between regions surrounding a vertex to accomplish segmentation was devised by Guzman in 1968 [1, 2].

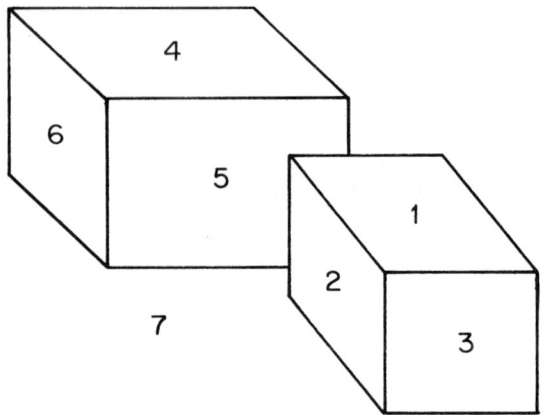

Figure 4-1: A simple scene

Guzman enumerated classes of vertices shown in Fig. 4-2. The type of a vertex is determined by the angular relationships between the lines forming the vertex. Each vertex provides evidence of whether regions surrounding it belong to the same body, as indicated by *links* between regions shown in Fig. 4-2. An absence of a link between two regions (as for a *T*-vertex) indicates that no connections between surrounding regions can be inferred.

Figure 4-3 shows a graph constructed from Fig. 4-1, by representing each region as a node and placing an arc between two nodes as indicated by Fig. 4-2 and examining each vertex. All links to the background (region 7), which is assumed to be known, are ignored. This graph separates into two groups such that the nodes in each group are linked to other nodes in that group by at least two links. One group consists of nodes 1, 2, and 3, and the other of 4, 5, and 6. These two separate groups correspond to the two desired distinct bodies.

Guzman's technique has been successfully applied to fairly complex scenes, such as the one shown in Fig. 4-4. The basic method is to construct a graph as above and group the nodes such that a node in each group is connected to at least one other node in that group by two or more links. In complex scenes this may result in some isolated groups but also some groups connected to others by a single link. The latter groups are merged if additional evidence of connection by a *weak* link is available. A weak link is formed between two faces of an arrow vertex, in addition to a strong link, if this vertex is also a *leg* vertex. A leg vertex is an arrow vertex in which one of the sides bends to become parallel to the stem or the center line of the arrow; three examples are shown in Fig. 4-5. A group consisting of a single region and connected to another group is merged into the latter.

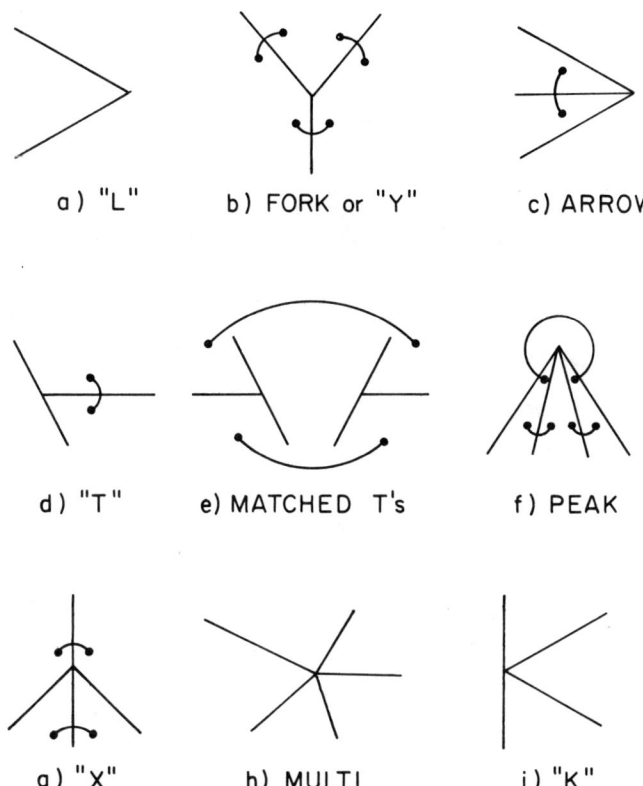

Figure 4-2: Vertex types and links

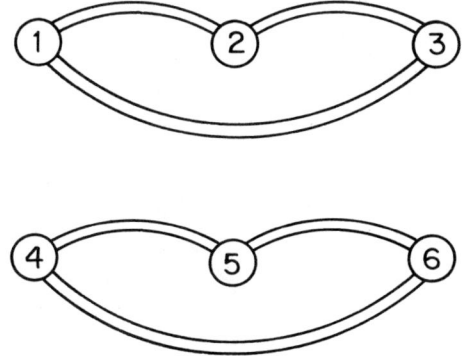

Figure 4-3: Region connectivity graph for scene of Fig. 4-1

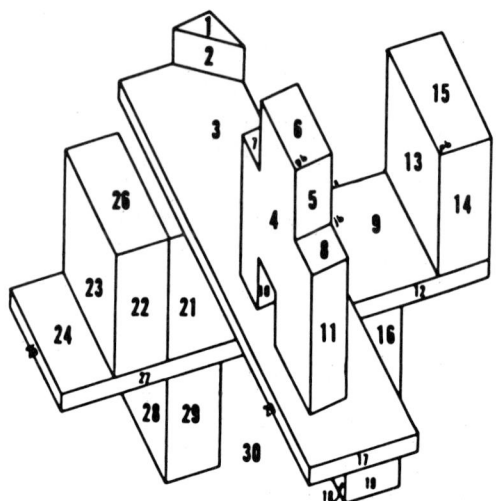

Figure 4-4: A "bridge" (from Guzman [2])

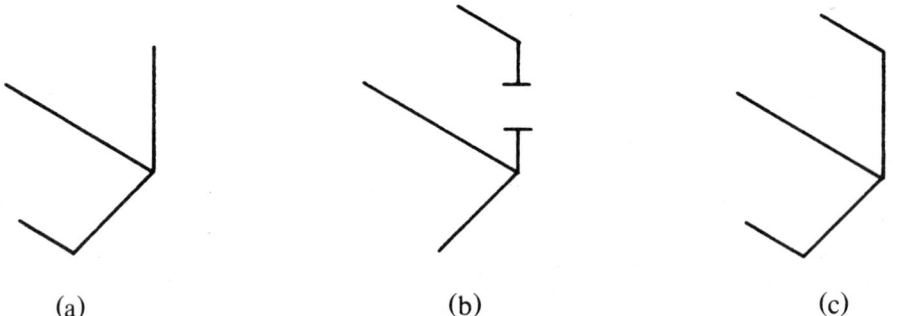

Figure 4-5: Three leg vertices

This simple strategy is sufficient to segment the scene in Fig. 4-4 satisfactorily and is a powerful demonstration of how global object characteristics can be inferred from rather local vertex characteristics. This technique is, however, ad hoc—hence its performance is difficult to predict and characterize. It is sensitive to certain accidental alignments and performs poorly on objects with holes. Note that perfect line drawings as input and complete absence of shadows are assumed. The reader may be interested in devising useful linking rules for more general scenes, such as the one shown in Fig. 4-6. An extension of Guzman's techniques for imperfect line drawings is given in [3].

Figure 4-6: Occluding curved objects

A formal study of polyhedral objects is presented next that justifies many of the heuristic rules used in Guzman's technique.

4.2 CLASSIFICATION OF LINES

Figure 4-7 shows three line drawings that seem to represent "impossible objects" in the sense that they cannot be the image of any solid polyhedral object, yet they are constructed of seemingly permissible and ordinary line and vertex structures. Actually, the object of Fig. 4-7(b) is possible, the other two are not. Huffman and Clowes, independently, studied the problem of describing lines and vertices such that whether a line drawing represents a solid object may be determined algorithmically [4-5]. Their classification scheme also provides a method for scene segmentation.

In this analysis, it is assumed that the objects are solid, and are viewed from a *general* position, defined to be one where a small change in viewing angle does not cause lines and vertices to appear or disappear—that is, there are no accidental alignments. Under these conditions, a line in a picture corresponds to an edge in an object formed by an intersection of two faces. This edge must be one of the

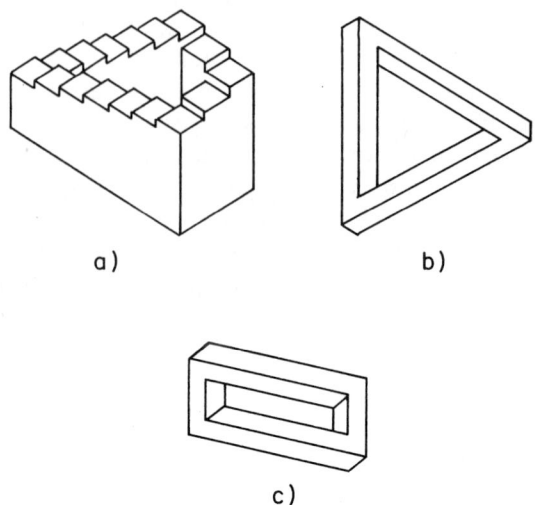

Figure 4-7: Three impossible-looking "objects"

following four types: a *convex* edge where the two faces recede away from the edge from the viewer's vantage point, a *concave* edge where the faces are toward the viewer, an *obscuring* edge where only one face is visible and the visible face is to the right of the edge and, finally, an *obscuring* edge where the visible face is to the left of the edge. Figure 4-8 shows an object with its edges labeled, where a "+" represents a convex edge, "−" a concave edge, and arrows the obscuring edges with the visible face to the right of the directed line.

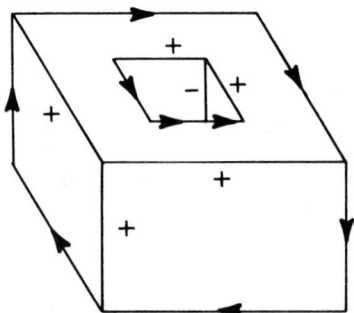

Figure 4-8: An object with labeled edges

Now, consider the vertices formed by the intersection of the faces of a polyhedron. Let the objects be restricted to be trihedral; that is, each vertex is formed by intersection of exactly three faces. If objects

COMPLEX SCENES OF POLYHEDRA   47

are viewed from a general position, defined to be such that the vertex and the line formations do not change with small changes in the viewing angle, then only arrow, fork, L, and T types of vertices can occur.

The major observation of the Huffman-Clowes discovery is that the lines at different vertices are not allowed to have all combinatorially possible labels, but are constrained to be one of the configurations shown in Fig. 4-9. These configurations can be derived by considering the three planes forming a vertex to divide space into octants. Now the solid object may fill one or more of these octants. However, strictly speaking, the objects filling an even number of octants do not form trihedral vertices. Typical object vertices with 1, 3, 5, and 7 octants filled are shown in Fig. 4-10. The possible visible vertex configurations are derived by viewing the four different types of vertices from all eight octants (each view does not necessarily give a distinct configuration).

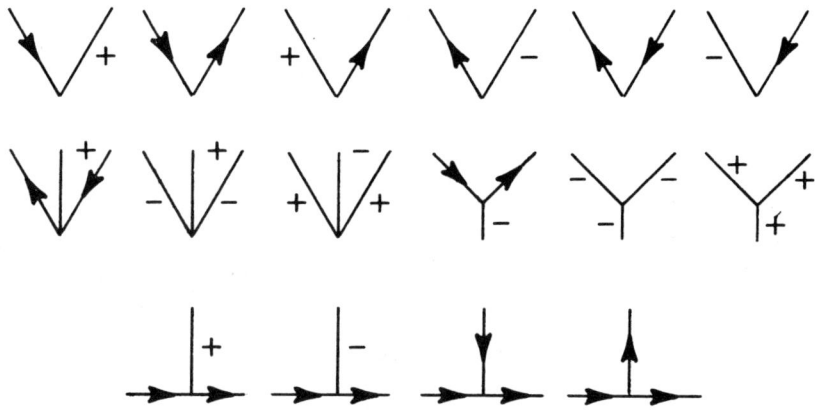

Figure 4-9: Allowed junction labels

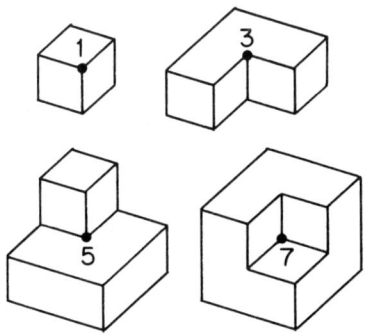

Figure 4-10: Four types of vertices with numbers indicating the number of filled octants (after Huffman [4])

A necessary condition for a line drawing to represent a possible object then is that its lines be labeled so that the vertices are labelled as in Fig. 4-9. It is clear that the label of a line cannot change between vertices. For some objects, multiple labelings are possible; such objects are ambiguous. The labeling for the object shown in Fig. 4-8 is consistent and hence it may be possible. However, no consistent labelings can be found for the line drawing in Fig. 4-11 and it cannot represent a possible solid object (to prove this, note that the lines on the outer boundary must be labeled as obscuring edges). These consistent labeling requirements are, however, only the *necessary* and not *sufficient* conditions. (The sufficient conditions are described in Section 4.3.)

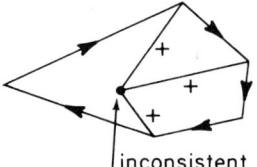

Figure 4-11: An object with no consistent labels

For a scene consisting of multiple objects, the line labels provide a straightforward segmentation; all regions connected by a line having a "+" or a "−" labeling must belong to the same body (for example, try to label Fig. 4-1). It is interesting to see that this theory supports the heuristic rules in Guzman's segmentation scheme. The center line of the arrow vertices in Fig. 4-9 has the label of "+" or "−" only. This implies that the two surrounding regions actually intersect and must belong to the same body. Similarly, two of the three fork configurations support Guzman's linking rules, but the existence of a third configuration is a possible source of errors (in Guzman's experiments, arrows were found to be more reliable than forks). The requirement of two links in Guzman's programs is also justified, as a line cannot change its label between vertices and must produce a similar linking evidence on both ends.

4.2.1 Inclusion of Shadows

Waltz [6,7] extended the types of line labels by including *crack* and *shadow* edges, as shown in Fig. 4-12. The crack edges are marked by a *C* along them and shadow edges by an arrow across them, with the dark region toward the arrowhead. Waltz also differentiated between subclasses of some types of lines. For example, a concave edge may be formed by two faces belonging to the same body or to two different bodies. The latter case is further distinguished by whichever of the two

COMPLEX SCENES OF POLYHEDRA

objects, if any, supports the other. Further distinctions are added by including illumination information for the regions on two sides of a label. A region is either illuminated, or in the shadow of another object or another face of the same body. With such distinctions, 59 separate line labels were enumerated.

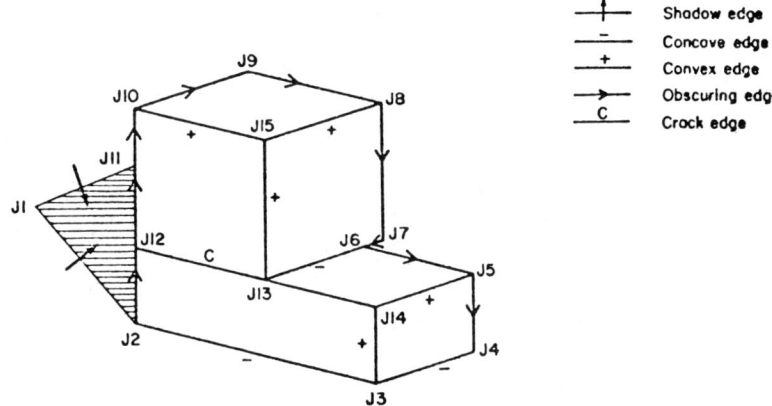

Figure 4-12: An object with cracks and shadows (from Waltz [7])

Again, not all combinationally possible sets of line labels at a vertex are physically possible. As a simple example, a shadow edge cannot occur at a type 1 vertex (the object occupying one octant). Waltz enumerated several thousand physically possible configurations for different types of vertices, including some caused by accidental alignments (such as K and multi). This number is a very small fraction of the combinationally possible labelings, which number in the tens of millions.

With this expanded set, certain types of vertices may have labels numbering in the hundreds, and finding a consistent set of labels for a complex line drawing might seem to be a computationally hopeless task. However, surprisingly, a simple algorithm described below has been found to converge remarkably rapidly.

Consider three vertices A, B, and C as shown in Fig. 4-13, which are part of a larger line drawing. Three sets S_A, S_B, and S_C of possible line configurations may be initially assigned to the three respective vertices. However, the line AB, must have the same label at the vertices A and B and hence those labels in S_A and S_B which do not assign a common label to the line in between them may be deleted from further consideration. The same procedure is now applied to the line BC and sets S_B and S_C. If any labels are deleted from the set S_B in this process, then more labels from S_A may now become ineligible. This process propagates to all connected vertices, considering one pair of

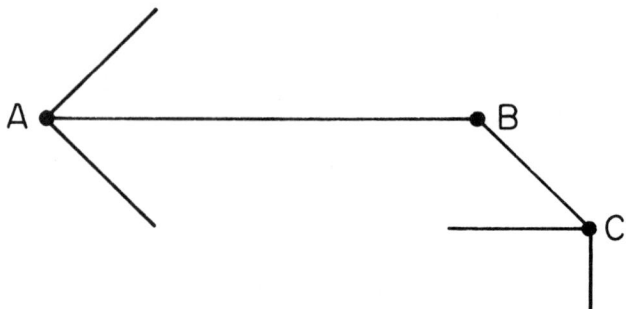

Figure 4-13: Part of a line drawing showing three vertices

vertices at a time.

In the example of Fig. 4-13, three labels can be assigned to each of the vertices A and C, and six labels to the vertex B without considering consistency with their neighbors. However, the labels of vertex A eliminate the possibility of line AB being occluding, and only two labels at vertex B can be retained, one with line AB being marked "+" with an arrow pointing from C to B, the other with line AB being "−" and an arrow pointing from B to C. However, only the latter is consistent with allowed labels of C. This comparison results in a unique label for both vertices B and C. This in turn also forces a unique label on vertex A, requiring AB to be "−".

It was found that the above simple algorithm applied iteratively to all vertices in a line drawing converged very fast, the number of possible labels decreased rapidly, and a unique labeling for lines was obtained in non-ambiguous figures. Thus, pairwise consistency of vertices results in global scene consistency. This agrees with our intuitive notion that a vertex does not affect the scene content very far away from it. Waltz's algorithm was successful in correctly labeling scenes of the complexity shown in Fig. 4-14. This labeling algorithm is also called *relaxation labeling*.

Labeling constraints for nonsolid objects such as wire frame objects, and objects with walls that are arbitrarily thin, have also been derived [8-10]. However, all such analysis assumes that the given line drawings are perfect and contain no missing or extra lines. Such line drawings are extremely difficult, if not impossible, to obtain even from pictures of carefully prepared, simple, homogeneous-surfaced objects. The practical utility of these procedures, even for polyhedral objects, has thus been limited. A very different technique for imperfect line drawings, using properties of a group of lines and vertices of specific objects known to be present in the scene, is described in [11].

COMPLEX SCENES OF POLYHEDRA

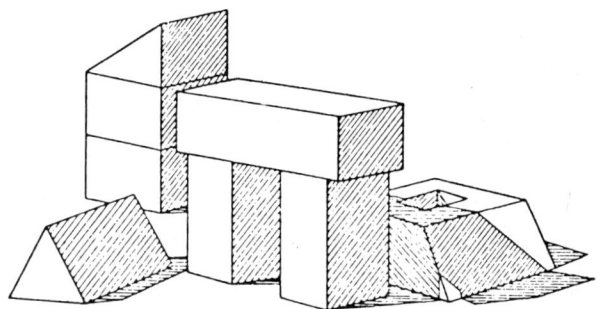

Figure 4-14: A complex scene (from Waltz [7])

4.3 GEOMETRICAL CONSTRAINTS FOR POSSIBLE OBJECTS

The Huffman-Clowes labels provide a way of verifying if a given line drawing is physically realizable. However, they provide only a necessary condition. The line drawing in Fig. 4-15 can be labeled consistently but is still not realizable as a trihedral object, as the three lines *AB*, *CD*, and *EF* do not meet in a point. We need to place some geometrical constraint on the line drawings, in addition to the syntactic constraints. The use of *dual graphs* for this purpose was suggested by Huffman [4] and further developed by Mackworth [12].

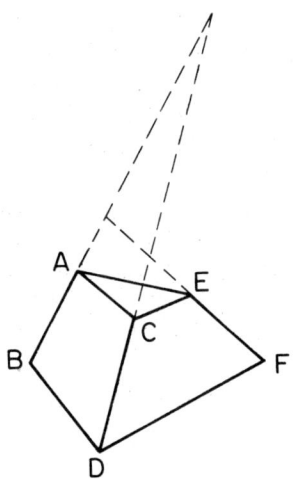

Figure 4-15: An "impossible" pyramid

4.3.1 Gradient Spaces and Dual Graphs

A convenient representation of the orientations of the surfaces of an object is needed for expressing the necessary constraints for these surfaces to belong to a possible object. The orientation of a plane defined by the equation

$$ax + by + cz + d = 0 \qquad (4\text{-}1)$$

is given by the direction numbers (a, b, c) of its normal. However, a more useful representation can be derived by rewriting Eq. (4-1) as

$$-z = \left(\frac{a}{c}\right)x + \left(\frac{b}{c}\right)y + \frac{d}{c} \qquad (4\text{-}2)$$

assuming c is not 0. Now let G_x and G_y be defined as below:

$$G_x = \frac{\partial z}{\partial x} = -\frac{a}{c} \qquad (4\text{-}3)$$

and

$$G_y = \frac{\partial z}{\partial y} = -\frac{b}{c} \qquad (4\text{-}4)$$

G_x and G_y are the gradients of the z components of the points in the plane in the x and y directions, respectively. (G_x, G_y) may be viewed as a two-dimensional *gradient space*; the orientation of each plane in the (x, y, z) space is uniquely represented by a point in the gradient space (except when c is 0). A point at the origin of the gradient space represents a plane parallel to the (x, y) plane and a point on one of the axes of the gradient space represents a tilt of this plane along the x or the y axes.

Most of the useful properties of the gradient space derive from a dual relation between the (x, y, z) space and a dual (u, v, w) space. These relationships are described as background in the next two paragraphs, and they may be skipped without loss of continuity.

A dual of the plane given by Eq. (4-1) in the (u, v, w) space is defined to be the point (a, b, c). The dual of a point (d, e, f) in the (x, y, z) space is defined to be the plane $du + ev + fw + 1 = 0$ in the (u, v, w) space. A straight line in the (x, y, z) space can be viewed as the intersection of a number of planes containing this line. The dual of this line in the (u, v, w) space is another straight line, passing through the points that are the duals of the planes determining the straight line in the (x, y, z) space.

A picture of a solid object is a projection from three-dimensional space onto a picture plane. In the following we restrict the projection to be orthographic. (Orthographic projection is equivalent to a perspective projection with the viewing point at an infinite distance. For object sizes much smaller than the viewing distances, the two projections are very similar.) An interesting correspondence exists between the picture and the projection of the dual space onto a specially chosen plane called the gradient plane, or the gradient space. We state, without proof, these relations between the lines and points in a picture with their dual representations in the gradient space.

A plane (polygon) in the picture plane corresponds to a point in the gradient space (G_X, G_Y). The location of this point in gradient space is determined by the gradient of the plane in the three-dimensional space along the X and Y axes, respectively, the picture projection being along the Z axis. A line in the picture plane corresponds to a line in the gradient space such that the two lines are perpendicular to each other (assuming that the axes of the two spaces are aligned).

An example of a vertex with three lines and three faces surrounding it is shown in Fig. 4-16(a), and its dual is shown in Fig. 4-16(b). The dual of the plane A is an arbitrarily chosen point A'. B', dual of B, must line on a line $A'B'$ normal to line 1. For line 1 to be convex, $A'B'$ must be in the same orientation along line 1' as A and B are across line 1—that is, left to right in this example (conversely for a concave edge). Length of line $A'B'$ determines the precise relative orientations of the planes A and B and cannot be determined from the line drawing. However, once A' and B' have been chosen, C', the dual of the plane C, is uniquely determined as it must lie on line 2' through B normal to 2 and line 3' through A normal to line 3. Note that for a consistent dual to exist, all three edges must be either all convex or all concave; the convex case being shown in Fig. 4-16 (the size of the triangle $A'B'C'$ can, under certain conditions, be determined by using the intensity values of the three faces. See Section 9.3 and [13] for more details.)

The geometrical condition for an object to be physically realizable is simple—it should be possible to construct a consistent dual for the object in the picture. This is both a necessary and a sufficient condition. For example, consider the object in Fig. 4-17(a). It appears, to us, to be a tetrahedron with two obscured faces. For simplicity, we will construct a dual in the gradient space assuming that the background plane, A, is also one of the hidden surfaces.

Duals of the planes A, B, and C are given by A', B', and C', forming a triangle as in Fig. 4-16. The position and the size of the triangle can not be fixed. Also, we are assuming that edges 1 and 4 are

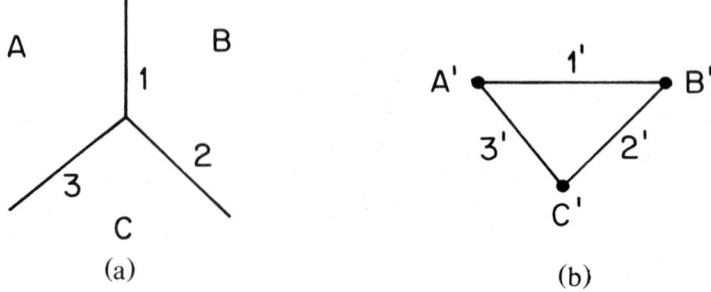

Figure 4-16: Three planes at a vertex and their dual graph

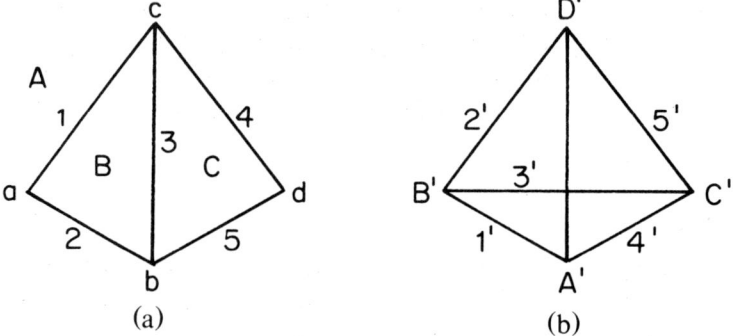

Figure 4-17: An object and its dual graph

concave and 3 is convex (one of the few possible and consistent interpretations). This interpretation implies that edges 2 and 5 must be occluding. It is interesting to determine if the occluded planes for these two edges could be the same! For this, the dual of the hidden plane, say D, must lie at the intersection of line $B'D'$ normal to line 2 and line $C'D'$ normal to line 5. Additionally, line $A'D'$ must be normal to line ad, as the plane D must also intersect the plane A along line ad, as is the case for this example. (A dual for the interpretation where A is a background plane and another plane E is another hidden surface of the tetrahedron is easily constructed replacing A' with E' in Fig. 4-17 and a new A' as an isolated point.)

This ability to impose constraints on invisible surfaces is quite remarkable. Mackworth has implemented a computer program to hypothesize the hidden surfaces, where possible by using reasoning such as given above [12]. The reader may find it instructive to verify that a consistent dual can not be constructed for the pyramid of Fig. 4-15 by assuming just one hidden plane intersecting line AE (but can be by using two hidden planes in the back).

4.4 DESCRIPTIONS OF OBJECT ASSEMBLIES

A *description* of a given scene is a major objective of the machine-perception process. A description of a scene should include the number and the type of objects in it and their relationships to each other. As an example, the scene of Fig. 4-18 may be described as consisting of three rectangular parallelepiped blocks (bricks), with the block *A* supported by the blocks *B* and *C*, and with the block *B* to the left of block *C*. Each block may in turn be described in terms of its components, such as its faces.

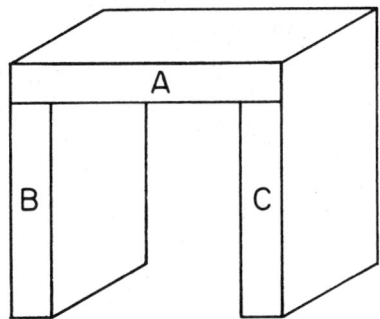

Figure 4-18: An arch

Such descriptions can be conveniently represented as a graph structure, with the objects (or components) being nodes of the graph and relationships between them being arcs of the graph. The graph representation of the above description of the scene in Fig. 4-18 is shown in Fig. 4-19. Such descriptions are useful for recognition of object assemblies.

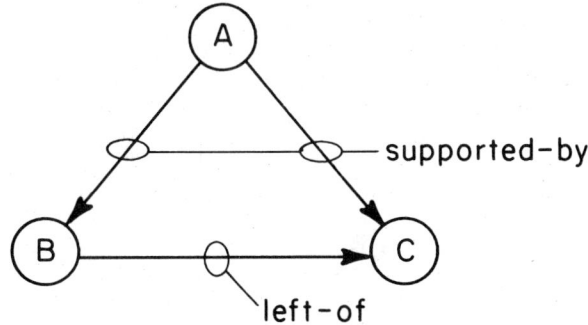

Figure 4-19: A simple graph description of the arch of Fig. 4-18

4.4.1 Computation of Descriptions

Computation of descriptions that require inference of relationships among objects is difficult. Relationships such as support are easy for us to infer, but difficult to give algorithms for. Techniques for inferring such relationships are not well developed and are, in general, heuristic in nature. A few such techniques were suggested by Winston [14, 15] and are discussed below. In the following, it is assumed that the individual objects of a scene have been separated by one of the previously described schemes.

Support. To infer that an object A is supported by another object B, object A must obscure some part of B. Also, assuming a normal viewing position, B will usually appear to be below A. Winston suggests that if the "bottom lines" of an obscuring object form an arrow vertex and share regions with the obscured object, then it may be inferred that the latter object supports the former (see Fig. 4-20). (This is easily extended to X or K vertices.) The bottom lines are those belonging to the lower vertices of the interior lines.

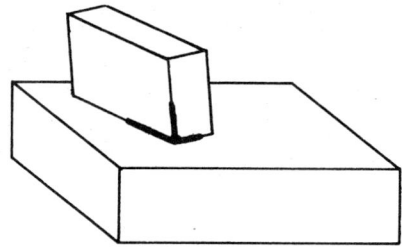

Figure 4-20: Evidence for support relation

Note that gravity and stability of objects have not been explicitly used, and the above algorithm is likely to lead to occasional errors. It is likely that these concepts play an important part in our inference of support relationships. However, they are difficult to compute from two-dimensional images.

Left and Right. Figure 4-21 shows various examples of two blocks in a scene. Some of the examples clearly depict a left-right relationship, while the others may appear to be front-behind relations. Based on these examples, we may define an object A to be to the left of A if the center of area of A is left of the leftmost point of B and the rightmost point of A is left of the rightmost point of B. The definition for A to be right of B is similar. (This definition is not necessarily symmetric; that is, A may be left of B, but B not right of A.) For ambiguous cases, such as in Fig. 4-21, it may be desirable to generate

COMPLEX SCENES OF POLYHEDRA

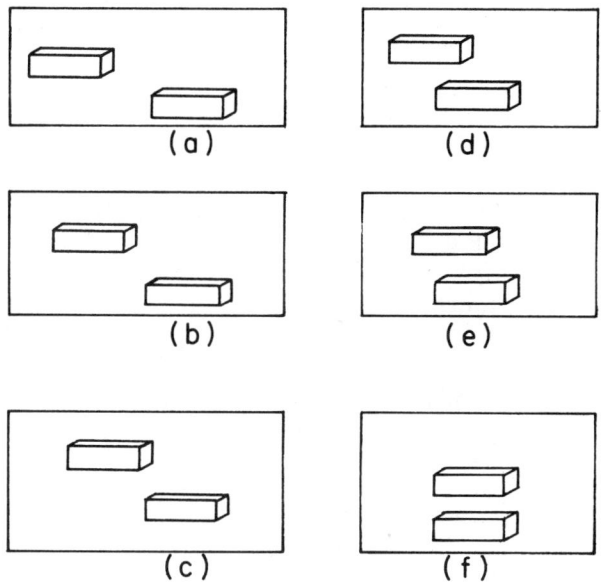

Figure 4-21: Left-right relations (after Winston [15])

more than one alternative description.

Groups of objects. A set of objects form a group if they are similar in some respects and share common relationships with others. In Fig. 4-22, blocks A, B, and C can be considered to belong to a group, as they are similar and are supported similarly. The latter relationship can be inferred from the chain of supported-by pointers. As another example, the four legs of a four-legged table may be considered to belong to a group. Here, the four legs must be similar, and they share the same relationship with the table top, namely that of supporting it.

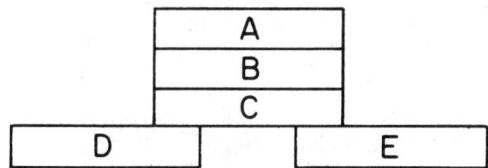

Figure 4-22: Example for a similarity relation

The relationships described above are only a subset of the relations used, by humans, and the description algorithms are far from being adequate. However, such descriptions are still useful for recognizing object assemblies. An interesting application to learning of structures was demonstrated by Winston and is described next.

4.4.2 Learning of Structural Descriptions

Suppose that a program is capable of generating the description shown in Fig. 4-19 from the scene of Fig. 4-18. If this program is next shown the scene in Fig. 4-23, it will generate a description similar to that of Fig. 4-19, with an additional link between nodes B and C indicating that they touch. A simple program that compared two graph descriptions would discover this similarity and difference (graph-matching techniques are discussed later in Chapter 5). If now the program is told that Fig. 4-23 is not acceptable as an arch, its concept of arch can be modified to contain the information that the supporting blocks B and C must not touch.

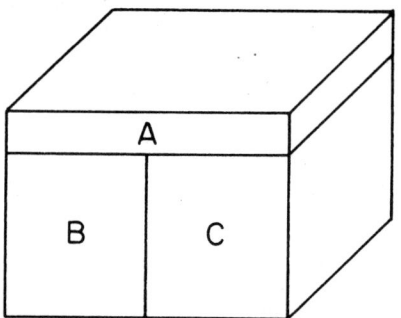

Figure 4-23: Almost an arch

The concept of an arch can be further elaborated by showing examples of other near-miss arch scenes—for example, the block A not being supported by the other two. On the contrary, if the top block is a pyramid and the structure is still called an arch, then the constraints on this object can be relaxed.

This type of concept learning should be distinguished from parameter learning in classical pattern recognition techniques, where only the weights of a decision function are modified. The learning described here results from a careful choice of near-miss sample sequences. It may be easier to teach a machine in this way than by reprogramming, but such learning is far from the usual notion of discovery with little or no help from a teacher.

4.5 SUMMARY

This chapter concludes our treatment of the analysis of scenes of polyhedra. In the analysis of the previous two chapters we assumed that the input to the programs was a perfect line drawing. Such line drawings are rarely available, and the techniques required for the analysis of imperfect or incomplete line drawings may need to be very different from those discussed previously. The described techniques are, thus, for the analysis of line drawings rather than for the analysis of polyhedral scenes. Also, the techniques are specific to polyhedra and may not extend to a more general class of objects.

Nonetheless, some useful lessons can be learned from the study of these techniques. The problem of three-dimensional scene analysis has proved to be much more difficult than anticipated and seems to require a deep understanding of the problem domain. It seems that general techniques that ignore the semantics of scenes are inadequate, even for simple scenes. The more knowledge one can incorporate in a program, the better is the performance (for example, Waltz's program can analyze more complex scenes than Guzman's). Finally, the description of scenes seems to require extensive knowledge of physical principles to adequately infer simple relations such as support and stability.

REFERENCES

[1] A. Guzman, "Computer Recognition of Three-Dimensional Objects in a Scene," MIT Report MAC-TR-59, December 1968.

[2] A. Guzman, "Decomposition of a Visual Scene into Three-Dimensional Bodies," *AFIPS Proceedings Fall Joint Comp. Conf.*, Vol. 33, 1968.

[3] G. Falk, "Interpretation of Imperfect Line Data as a Three Dimensional Scene," *Artificial Intelligence*, Vol. 3, Issue 2, 1972.

[4] D. A. Huffman, "Impossible Objects as Nonsense Sentences," in *Machine Intelligence 6*, B. Meltzer and D. Michie (eds)., Edinburgh University Press, Edinburgh, 1971.

[5] M. B. Clowes, "On Seeing Things," *Artificial Intelligence*, Vol. 2, Issue 1, 1971, pp. 79-116.

[6] D. L. Waltz, "Generating Semantic Descriptions from Drawings of Scenes with Shadows," MIT Report AI-TR-271, November 1972.

[7] D. L. Waltz, "Understanding Line Drawings of Scenes with Shadows," in *The Psychology of Computer Vision*, P. H. Winston (ed.), McGraw-Hill, New York, 1975, pp. 19-91.

[8] P. V. Sankar, "A Vertex Coding Scheme for Interpreting

Ambiguous Trihedral Solids," *Computer Graphics and Image Processing*, Vol. 6, 1977, pp. 61-89.

[9] T. Kanade, "A Theory of the Origami World," *Artificial Intelligence*, Vol. 13, 1980, pp. 279-311.

[10] K. Sugihara, "Picture Language for Skeletal Polyhedra," *Computer Graphics and Image Processing*, Vol. 8, 1978, pp. 382-405.

[11] G. R. Grape, "Model Based (Intermediate-level) Computer Vision," Stanford Artificial Intelligence Laboratory, Memo AIM-201, May 1973.

[12] A. K. Mackworth, "Interpreting Pictures of Polyhedral Scenes," *Artificial Intelligence*, Vol. 4, 1973, pp. 121-137.

[13] B. Horn, "Understanding Image Intensities," *Artificial Intelligence*, Vol. 8, 1977, pp. 201-231.

[14] P. H. Winston, "Learning Structural Descriptions from Examples," MIT Report MAC-TR-76, September 1970.

[15] P. H. Winston, "Learning Structural Descriptions from Examples," in *The Psychology of Computer Vision*, P. H. Winston (ed.), McGraw-Hill, New York, 1975, pp. 157-209.

5

SHAPE ANALYSIS
AND RECOGNITION

Scenes of interest rarely contain solely polyhedral objects. The motive in studying the problems of the blocks world was to better understand some aspects of the perceptual process. The main problems encountered were of the low-level processes to obtain object boundaries, segmentation of scenes containing multiple occluding objects, recognition of objects under the changes of scale, rotation, perspective, and varying amounts of occlusion, and descriptions of object assemblies. We now examine the generalization of these processes for nonpolyhedral objects, concentrating on the problems of shape analysis and recognition based on these descriptions.

Boundary-extraction techniques of polyhedral objects generalize to other objects, provided that the surfaces of objects are still homogeneous and shading of the surfaces due to curvature is not strong. These techniques must now be more local, as boundaries are not necessarily straight. If the objects or the background are textured, boundary extraction becomes a complex problem (for polyhedral objects as well). These low level processes will be discussed in detail in the succeeding chapters. For now, we assume that perfect boundaries, corresponding to discontinuities in the object surfaces or their slopes, are available.

Segmentation techniques for polyhedral objects were based on effective utilization of the knowledge of constraints placed on the images by the nature of the objects and the image-formation process.

Huffman-Clowes-Waltz techniques used generic knowledge common to trihedral objects, whereas Roberts' technique required knowledge of specific potential objects in a scene (the segmentation being performed simply by recognition). Huffman has generalized his line-labeling theories to apply to arbitrary polyhedral objects and also to objects of zero-Gaussian-curvature surfaces [1]. Chien and Chang have attempted to generate a catalog of vertex types for scenes of simple curved objects such as circular cylinders and cones [2]. However, no similar segmentation techniques have been developed for more general objects.

Scene segmentation is greatly simplified if three-dimensional positions of points on the *visible* surfaces of the objects are available. Such information, sometimes known as *two-and-a-half* dimensional data, can be obtained from multiple views of a scene, as in stereo vision, artificial range measuring devices, and to a certain extent from examination of the variations in surface brightness. These techniques are discussed in Chapter 9. Availability of such information is assumed in some of the techniques described in this chapter.

For most of the remainder of this chapter we assume that perfect object boundaries are available, and that the objects have been segmented or are to be segmented by recognition (that is, knowledge of specific objects is available). 3-D information of the visible surfaces will be assumed where indicated. In this chapter we will concentrate on descriptions of the shape properties of an object and their recognition, based solely on these shape descriptions. 2-D shape analysis is also included for completeness.

5.1 REPRESENTATION OF COMPLEX SHAPES

A good shape representation should allow recognition from partial views of an object, and small changes in object shape should cause only small changes in the shape description. Representation of articulation of parts of an object should be convenient, and the representation should allow a comparison of differences and similarities of two objects rather than just simple classification. The latter property is important if the machine must deal with new objects that are similar to previously seen objects. An encounter with a purple, five-legged "cow" should result in just such a description of differences and not simply an answer that this object is unknown.

The above requirements are largely satisfied if the complex objects are represented by segmentation into simpler parts and the interrelationships of these parts. As example, a human shape could be described to consist of various limbs such as head, arms, body and legs, and the manner in which they are connected to each other. Each limb may again be described in more detail in a similar fashion—for example, the arms consisting of an upperarm, forearm, and a hand, and the hand in turn being made of a palm and the fingers, and so on. It is sometimes useful to view such descriptions as comprising a graph structure with the parts being the nodes of the graph and relations between the parts being the arcs of this graph. The relations may be of part/whole and connectivity or the more complex relations such as similarities of some parts, for example, left and right arms, or similarities of groups of parts such as bilateral symmetry of a human shape. Such descriptions are also called *relational descriptions* or *structural descriptions*.

Recognition is by matching of two relational descriptions. Partial views of an object generate description graphs that are subgraphs of complete object descriptions and can be accommodated in the matching process. The variations of an object, such as extra parts or articulation of parts, are described naturally.

Such descriptions should be contrasted with representations based on properties of the complete surfaces, such as a Fourier series or moments expansion of a surface. Changes caused by partial views in such descriptions are not easily described, nor do they allow a useful comparison of similarities and differences between two objects. However, they are easily computed and are useful for applications where the above considerations are not important.

In the following, various representations, both segmented and otherwise, are discussed for line, area, and volume shapes.

5.2 LINE DESCRIPTIONS

Descriptions of curves are important for special objects such as the characters of an alphabet, and also for objects in three-dimensional scenes such as roads in an aerial photograph. Further, shape descriptions of three-dimensional objects are sometimes reduced to "skeleton" line structures, as described in Sections 5.3 and 5.4.

5.2.1 Storage of Lines

A line is most easily described by an ordered list of the coordinates of the successive points along it. A significant savings in storage can be obtained if only the coordinates of the starting point and incremental changes for the successive points are stored. A popular technique due to H. Freeman [3], known as chain coding, operates by assigning an integer code to each of the eight neighbors of a pixel as shown in Fig. 5-1. An arbitrary curve is described by a starting point and the code corresponding to each successive point on the curve. The chain code of the line shown in Fig. 5-2, for example, is 0, 1, 2, 2, 3, 2.

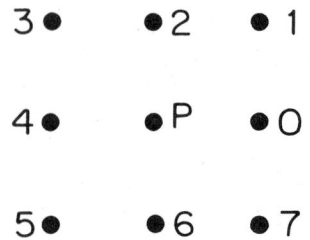

Figure 5-1: Chain codes of the eight neighbors of a pixel

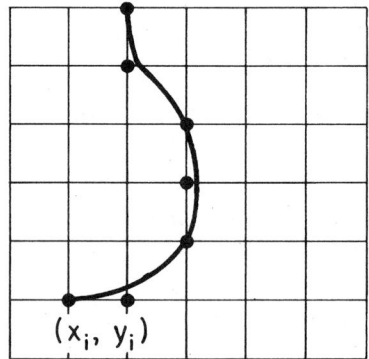

Figure 5-2: A chain-coded curve

Similarities of two curves with chain codes of $\mathbf{a} = (a_1, a_2, ... a_n)$ and $\mathbf{b} = (b_1, b_2, ..., b_n)$ can be defined by

$$C_{ab} = \frac{1}{n} \sum_{i=1}^{n} a_i \cdot b_i \qquad (5\text{-}1)$$

where $a_i \cdot b_i = \cos(\text{angle}(a_i) - \text{angle}(b_i))$, where angle (α) stands for the angle denoted by code α. This measure is useful only if the two curves are of the same scale, length, and orientation but may have different starting positions. Similarity of two curves of different length can be measured by "sliding" one curve with respect to another and choosing the maximum value of the above similarity measure—that is, picking the maximum value of $C_{ab}(j)$ for all values of j where

SHAPE ANALYSIS AND RECOGNITION

$$C_{ab}(j) = \frac{1}{k} \sum_{i=1}^{n} a_i \cdot b_{i+j} \qquad (5\text{-}2)$$

where k is the length of the smaller curve.

5.2.2 Line Approximations

Compact and structured descriptions of a curve are obtained by approximating it by expansion in an orthogonal series of functions or by piecewise segments of simpler curves. Approximation by piecewise linear segments is common, and splines, which are piecewise polynomials with continuity conditions defined at the junctions, are a generalization.

A very simple and effective technique for piecewise linear segment approximation is that of *iterative end-point fitting*, which operates by connecting the end points of a given curve by a straight line and searching for the point on the curve that is farthest from this line. If this distance is unacceptably large, the curve is segmented in two at the point of the maximum excursion and the process iterated for the two segments, as shown in Fig. 5-3. To apply this technique to closed curves, an initial segmentation into two parts, usually derived arbitrarily, is needed. Implementation of piecewise linear approximations is described in [4-7]. Details of spline approximations may be found in [8].

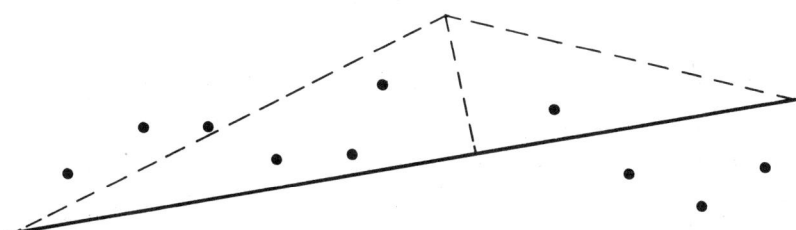

Figure 5-3: Iterative end-point fit

The above technique does not always produce segmentation points or corners that correspond to the human perception. For our perception, the most natural points of segmentation seem to be the points of maximum curvature. To be useful, computation of curvature in a digital curve requires differencing and averaging over a range. A comparative survey of corner-finding methods is given in [9].

Qualitative descriptions of a curve can be generated in terms of its segmentation, by using the number of corners and inflection points, and descriptions of the simpler segments such as being straight or circular.

5.2.3 Analytical Line Shape Measures

The coefficients associated with an analytical approximation of a curve can be used as shape features. Curves of different shape will have different coefficients. However, variations with scale, rotation, and occlusion may alter the coefficients in complex ways. Hence, such measures are useful only if the number of curves and the expected variations in them are small.

A plane curve is generally a multivalued function of two variables [for example, $f(x, y) = 0$]. Analytical approximation of a curve is simplified by transformation to a related single-valued function. One such transformation is a new function $\theta(s)$, defined to be the rotation of the tangent at a point on a curve with the arclength, s, in comparison to the tangent at the starting point, as shown in Fig. 5-4. (An arbitrary starting point may be chosen for a closed curve.) Note that $\theta(0) = 0$ and $\theta(L) = -2\pi$, for a closed curve, where L is the arclength of the curve. A modified function given by Zahn and Roskies [10] is defined as follows:

$$\theta'(t) = \theta\frac{Lt}{2\pi} + t \qquad (5\text{-}3)$$

where t is in range $[0, 2\pi]$ and related to s by $t = (2\pi/L)\, s$.

$\theta'(t)$ is invariant to translation, rotation, and scaling of the curve. Analytic shape measures can now be obtained by approximating this function; a common approach is to expand in a Fourier series and use the lower-order coefficients (for example, see [10]). Curvature of the curve, $K(s)$, provides an alternative transformation. However, this function is ill-behaved for curves with corners.

Another transformation for a closed curve is a function $\phi(s)$, defined to be the angle made by line joining a point on the curve with its centroid, where s is the arclength as before (see Fig. 5-5). This transformation is convenient to use only if the resulting $\phi(s)$ is single-valued.

A curve can also be represented parametrically by two equations of the form $x = f(t)$, $y = g(t)$ and the two functions approximated directly. Again arclength s is a suitable parameter.

SHAPE ANALYSIS AND RECOGNITION

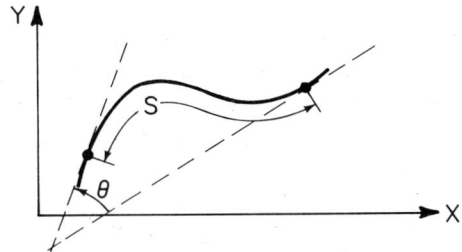

Figure 5-4: Arc length and rotation of the tangent of a curve

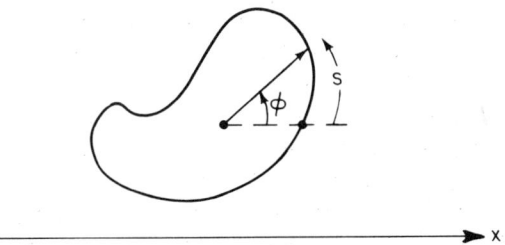

Figure 5-5: Polar transformation of a closed curve

5.3 AREA DESCRIPTIONS

The shape of a plane figure can, of course, be described by its enclosing boundary using the methods of the previous section. This section covers the techniques of describing a figure using the points in its interior and not just on the boundary. Such descriptions are likely to be more robust, as small changes in area can cause rather large changes in the boundary (imagine a jagged boundary rather than a smooth one).

5.3.1 Simple Shape Measures

Rough measures of the shape of a plane figure can be obtained simply from its area and perimeter. *Area/(perimeter)^2* is a measure invariant with the size, position, and orientation of a figure. This measure is maximum for a circle and becomes smaller for elongated shapes. However, this ratio is not necessarily different for two different shapes (the reader may try to construct examples). A better measure for elongation is the ratio of major to minor axes of the minimal bounding rectangle of a figure, defined to be a rectangle completely enclosing the figure but not itself enclosed in any other such rectangle (see Fig. 5-6).

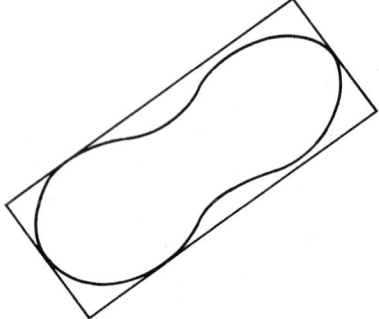

Figure 5-6: Minimum bounding rectangle

An improved approximation to the figure shape is by its *convex hull*, defined to be the minimal convex figure enclosing the given figure. The original figure is now described by the shape of the convex hull and by the number and the shapes of the concavities or the *concave deficiencies* in the figure (see Fig. 5-7). Qualitative shape measures can also be based on the topology of the figure and include the number of connected components and holes.

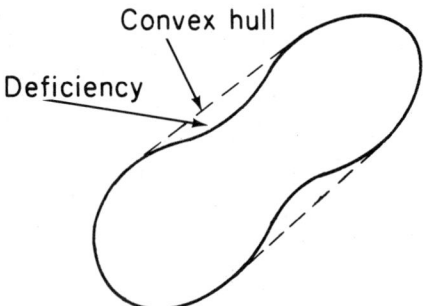

Figure 5-7: Convex hull of a figure

The simple shape measures described here can be expected to differentiate only among a small number of widely different shapes and do not account for the changes caused by perspective and occlusion, if the figure is a projection of a 3-D object.

5.3.2 Analytical Measures

As in the case of line descriptions, the coefficients obtained by expansion or approximation of a figure in terms of some basis functions, such as, 2-D Fourier series, may be used as analytical shape measures. For some basis functions, it is possible to combine the coefficients to obtain invariance to scale, position, and rotation (but not to perspective or occlusion changes). These methods have been extensively applied to recognition in limited domains, mainly character recognition of the English alphabet. Use of approximations by moments is considered in detail below.

The *pq*th order moment of given figure, R, is defined to be

$$m_{pq} = \sum_{x,y \in R} x^p y^q \qquad (5\text{-}4)$$

where (x, y) is a point in or on the boundary of R. The zero order moment, m_{00}, is simply the number of points in the figure (that is, the area) and m_{10} and m_{01} give the position of the centroid. The moments can be made invariant to position of the figure by translating the origin to the centroid and defining new coefficients as

$$\mu_{pq} = \sum\sum_{x,y \in R} (x - \bar{x})^p (y - \bar{y})^q \qquad (5\text{-}5)$$

where $\bar{x} = m_{10}/m_{00}$ and $\bar{y} = m_{01}/m_{00}$. Note that $\mu_{10} = \mu_{01} = 0$ and μ_{11}, μ_{02}, and μ_{20} are the usual moments of inertia.

Invariance to scale can be obtained by using

$$\mu'_{pq} = \frac{\mu_{pq}}{\mu_{00}^{((p+q)/2) + 1}} \qquad (5\text{-}6)$$

Invariance to rotation can be obtained by rotating the coordinate axes by an angle θ, where

$$\tan 2\theta = \frac{2\mu_{11}}{\mu_{20} - \mu_{02}} \qquad (5\text{-}7)$$

A set of functions of the second- and third-order moments, invariant to rotation and reflection, are given below (from [11]). (The last M_7 is invariant to reflection in magnitude only.)

$$M_1 = (\mu_{20} + \mu_{02})$$
$$M_2 = (\mu_{20} - \mu_{02})^2 + 4\mu^2_{11}$$
$$M_3 = (\mu_{30} - 3\mu_{12})^2 + (3\mu_{21} - \mu_{03})^2$$
$$M_4 = (\mu_{30} + \mu_{12})^2 + (\mu_{21} + \mu_{03})^2 \qquad (5\text{-}8)$$
$$M_5 = (\mu_{30} - 3\mu_{12})^2(\mu_{30} + \mu_{12}) \cdot [(\mu_{30} + \mu_{12})^2 - 3(\mu_{21} + \mu_{03})^2]$$
$$+ (3\mu_{21} - \mu_{03})(\mu_{21} + \mu_{03}) \cdot [3(\mu_{30} + \mu_{12})^2 - (\mu_{21} + \mu_{03})^2]$$
$$M_6 = (\mu_{20} - \mu_{02})[(\mu_{30} + \mu_{12})^2 - (\mu_{21} + \mu_{03})^2]$$
$$+ 4\mu_{11}(\mu_{30} + \mu_{12})(\mu_{21} + \mu_{03})$$
$$M_7 = (3\mu_{21} - \mu_{03})(\mu_{30} + \mu_{12}) \cdot [(\mu_{30} + \mu_{12})^2 - 3(\mu_{21} + \mu_{03})^2]$$
$$- (\mu_{30} - 3\mu_{12})(\mu_{21} + \mu_{03}) \cdot [3(\mu_{30} + \mu_{12})^2 - (\mu_{21} + \mu_{03})^2]$$

Dudani et al. used these moment functions for the recognition of different aircraft shapes [12]. The perspective changes were accommodated by storing the seven moment values for each separate view every few degrees apart.

5.3.3 A Medial Axis Transform

An intuitive description of area shape is by a curve in the "middle" of the figure and the varying width of the figure along this curve. Blum formalized this notion by defining a *medial axis transform* [13]. The transform is most easily explained by imagining the given figure to consist of flammable grass and a fire started at its perimeter. Those points in the interior at which two fire fronts meet and extinguish each other are the desired points of a medial axis (see Fig. 5-8). The time of fire extinction, for a given velocity, gives the "width" or the distance from the axis of the figure at that point. From such an axis and distance function, the original figure can be reconstructed accurately.

Two equivalent and precise definitions for the transform are as follows:

1. The points on the medial axis are the centers of the maximal circular neighborhoods totally contained in the figure—that is, those neighborhoods not entirely contained within any other circular neighborhood. The radii of the circles give the distance

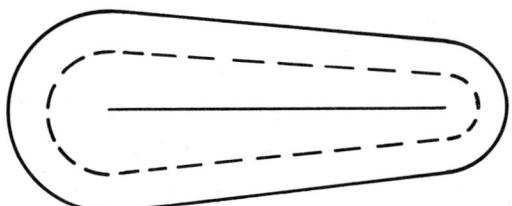

Figure 5-8: Medial axes by Blum transform

function. In Fig. 5-9, the points A and B are centers of such neighborhoods, but not the points C and D.

2. For each point x in the interior of the figure, let a quench function, q, be defined to be

$$q(x, \mathbf{B}) = \min(d(x, y)), y \text{ in } \mathbf{B}$$

where y is another point on the boundary $\mathbf{B}$, and d is the Euclidean distance between x and y. Each point x in the interior for which $q(x, \mathbf{B})$ is nonsingular (that is, two points on the boundary are at equal minimum distance from x) belongs to the medial axis, and the quench function is also the desired distance function.

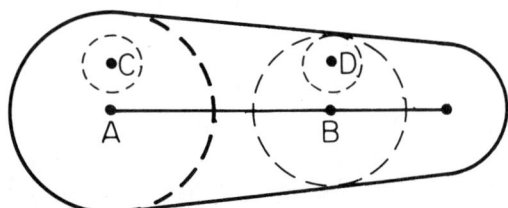

Figure 5-9: Maximal circular neighborhoods

Blum's medial axis transform gives intuitively agreeable descriptions for smooth objects but suffers from some deficiencies. The axes for a rectangle, for example, are as shown in Fig. 5-10, rather than a single line along the major axis. Even more serious is the effect of small changes in the boundary on the derived descriptions, as shown by the axes of a rectangle with a small notch in Fig. 5-11. These problems can be partially alleviated by removing those points along the axis where the speed of quenching is high—that is, the points with large values of

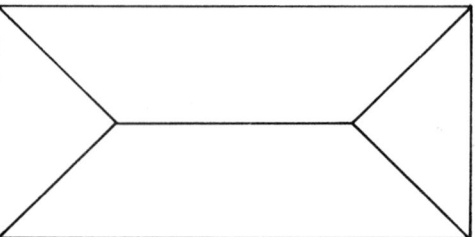

Figure 5-10: Medial axes of a rectangle

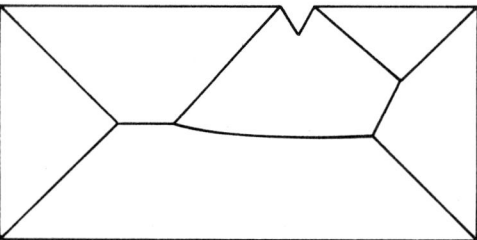

Figure 5-11: Medial axes of a rectangle with a notch
(after Agin [23])

$\Delta s/\Delta q$, where s is the distance along the axis. Computational algorithms for the Blum medial axis transform and its modifications may be found in [14-16]. Another medial-axis-like representation using *generalized cones* that avoids these problems, and which also applies to 3-D objects, is described in Section 5.4.

If the figure is subject to changes caused by occlusion and the representation is to meet the other requirements of Section 5.1, it should be described by segmentation into simpler shapes. One criterion is to segment into parts that are convex. Another technique of segmentation into simple generalized cones is described in the next section. Other descriptions based on detecting symmetry may be found in [17].

5.4 DESCRIPTIONS OF 3-D OBJECTS

Shape description of 3-D objects, may be in terms of their exterior surfaces or the volume enclosed by these surfaces. (Holes can be described as negative volumes.) Volume descriptions are likely to be more robust, as relatively large surface changes, such as a nick or a fold, may result only in small changes in volume and the perceived shape. For certain objects, however, primarily those constructed of thin sheetlike material, such as clothing or pressed metal objects, surface descriptions may be more natural.

An additional difficulty with 3-D object descriptions is that the 3-D surfaces or volumes need to be inferred from a 2-D image. If the 3-D positions of the visible surfaces are available, partial surface descriptions can be derived directly, but volume descriptions still require inferences about the invisible surfaces.

Surface description, given 3-D positions, can be viewed as a problem of approximation and segmentation by simpler surfaces, such as planes or multi-dimensional splines. A method using surface patches, called Coons surfaces, is given in [18]. Surface descriptions are common for computer graphics applications, and details may be found in [19, 20]. Volume descriptions, given 3-D positions of *all* surface points, could proceed by analogous volume approximation techniques, say by polyhedra. We will concentrate on the problem of volume descriptions from a 2-D image, with or without the 3-D positions of the visible points, as it is most common in normal perception.

5.4.1 Generalized Cones

A *generalized cone* is a volume generated by sweeping an arbitrarily shaped planar figure, called a cross section, along an arbitrary 3-D space curve called the axis. The axis passes through the centroids of the cross sections and is normal to them. The size and the shape of the cross section may change along the axis, as-specified by a cross section function. These cones may be viewed as a generalization of regular, right circular cones which are generated by sweeping a circular cross section along a straight line axis, the cross section function being a linear scale change. Generalized cones were introduced by Binford [21].

While a single generalized cone can describe an arbitrary volume, complex shapes are more naturally described by segmentation into a number of simpler generalized cones. For example, the screwdriver shown in Fig. 5-12 is described by four generalized cones, one corresponding to the blade with a varying rectangular cross section, a stem with constant circular cross section and the handle consisting of two generalized cones, as shown. Criteria for simplicity of a generalized cone may be no abrupt change in the size or shape of the cross section, or in the direction of its axis. Techniques for segmentation are discussed later.

Generalized cones give simple descriptions for many natural shapes, such as, animals and tree trunks and also manufactured objects.

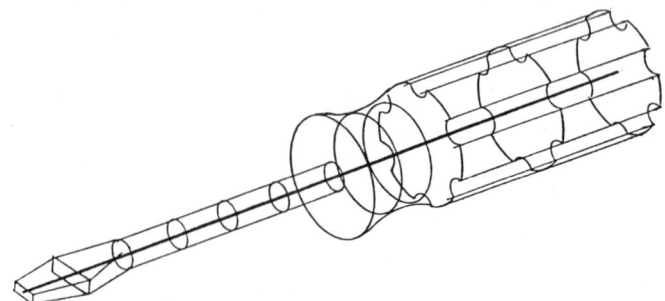

Figure 5-12: Generalized cone representation of a screwdriver (from Agin [23])

Manufacturing processes of extrusion and turning have natural correspondences to generalized cones. Fastening of parts is like cutting and pasting of generalized cones. Generalized cones are not well suited to descriptions of non-elongated objects, such as, spheres which have no preferred axis, or objects of arbitrarily deformed surfaces enclosing little volume.

Simplified generalized cone descriptions still retain many of the important shape properties. Simply a "stick figure" composed of cone axes is adequate for gross shape recognition, without any knowledge of the cross sections along it. For example, humans have little difficulty recognizing the shapes of the figure shown as a stick figure in Fig. 5-13. More subtle distinctions, say between animals of similar skeletal shape, may require detailed knowledge of the cross sections. The cross sections themselves may be represented by 2-D generalized cones; here the axis is a curve in a plane and the cross sections simply straight-line segments normal to the axis.

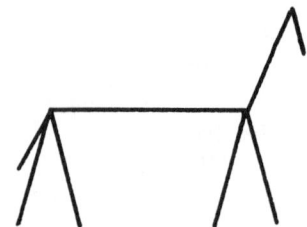

Figure 5-13: A stick figure

The structure of the axes offers some invariance to perspective changes. The relative lengths of the axes change, and not all of the parts of an object are always visible, but the connectivity of axes remains largely unchanged, except for widely different views, such as a horse viewed from the side, from the front, or the top. In such cases, multiple models for an object need to be stored, but the number of such views is small.

Marr argues that a generalized cone interpretation may be implicit in our normal perception of 2-D line drawings [22]. Two reasonable assumptions in perceiving 2-D contours as 3-D objects are that the contiguous positions of contours arise from contiguous parts of the viewed surfaces (that is, there are no invisible occluding edges) and that the convexities and concavities correspond to real properties of the viewed surfaces. These two assumptions are shown to be equivalent to assuming the viewed surfaces to be generalized cones with fixed-shape cross sections.

The axis and cross-section representation of generalized cones has similarities with Blum's medial axis transform, for 2-D figures. However, the 3-D generalization of the Blum transform, requiring axes to consist of centers of maximal spherical neighborhoods, yields axes that are surfaces rather than curves. Also, small boundary irregularities, have only small effects on generalized cone representations; for example, the notch in the rectangle of Fig. 5-11 causes only a small dip in the generalized cone axis and a small local change in the cross-section width.

First implementations of the generalized cone representation were by Agin and Binford [23, 24], and Nevatia and Binford [25, 26]. Marr and Nishihara also discuss their use as general shape descriptors [27]. Hollerbach used them to describe pottery patterns for anthropological descriptions [28], and Soroka has applied them to biological cell descriptions [29].

5.4.2 Computation of Generalized Cones

The generalized cone representation is not a transform representation, and many alternative descriptions are possible for the same input. We need to choose one or more preferred descriptions among the alternatives. A unique choice is not necessary, and a small number of multiple descriptions may be carried to higher levels for recognition. Some alternative techniques of computing generalized cone descriptions are given below.

Fitting surface data. Optimal generalized cones can be fitted, given 3-D positions of visible surface, and restrictions on the axis and the cross section shapes. A simple iterative solution is possible for cross sections of known shape. Consider a straight circular cylinder. Initially, the orientations of the axes and the cross sections are unknown. Choosing an arbitrary orientation, elliptical cross sections can be fitted to the visible surface. An axis passing through the centroid of these cross sections is not necessarily normal to them. New cross sections can now be constructed normal to the derived axis and the process repeated until only small changes are observed. For straight, circular cylinders and cones the process converges rapidly. Convergence for arbitrary shapes is unclear. This technique was used by Agin and Binford, assuming cross sections could be approximated by ellipses [24].

Using object boundaries. 2-D cones can be computed from the object boundaries. If the 2-D contours are the projection of a 3-D object, the computed cones are the projections of the desired 3-D cones. A brief description of a technique developed by Nevatia and Binford is given below; details may be found in [25, 26]. (Another technique using concavities in the boundary is given in [27].)

In the Nevatia-Binford technique; local cones with straight axes are computed first; these cones are then extended by allowing smooth curving of the axes, and preferred cones are chosen among the various alternatives. Structured descriptions are generated from the properties of the computed cones and their connectivity.

The local cones are computed simply by choosing various directions (say eight equally spaced directions) and examining if any parts of the boundary fit the requirements of the generalized cones. These requirements are that the chosen axis direction pass through midpoints of the cross sections, defined by lines perpendicular to the axis, and that the width of the cross sections be continuous. Figure 5-14 shows an object and the local cone axes in eight directions (note that the object is rotated for the eight views).

These local cones are then extended by extrapolating the axes of the local cones and constructing new cross sections. The midpoint of the new cross section defines a new point on the axis (see Fig. 5-15). This process allows the axis to curve smoothly. Extension of cones terminates by defined criteria of axis and cross-section continuity.

This process may result in the same parts of an object being described by more than one cone. Preferred descriptions are selected by choosing elongated and cylindrical descriptions over less elongated and more conical descriptions.

Figure 5-16 shows the cones computed from the boundary of a doll using the above technique (from [26]). Note that one of the legs is segmented into two cones (*P5* and *P6*), which are merged at this level to generate an alternative description.

The segmented generalized cones, representing parts or pieces of an object, and their connectivity relations constitute structured

SHAPE ANALYSIS AND RECOGNITION 77

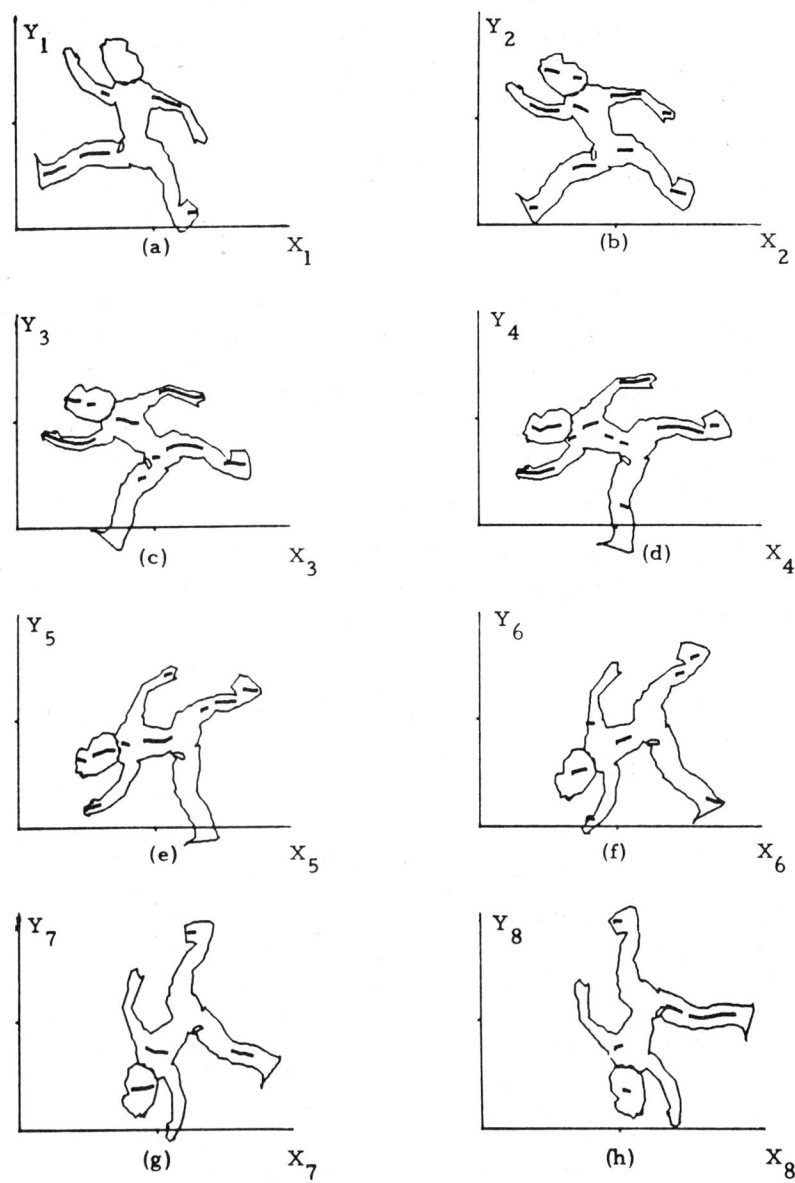

Figure 5-14: Axes of local cones in eight directions for a doll (from Nevatia [26])

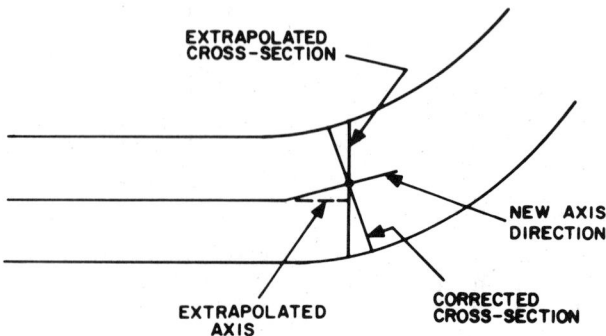

Figure 5-15: Extension of a local cone

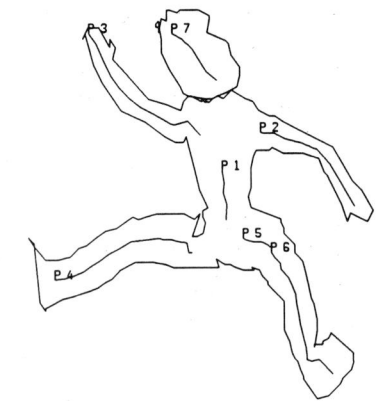

Figure 5-16: Selected cones in a doll

descriptions of the object. This description may be viewed as a graph with joints as nodes and pieces as arcs or vice versa. Figure 5-17 shows the graph corresponding to the segmentation of Fig. 5-16 (assuming *P5* and *P6* were merged).

The structured descriptions also include summary descriptions of the parts and their joints. The part descriptions may include the approximate axis shape, the length of axis to average cross-section width ratio, and approximation of the cross-section function. Joints are characterized by the parts connected to them and the interrelationships of these parts. Some joint types are shown schematically in Fig. 5-18. Additional descriptions may include properties relating to the whole structure - for example, bilateral symmetry and the axis of this symmetry. Recognition of objects from such descriptions is described in the next section.

SHAPE ANALYSIS AND RECOGNITION

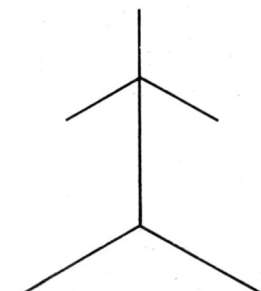

Figure 5-17: Graph representation of the doll axes

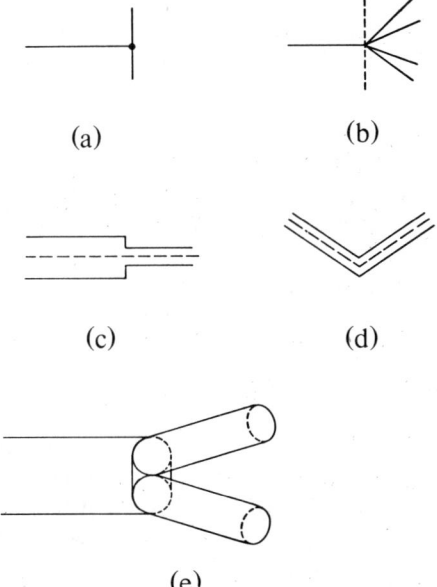

Figure 5-18: Some types of joints: (a) T, (b) fork, (c) neck, (d) elbow, (e) cross-section-conserving

5.5 RECOGNITION OF OBJECTS

Objects, or structures consisting of several objects, can be recognized by comparing their descriptions with the descriptions of models stored in a memory. The models may be acquired by storing machine descriptions of them from a previous encounter, by a directed *learning* sequence of a number of views, as in Winston's method of Section 4.4.2, or they may be simply supplied by a human operator.

If object descriptions are just a list of properties—that is, a feature vector—recognition can use standard mathematical pattern-recognition techniques (as in Chapter 2). For structured descriptions, more elaborate matching techniques are required. Additionally, it is undesirable to match a description with each stored model in a large memory, and *indexing* to select a suitable subclass without complete matching is needed.

5.5.1 Graph Matching

Structured descriptions may be viewed as graphs (or networks). We are interested in evaluating the similarity of two graphs. Some measures of similarity are introduced below.

Let a graph **G**: $<$**N, P, R**$>$ be defined to consist of a set of nodes **N** (representing parts of an object), a set of properties **P** of these nodes, and a set of relations **R** between the nodes. Given two graphs **G**: $<$**N, P, R**$>$ and **G'**: $<$**N', P', R'**$>$, nodes n in **N** and n' in **N'** are said to form an *assignment* if and only if $P(n)$, property of node n, is similar to $P'(n')$, property of node n', by a given similarity measure. Two assignments (n_1, n_1') and (n_2, n_2') are said to be *compatible* if $r(n_1, n_2) = r'(n_1', n_2')$, for all relations r in **R** and r' in **R'** (relations are assumed to be binary).

The two graphs **G** and **G'** are said to be *isomorphic* if there exists a one-to-one assignment of nodes in **G** and **G'** such that all assignments are mutually compatible. [We also require $P(n) = P'(n')$ if (n, n') is an assignment]. **G** and **G'** are said to be subisomorphic if a subgraph of **G** is isomorphic to a subgraph of **G'**.

Graph isomorphism could be determined by an exhaustive search of all assignments and a test of their mutual compatibilities. Subgraph isomorphism could be determined by computing the isomorphism of all subgraphs. A more efficient technique is given in [30]. (Note that the graph-isomorphism problem belongs to the computational complexity class of *NP*-complete problems.)

For application to object recognition the isomorphism or sub-isomorphism measures are likely to be too stringent, as errors are

SHAPE ANALYSIS AND RECOGNITION

made at the various levels of the decription processes. Some applications of these techniques to object recognition are given in [31].

A less stringent measure is that of determining *maximal cliques*. From the two graphs to be matched, let us define a new graph, called the match graph, such that the nodes of the match graph consist of an assignment of a pair of nodes from **G** and **G'**, and an arc exists between two nodes of the match graph if the two corresponding assignments are compatible. A clique (of the graphs **G** and **G'**) is a totally connected subgraph of the match graph. A clique is *maximal* if it is not included in any other clique.

Figures 5-19(a) and (b) show two graphs to be matched. Three types of nodes are present, those marked with light circles, dark circles, and a square. Only like nodes can be matched. The two graphs are quite similar and would be isomorphic if nodes *B* and *D* were of the light circles type rather than the rectangle type. However, the only isomorphic connected subgraphs are the isolated nodes. Maximal cliques can help find larger compatible matching sub-structures. Figure 5-20 shows the matching graph for the two graphs of Fig. 5-19. Two cliques are present, one with the match $((A, 1), (C, 3), (E, 5))$ and the other $((A, 5), (C, 3), (E, 1))$.

Figure 5-19: Two graphs to be matched

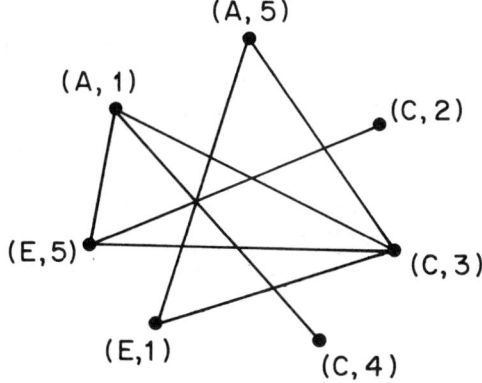

Figure 5-20: Match graph for Fig. 5-19 graphs

A simple procedure to find maximal cliques is given below (from [32]). A function clique (X, Y) generates the set of all cliques that include nodes in clique X and are included in the set Y. Cliques $(0, N)$, N being the set of all nodes, will find all cliques. It is defined as:

cliques $(X, Y) :=$ *If* no node in $Y - X$ is connected
to all elements of X
then $\{X\}$
else cliques $(X \cup \{y\}, Y) \cup$ cliques $(X, Y - \{y\})$
where y is such a node

A clique of a minimum size k can be found by stopping the recursion if the size of X plus the number of nodes in Y-X connected to all of X is less than k. To find maximal cliques, start with large k and reduce k by one until some cliques are found.

In a worst case, the maximal-clique computation can be expensive, and the number of maximal cliques can be as large as $(n/2)^{n/2}$, n being the number of nodes. The maximal-clique technique can be modified to include nonbinary relationships, by defining a modified compatibility criterion.

5.5.2 Relaxation Labeling

A labeling problem can be defined to be assignment of a set of labels to a set of nodes (or units) such that the label assignments are consistent according to given constraints. Such labeling has many applications and includes the problem of graph matching (the labels are now nodes of the other graph).

Let **N** be the set of nodes to be labeled and **L** be the set of allowed labels. To each node n_i we wish to assign a set of labels $\mathbf{L}_i$, such that $\mathbf{L}_i$ is a subset of **L**, and the labels are consistent according to the given constraints. For unambiguous cases, each set $\mathbf{L}_i$ contains one element only. Simplest constraints are *unary*, restricting the labels that may be assigned to a certain node, without consideration of the other nodes in the network. *Binary* constraints specify relations between labels of a pair of nodes. A set of labels $\mathbf{L}_i$ for node n_i may be said to be consistent with a set of labels $\mathbf{L}_j$ for node n_j if each label in $\mathbf{L}_i$ is consistent with at least one label in $\mathbf{L}_j$ and vice versa. Such consistency is called *arc consistency*.

In general, the constraints are n-ary, and arc consistency may not result in global consistency. Figure 5-21 shows an example (from [32]), where the unary constraints are that each node be labeled red or green, and that adjacent nodes be of a different color. For each assignment of

SHAPE ANALYSIS AND RECOGNITION

red or green to one node, we can assign a consistent label to the neighboring nodes, but we can not satisfy the global constraint simultaneously at the three nodes.

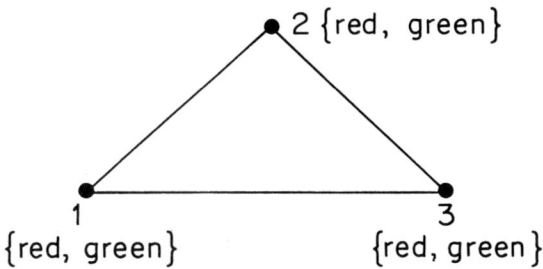

Figure 5-21: An arc-consistent but globally inconsistent labeling

A more powerful constraint is that of *path consistency*. Two nodes n_i and n_j with labels l_k and l_l are path inconsistent, if there exists a path in the network from n_i to n_j, such that there is no set of labels, one for each node along the path, that is simultaneously consistent (in a binary way) with the labels l_k and l_l at the two ends. Note that the network of Fig. 5-21 is not path consistent.

However, path consistency also does not guarantee global consistency. The problem of global consistency is computationally expensive (*NP*-complete), though efficient solutions may be achieved for some networks. In the following we will consider only arc consistency, as it is often helpful in reducing the number of alternatives; more complex labeling methods may be found in [33-36].

Rosenfeld, Hummel, and Zucker have described an iterative *relaxation* scheme for computing arc-consistent labels [37]. Initially, all labels satisfying unary constraints are assigned to each node. At any iteration of the algorithm, those labels of a node that are not arc consistent with the other nodes are removed. Note that removal of some labels may create new inconsistencies that are removed at the next iteration. It can be shown to converge to a consistent labeling, if one exists. It is a generalization of the Waltz labeling method described in Chapter 4 and can be implemented as a parallel algorithm.

Rosenfeld, Hummel, and Zucker have also described a probabilistic or stochastic version of the relaxation labeling, in an effort to account for the variations that are common in image descriptions. A weight or probability is associated with each label assigned to each node. The compatibility between the labels of two nodes is also given by a range of values. At each iteration of the algorithm, the probability of each assignment is updated, based on their compatibility with the neighboring assignments. Generally, the probability of a label should be increased if other high-probability labels are highly compatible with it. Let $P_i^t(k)$ be the probability of label l_k being assigned to node n_i, at the tth iteration, such that

$$\sum_k P_i^t(k) = 1 \qquad (5\text{-}9)$$

These probabilities may be updated based on labels of other nodes by the following expression (according to [38]):

$$P_i^{t+1}(k) = \frac{P_i^t(k)[1 + q_i^t(k)]}{\sum_k \{P_i^t(k) \cdot (1 + q_i^t(k))\}} \qquad (5\text{-}10)$$

where $q_i^t(k)$ gives the correction to the assignment probability and the denominator guarantees that the new probabilities still sum to one. $q_i^t(k)$ is defined by

$$q_i^t(k) = \sum_j d_{ij} [\sum_{k'} r_{ij}(k, k') \cdot P_j^t(k')] \qquad (5\text{-}11)$$

d_{ij} is a weight to determine the effect of node j on node i. $r_{ij}(k, k')$ is a measure of compatibility between the nodes i and j having labels k and k', respectively. Statistical correlation between the two labels has been suggested as one appropriate measure.

Hopefully, in an unambiguous case, the various assignment probabilities will converge to a value of 1 or 0. However, the convergence of this process is not guaranteed for the probabilistic case, as it was for the discrete case. Performance of the algorithm is likely to be highly dependent on the choices of the weights and the compatibility measures.

Experiments with different compatibility measures and updating functions are given in [37, 38]. An approach, that seeks to maximize a certain function, and thus is converging by definition, is described in [39]; an application to labeling of aerial images is given in [40]. Another approach to using nonbinary weights for relaxation may be found in [41].

5.5.3 Multilevel Matching

Graph-matching and scene-labeling techniques discussed above are general. However, they do not provide satisfactory descriptions of similarities and differences. Use of numerical weights, combining unrelated features, such as , color and size, may be meaningless. An alternative is multilevel matching. Here, the result of matching two descriptions is itself a description of their similarities and differences, as, for example, in Winston's learning program (Chapter 4). Of course, eventually a decision for recognition must be made, but the results of matching can now be examined with more context; for example, the particular model may have associated information as to the relative importance of color and size. If matching with two models yields similar differences, the scene may now be reexamined to find specific finer details. Marr has argued that deferrng of decisions, by carrying along additional information, until more contextual information is available is an important organization rule for visual processes; he has called this the "principle of least commitment" [42].

Nevatia and Binford [25, 26] used such an approach for recognizing objects by matching generalized cone descriptions, as in Section 5.4.1. The matching was facilitated by marking the wide pieces (the body and the head) as being *distinguished* and matching them to other distinguished pieces only. Alternative matches of parts, each consistent with the connectivity relations, produces a difference description. Some matches are clearly inferior to others, such as those containing more pieces in the observed object than the model, and are discarded.

In some cases two models (for example, a doll and a horse) may have similar connectivity. In such cases the models may be distinguished by properties of individual parts. In general, a more detailed analysis may be required, such as looking at the limb extremities in the above example.

When the number of models is large, matching with each model is prohibitive, and indexing into memory to retrieve only a small number of likely models is required. Indexing may be by use of context, such as the knowledge of observer location and expected objects in the environment. However, humans are able to quickly perceive objects out of context as well, as in a collage of unrelated objects, and indexing in such cases seems to be based solely on object descriptions.

An indexing procedure must accommodate the usual changes in object descriptions due to different viewing conditions and also the variability caused by the description processes themselves. Indexing is largely ignored, as most systems usually deal with a small number of objects only. An indexing procedure using the properties of distinguished pieces in a generalize cone description is described in [25, 26]. Variability in the descriptions is accommodated by indexing with the observed descriptors as well as by perturbing these descriptions according to expected changes.

5.6 SUMMARY

In this chapter we have considered analysis of nonpolyhedral objects and concentrated mostly on shape analysis. The described techniques should be adequate for a wide range of applications, if the number of objects is small and perfect boundaries are available. However, as will be seen in the next few chapters, perfect boundaries are difficult to extract from a single image of a 3-D scene, and the description mechanisms need to be modified to work with imperfect data. Some examples of systems that operate on real data are given in Chapter 10.

REFERENCES

[1] D. A. Huffman, "Curvature and Creases: A Primer on Paper," *IEEE Transactions on Computers*, Vol. 25, 1976, pp. 1010-1019.

[2] R. T. Chien, and Y. H. Chang, "Recognition of Curved Objects and Object Assemblies," *Proceedings of the Second International Joint Conference on Pattern Recognition*, Copenhagen, 1974, pp. 496-510.

[3] H. Freeman, "On the Encoding of Arbitrary Geometric Configurations," *IRE Transactions on Electronic Computers*, June 1961, pp. 260-268.

[4] T. Pavlidis, *Structural Pattern Recognition*, Springer-Verlag, New York, 1977.

[5] T. Pavlidis and S. L. Horowitz, "Segmentation of Plane Curves," *IEEE Transactions on Computers*, Vol. 23, No. 8, August 1974, pp. 860-870.

[6] U. Ramer, "An Iterative Procedure for the Polygonal Approximation of Plane Curves," *Computer Graphics and Image Processing*, Vol. 1, 1972, pp. 244-256.

[7] L. Davis, "Shape: Angles and Sides," *IEEE Transactions on Computers*, March 1977, pp. 236-242.

[8] C. de Boor, "On Calculating with B-Splines," *Journal of Approximation Theory*, Vol. 6, 1972, pp. 50-62.

[9] W. S. Rubkowski and A. Rosenfeld, "A Comparison of Corner-Detection Techniques for Chain-Coded Curves,"

University of Maryland, Computer Science Department, Report TR-623, January 1978.

[10] C. T. Zahn and R. Z. Roskies, "Fourier Descriptions for Plane Closed Curves," *IEEE Transactions on Computers*, Vol. 21, March 1972, pp. 269-281.

[11] M. K. Hu, "Visual Pattern Recognition by Moment Invariants," *IRE Transactions on Information Theory*, February 1962, pp. 179-187.

[12] S. A. Dudani, K.J. Breeding, R. B. McGhee, "Aircraft Identification by Moment Invariants," *IEEE Transactions on Computers*, Vol. 26, No. 1, January 1977, pp. 39-46.

[13] H. Blum, "A Transformation for Extracting New Descriptions of Shape," in *Symposium on Models for Perception of Speech and Visual Form*, W. Wathen-Dunn (ed.), MIT Press, Cambridge, Mass., 1967, pp. 362-380.

[14] A. Rosenfeld and J. L. Pfalz, "Distance Functions on Digital Pictures," *Pattern Recognition*, Vol. 1, July 1968, pp. 33-62.

[15] U. Montanari, "A Method for Obtaining Skeletons Using a Quasi-Euclidean Distance," *Journal of the ACM*, Vol. 15, October 1968, pp. 600-624.

[16] U. Montanari, "Continuous Skeletons from Digitized Images," *Journal of the ACM*, Vol. 16, October 1969, pp. 534-549.

[17] L. S. Davis, "Understanding Shape: Symmetry," University of Maryland, Computer Science Department, Report TR-441, February 1976.

[18] S. A. Coons, "Surfaces for Computer Aided Design of Space Forms," MIT Project MAC, MAC-TR-41, June 1967 (AD 663504).

[19] W. M. Newman and R. F. Sproull, *Principles of Interactive Computer Graphics*, 2d ed., McGraw-Hill, New York, 1979.

[20] D. F. Rogers and J. A. Adams, *Mathematical Elements for Computer Graphics*, McGraw-Hill, New York, 1976.

[21] T. O. Binford, "Visual Perception by a Computer," *IEEE Conference on Systems and Controls*, Miami, Florida, December 1971.

[22] D. Marr, "Analysis of Occluding Contour," *Proceedings Royal Society of London*, B200, 1977, pp. 441-475.

[23] G. J. Agin, "Representation and Description of Curved Objects," Stanford Artificial Intelligence Laboratory Memo AIM-173, Ph.D. Thesis (1972).

[24] G. J. Agin and T. O. Binford, "Computer Description of Curved Objects," *IEEE Transactions on Computers*, Vol. 25, April 1976, pp. 439-440.

[25] R. Nevatia and T.O. Binford, "Description and Recognition of Curved Objects," *Artificial Intelligence*, Vol. 8, No. 1, February 1977, pp. 77-98.

[26] R. Nevatia, *Computer Analysis of Scenes of 3-D Curved Objects*, Birkhauser-Verlag, Basel, Switzerland, 1976.

[27] D. Marr and K. Nishihara, "Representation and Recognition of the Spatial Organization of Three-Dimensional Shapes," *Proceedings Royal Society of London*, B200, 1977, pp. 269-294.

[28] J. M. Hollerbach, "Hierarchical Shape Representation of Objects by Selection and Modification of Prototypes," MIT AI-TR-346, November 1975.

[29] B. I. Soroka, "Generalized Cones from Serial Sections," *Computer Graphics and Image Processing*, Vol. 15, No. 2, February 1981, pp. 154-166.

[30] J. R. Ullman, "An Algorithm for Subgraph Isomorphism," *Journal of the ACM*, Vol. 23, January 1976, pp. 31-42.

[31] H. G. Barrow, A. P. Ambler, and R. M. Burstall, "Some Techniques for Recognizing Structure in Pictures," in S. Watanabe (ed.), *Frontiers of Pattern Recognition*, Academic Press, New York, 1972, pp. 1-29.

[32] A. P. Ambler, H. G. Barrow, C. M. Brown, R. M. Burstall, and R. J. Popplestone, "A Versatile Computer Controlled Assembly System," *Proceedings of the Third International Joint Conference Artificial Intelligence*, Stanford, California, August 1973, pp. 298-307.

[33] E. C. Freuder, "Synthesizing Constraint Expressions," *Communications of the ACM*, Vol. 21, 1978, pp. 958-966.

[34] U. Montanari, "Networks of Constraints: Fundamental Properties and Applications to Picture Processing," *Information Science*, Vol. 7, No. 2, April 1974, pp. 95-132.

[35] A. K. Mackworth, "Consistency in Networks of Relations," *Artificial Intelligence*, Vol. 8, No. 1, 1977, pp. 99-118.

[36] R. M. Haralick and L. G. Shapiro, "The Consistent Labeling Problem: Part 1," *IEEE Transactions on Pattern Analysis and Machine Intelligence*, Vol. 1, No. 2, April 1979, pp. 173-184.

[37] A. Rosenfeld, R. A. Hummel, and S. W. Zucker, "Scene Labeling by Relaxation Operations," *IEEE Transactions on Systems, Man and Cybernetics*, Vol. 6, No. 6, June 1976, pp. 420-453.

[38] L. Kitchen, "Relaxation Applied to Matching Quantitative Relational Structures," *IEEE Transactions on Systems, Man and Cybernetics*, Vol. 10, No. 2, February 1980, pp. 96-101.

[39] O. D. Faugeras and M. Berthod, "Scene Labeling: An Optimization Approach," *Proceedings of IEEE Conference on*

Pattern Recognition and Image Processing, Chicago, August 1979, pp. 318-326.

[40] O. D. Faugeras and K. Price, "Semantic Description of Aerial Images Using Stochastic Labeling," *IEEE Transactions on Pattern Analysis and Machine Intelligence*, November 1981.

[41] J. M. Tenenbaum and H. G. Barrow, "MSYS: A System for Reasoning about Scenes," SRI Technical Note 121, March 1976.

[42] D. Marr, "Early Processing of Visual Data," *Philosophical Transactions of the Royal Society of London*, B275, 1976, pp. 483-524.

6

PERCEPTION OF BRIGHTNESS AND COLOR

In previous chapters we addressed the problems of separating occluding objects, generating suitable descriptions for them, and recognizing them, *assuming* that the boundaries of the objects were known. We now turn our attention to early processing of visual information and the important problems associated with obtaining such boundaries. These processes include *figure-ground* separation or *scene segmentation*—that is, identifying the regions of an image that correspond to physical objects of interest.

For controlled scenes of polyhedral objects, scene segmentation is simple, at least in principle. The surfaces of the objects can be arranged to have continuous brightness values that are distinctly different from the backgrounds. However, in general, the images of our daily experience are much more complex. An object surface is not always characterized by a simple uniformity of, say, intensity or color. Rather, the patterns of intensity and color over one object surface seem to be different from those of others. For example, a grass field is not uniformly green, but the pattern of elongated blades in it is different from the patterns caused by waves in a nearby lake. We call such patterns the *texture* of a surface.

Human vision uses many sources of information to aid in the segmentation process. An important source is our ability to extract relative three-dimensional positions of objects using two eyes or even from a single view using the variations in the surface brightness and

PERCEPTION OF BRIGHTNESS AND COLOR

texture, and other cues. Many of these operations are poorly understood, and only weak mechanisms for machines to perform the same operations have been developed. Segmentation using different sources of information is discussed in Chapters 7, 8, and 9. In this chapter we first consider our perception of brightness and color, which in itself is a complex process.

6.1 BRIGHTNESS AND COLOR

Measurement of the brightness or the color of an isolated single pixel is relatively straightforward. However, our perception of the brightness (or color) of a part of an image is strongly influenced by the brightness (color) values of the neighboring parts. For example, see Fig. 6-1, which consists of a small square in each of the three larger squares. The leftmost small square *appears* to be much brighter than the rightmost small square, the center one having an intermediate value. In fact, the three small squares have the same intensity. (A similar effect is also observed for color perception.)

Figure 6-1: An example illustrating simultaneous contrast

Another important effect is the relative constancy of the perceived *lightness* and color of a surface under different illumination conditions. A grey piece of paper taken from inside a poorly lit room to the bright outside sunshine still appears grey, even though the reflected light from it is several orders of magnitude larger than from a white piece of paper indoors. Only a small part of the change is explained by the change in the size of the iris (the lens opening) of our eyes. Similarly, a surface of a certain color retains its perceived color under most conditions even when the color of illumination changes. These effects, known as brightness- and color-constancy phenomena, are clearly desirable properties for a perceiving machine to have. (The brightness and color constancies are only approximate, and they do break down under extreme conditions such as very dim light.)

6.1.1 The Human Eye

The human visual system may be simply thought of as consisting of two eyes that image the environment and pass the information to the cortex in the brain. Besides forming the image, some very important processing also takes place in the eye itself, before the information reaches the cortex. All descriptions presented here are highly simplified; much remains unknown about the human visual system.

A simple model of the human eye consists of a lenslike device that forms an image on a *retina*. The retinal surface is nearer to being spherical than planar, as for ideal camera systems of Chapter 3. The opening of the lens is adjusted by an iris. However, adaptability to wide variations in light intensity, say between night and day viewing, is accomplished by the variations in the sensitivity of the sensing elements, called *receptors*.

The human retina contains two types of receptors, called rods and cones. The cones are responsible for color vision, but the rods have a higher sensitivity to light. The spatial distribution of these receptors is not uniform over the retina. Most of the cones are concentrated in a central region known as the fovea. Thus, we have poor color vision in the dark and at the periphery of the field of view.

Under normal viewing, the fovea focuses on different parts of the scene in an apparently pseudo-random way, but concentrating on "interesting" parts. The points of focus seem to be the busy areas of the scene, but it is likely that the choices are based on more complex processing. The spatial resolution of the human system is extremely high (1/2 second of arc at the fovea). Each eye is estimated to have 6 million cones and 120 million rods. The light sensitivity of the rods is also amazingly high; it is estimated that a single photon of light activates a rod, and a few photons suffice for reliable detection of the presence of light. Details of the human visual sensory system may be found in [1, 2].

6.1.2 Local Measurements

Local measurement of the brightness of a small area of an image is made by a sensor whose response is proportional to the average light intensity in a small neighborhood. For the human system, these local measurements may be considered to be the responses of the individual rods and cones. The response, for the human system and also for many electronic sensors, is roughly proportional to the logarithm of the image intensity. The perceived brightness, however, is dependent on the intensities of the surrounding pixels and possibly even on the global context.

Perception of local color is more complex. Humans are able to distinguish between two homogeneous surfaces of different colors by three independent attributes: intensity, hue and saturation. *Intensity* is the attribute also used for noncolor or achromatic images (commonly called black-and-white or grey-level images). *Hue* is the common English language sense of color; for example, red, green, and blue are three different hues. *Saturation* is a measure of the amount of white mixed with a pure hue. Our color sensation can be viewed as requiring three independent parameters for its characterization.

For a monochromatic source of light, our perception of hue is directly dependent on the wavelength. However, in our normal viewing environments, objects of a certain hue, say red, do not reflect just the light of a single wavelength, but rather a broad spectrum that has a distribution different from that of the white light. Different hues are also obtained by mixing colors; for example, green hue is obtained by mixing blue and yellow, even though the mixed light may contain no green-wavelength component at all. It is known, from empirical data, that all colors distinguished by humans can be synthesized by a mixture of three *primary* colors. The commonly used primary colors are red, green, and blue, but the choice of primaries is not unique. Note that the sufficiency of the three primaries corresponds to the characterization of color by three independent components. The primary colors need not be monochromatic but may have a wide-spectrum distribution of light intensity. Broadcast television relies on standard primary color spectra in the three light sources of the receivers. The three primary distributions have peaks at the nominal red, green, and blue wavelengths and overlap.

The receptors in the human retina, or the color TV cameras, do not directly measure the perceived attributes of intensity, hue, and saturation. Instead, the measured attributes correspond to the intensity of the three primary color components in the viewed surface. For a color camera, the three measurements are from three sensors that respond to light according to the response curves for the standard primaries. Let the three intensity measurements be R, G, and B, corresponding to the nominal red, green and blue primaries. Similar measurements could be obtained from a noncolor camera by using three different color filters in front of the lens. For human vision, the cone receptors are believed to be of three types with three different spectral responses, as shown in Fig. 6-2. (This figure is not intended to give highly accurate psychophysical data, but only an illustrative estimate.)

There are many theories as to how the attributes of intensity, hue, a saturation are inferred from the brightness values for the three primaries—that is, the R, G, and B measurements. A simple method is

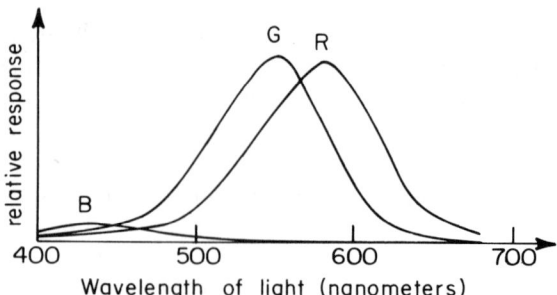

Figure 6-2: Relative responses of three color sensors in the human retina (illustrative data only)

presented here. The intensity I is given simply by a weighted sum of the three components:

$$I = c_1 R + c_2 G + c_3 B \tag{6-1}$$

The constants c_1, c_2, and c_3 depend on the choice of the primary colors and can be determined by measurements made on a white surface. (See [3] for details.) For a camera calibrated according to United States TV broadcast standards (known as N.T.S.C., the National Television Systems Committee Standards), the three constants in order are 0.299, 0.587, and 0.114.

To compute hue and saturation components, it is convenient to introduce two additional attributes T_1 and T_2 defined as follows:

$$T_1 = \frac{R}{R + G + B} \tag{6-2}$$

$$T_2 = \frac{G}{R + G + B} \tag{6-3}$$

The T_1-T_2 plane contains all of the chromaticity (non-brightness related) information. Note that the transformation is undefined when $R=G=B=0$; a detailed discussion of this singularity may be found in [4]. The three primary colors R, G, and B are at the three points in the T_1-T_2 plane as shown in Fig. 6-3. The triangle connecting these points is known as the *color triangle*; all observed colors must fall within this triangle. White is represented by the point $W(1/3, 1/3)$. For a given color represented by the point P in the color triangle, its distance Y from the point W, as shown in Fig. 6-3, determines its saturation and the angle θ of the line joining P to W with the T_1 axis determines the hue.

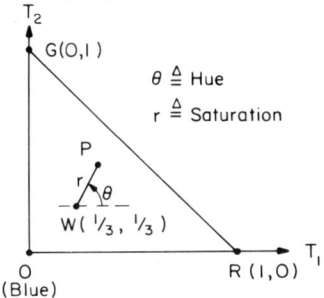

Figure 6-3: A color triangle

6.2 LATERAL INHIBITION AND LIGHTNESS COMPUTATION

In the human system, each receptor output does not go to the cortex in the brain. It is estimated that the outputs from about 120 million receptors in each eye are transmitted along only a million nerve fibers to the brain. This reduction in the member of output signals is a result of very important, and only partially understood, processing at the retina. The retina contains layers of cells in addition to the receptor cells and is capable of extensive computation. Only very simple models of processing at the retinal level are given below.

The most common model of interaction between receptors at the retina is that of *lateral inhibition*. Outputs from a small neighborhood of receptors, known as a receptive field, are combined by forming a weighted sum of the individual outputs. The receptors in a central excitatory neighborhood contribute positively and those in a larger surrounding inhibitory neighborhood have negative weights. Figure 6-4(a) shows a schematic receptive field and Fig. 6-4(b) shows the weights of the receptors along a diameter. The lateral inhibition operation may also be viewed as performing a 2-D bandpass filtering of the input signal. (The filter is the spatial Fourier transform of the lateral inhibition weighting function.) Such filtering explains the observed phenomenon of Mach bands, shown in Fig. 6-5. In this figure, near the center of the strip, the intensity changes linearly from dark to bright, but the reader should see a thin dark strip on the left side and a thin light strip on the right side of the area of change.

Lateral inhibition is also commonly used to explain the

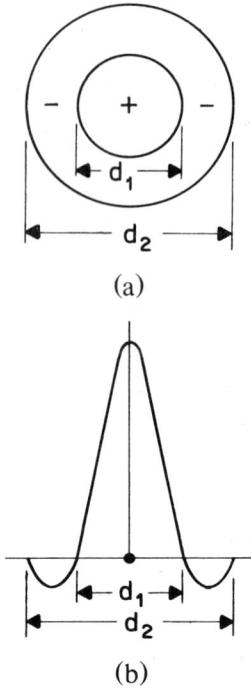

Figure 6-4: Lateral-inhibition operator: (a) receptive field, (b) weighted contributions of the receptors

Figure 6-5: An example of Mach bands effect

phenomenon of simultaneous contrast—that is, the dependence of perceived brightness on the surround, as in Fig. 6-1 (for example, see [1]). Modeling the receptor response as logarithmic, the lateral inhibition operation can be viewed as computing the ratio of central brightness with peripheral brightness. However, this only explains perceived brightness near the boundaries and not the perceived uniform brightness of each square in Fig. 6-1. Similar arguments also apply to lateral inhibition explaining the phenomenon of brightness constancy, where perceived brightness is again computed relative to those of other surrounding surfaces. We will later see, in Chapter 7, that an operation like lateral-inhibition is also useful for edge detection.

A better explanation for brightness constancy and simultaneous contrast is given by the *retinex* theory suggested by Land and McCann [5, 6]. The light intensity at the receptor, say $p'(x)$, is a product of the incident light, $s'(x)$, and surface reflectivity, $r'(x)$. Given an image and hence $p'(x)$, we seek to compute $r'(x)$ without a priori knowledge of $s'(x)$. Taking logarithms of p', s', and r', we get

$$p(x) = s(x) + r(x) \qquad (6\text{-}4)$$

where $p(x) = \log p'(x)$, and so on.

Taking derivatives, we get

$$d(x) = D(p(x)) = D(s(x)) + D(r(x)) \qquad (6\text{-}5)$$

Now, if we assume that the incident illumination $s(x)$ changes smoothly across the image whereas the reflectivity $r(x)$ changes abruptly at the object boundaries, then $D(s(x))$ is finite and $D(r(x))$ consists of infinite impulses at the object boundaries (see Fig. 6-6.) $D(r(x))$ can be easily separated from $D(s(x))$. In the discrete case, the derivative is approximated by a differential, and thresholding $d(x)$ gives $D(r(x))$. The reflectivity (or lightness) $r(x)$ can now be recovered by integrating the thresholded differential, except for a constant term. Note that in Fig. 6-6, lightness $l(x)$ has negative values. A constant of integration must be added to get physically realizable values.

Land and McCann's theory was formulated for continuous domain processing along a line. For 2-D processing, they suggest use of randomly selected lines. Horn has generalized the theory for 2-D directly by using a Laplacian operation instead of the derivative and approximating the Laplacian for discrete images [7]. Marr has given a neurological model for this computation in the human retina [8].

Computation of the lightness of a surface, independent of the illumination, explains brightness constancy. Simultaneous contrast is explained by perception of the differences in the logarithms of the lightness. Color constancy is explained by assuming that the lightness for the three components is first computed independently and that the ratios of the lightness values, rather than the intensity values, are used for chromatic perception. However, this model applies only to surfaces with uniform lightness (sometimes called Mondrian surfaces). It also fails to explain some of the other observed effects of human perception,

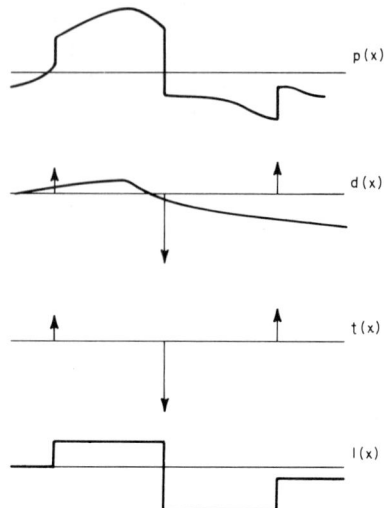

Figure 6-6: Steps in computing lightness

such as Mach bands.

Owing to the limitations of the human visual models, their use in machine processing is not widespread. Instead, only the single pixel brightness and color are frequently used for further processing.

6.3 SUMMARY

The perception of apparently simple properties, such as lightness and color, is seen to be rather complex and only partially understood. The major effects are due to the interaction with the neighboring cells. Two models, those of lateral inhibition and retinex, have been described.

REFERENCES

[1] T. N. Cornsweet, *Visual Perception*, Academic Press, New York, 1970.
[2] I. Rock, *Introduction to Perception*, Macmillan, New York, 1975.
[3] W. K. Pratt, *Digital Image Processing*, John Wiley & Sons, New York, 1978.
[4] J. Kender, "Saturation, Hue, and Normalized Color: Calculation, Digitization Effects and Use," Carnegie-Mellon University,

Department of Computer Science, Pittsburgh, November 1976.
[5] E. Land, "Experiments in Color Vision," *Scientific American*, May 1959, pp. 84-99.
[6] E. Land and J. J. McCann, "Lightness Theory," *Journal of the Optical Society*, Vol. 61, No. 1, January 1971, pp. 1-11.
[7] B. K. P. Horn, "Determining Lightness from an Image," *Computer Graphics and Image Processing*, Vol. 3, 1974, pp. 277-299.
[8] D. Marr, "The Computation of Lightness by the Primate Retina," *Vision Research*, Vol. 14, 1974, pp. 1377-1388.

7

EDGE AND CURVE DETECTION

Detection of object boundaries is an important part of the perception process. There is much psychological evidence, such as in our ability to understand cartoons, that boundaries are sufficient for perception of a broad class of objects. In this chapter, techniques for detecting boundaries by aggregating evidence from local discontinuities are described. A different approach will be discussed in the next chapter, that of finding areas in an image over which some attributes are constant.

Edge-detection techniques aim to find local discontinuities in some image attribute, such as intensity or color. These discontinuities are of interest because they are likely to occur at the boundaries of objects. But, local edges may also occur due to variations in surface characteristics of an object, changes in illumination and shadows, and the like. An important process of perception is to organize the local edges into aggregates that lead to a scene segmentation. Thus, the process of edge detection may be viewed as one stage of abstracting descriptions from the image data.

7.1 EDGE DETECTION

We first concentrate on the detection of local edge elements. An edge is said to occur at a point in the image if some image attribute changes in value discontinuously at that point. Here we will discuss intensity edges; edges in other attributes can be defined similarly.

An ideal edge, in one dimension, may be viewed as a step change in intensity. In real signals, the step change is likely to be mixed with "noise" caused by sensor, surface, or illumination variations, as shown schematically in Fig. 7-1. In two dimensions, the ideal step occurs along a line of certain length, the intensity values on the two sides of the line being different. Also, edges of interest are not necessarily limited to step edges.

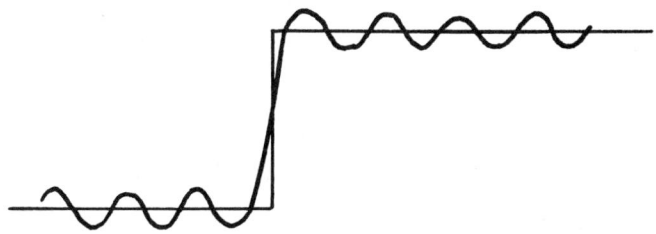

Figure 7-1: A one-dimensional edge

Detection of ideal step edges, without noise, would be simple. In real images, with noise and surface imperfections, a compromise must be achieved between maximizing the detection of the desired edges and minimizing the detection of the undesired noise edges. (Some of the "undesired" edges are due to legitimate surface variations, such as texture, and the local edge detection process is not intended to discriminate against them.)

The literature on techniques of edge detection is rather large. Only the prominent classes of techniques are discussed below. Good surveys of edge-detection techniques are also given in [1, 2].

7.1.1 Edge Enhancement and Differentiation

If an operator enhances the edges in a picture—that is, it outputs higher values for points at the desired edges than for the other points, then edge-detection can be performed by simple thresholding of the enhanced picture. While enhancement can be by any general operator, linear filtering techniques, such as Wiener filtering applied uniformly to the entire image, are often suggested. The difficulty with the use of a global filtering technique is in the choice of proper enhancing functions. As objects in a given picture may be of different sizes and at different ranges, it is unlikely that a uniform filter function for the entire picture is appropriate.

Differentiation may also be viewed as a local edge enhancement operator. For application to two-dimensional images, an appropriate derivative operation is that of the gradient. Robert's gradient operator, using a 2-by-2 neighborhood, was described in Section 3.1.1 [3]. Better immunity to noise is achieved if a larger neighborhood is used for approximating the magnitude of the gradient.

Consider a 3-by-3 neighborhood of a certain pixel, say (i, j), with intensity values as shown in Fig. 7-2. We can define the magnitude of the gradient by

$$S = \sqrt{S_x^2 + S_y^2} \tag{7-1}$$

where

$$S_x = (a_2 + ca_3 + a_4) - (a_0 + ca_7 + a_6) \tag{7-2}$$

$$S_y = (a_6 + ca_5 + a_4) - (a_0 + ca_1 + a_7) \tag{7-3}$$

and c is constant. c was chosen to be 1 in an edge detector described by Prewitt [4] and 2 by Sobel. (No published source is available for Sobel operator, but the described operator is generally associated with this name.)

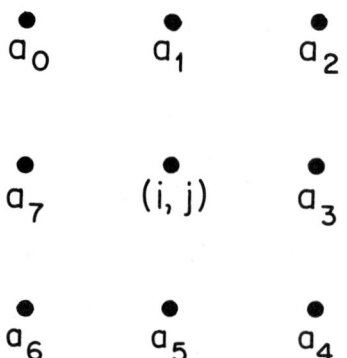

Figure 7-2: A pixel and its eight neighbors

The direction of the edge, θ, in these operations is given by

$$\theta = \tan^{-1}\left(\frac{S_x}{S_y}\right) \tag{7-4}$$

Note that these operators are not perfectly isotropic; that is, edges of the same strength but differing directions give different edge magnitude outputs.

7.1.2 Edge Fitting

Another approach to edge detection is to have models of ideal edges and to determine how closely these models fit to a given image neighborhood. A popular analytical procedure due to Hueckel is described below.

Hueckel operator. A simplified model of an ideal edge used in this operator is as shown in Fig. 7-3, where an edge at an angle θ and distance r from the center separates two regions of brightness b and $b + h$. We desire to compute the ideal step function that matches best with the picture function by varying the position, orientation, and intensity values of the ideal step—that is, b, h, r, and θ of Fig. 7-3—comprising a vector ξ. Define the difference, N, between a neighborhood of an image and the ideal step by

$$N^2 = \sum_{\mathbf{x} \in \mathbf{R}} (A(\mathbf{x}) - S(\mathbf{x}, \xi))^2 \tag{7-5}$$

where $A(\mathbf{x})$ is the image intensity at point $\mathbf{x}$ and $S(\mathbf{x}, \xi)$ is the intensity of the ideal step function for a chosen vector of parameters ξ. The sum is to be computed over the entire neighborhood, $\mathbf{R}$, of the ideal step. ξ is to be chosen such that N^2 is minimized. The decision as to the presence of an edge is based on N being small and the step height, h, being large.

To simplify this minimization computation, Hueckel suggested approximating the $A(.)$ and $S(.)$ functions by an orthogonal series of functions, say $H(.)$. The series chosen was a radial Fourier series where only the first nine functions shown in Fig. 7-4 were used. We now wish to minimize

$$N'^2 = \sum_{i=0}^{8} (a_i - s_i(\xi))^2 \tag{7-6}$$

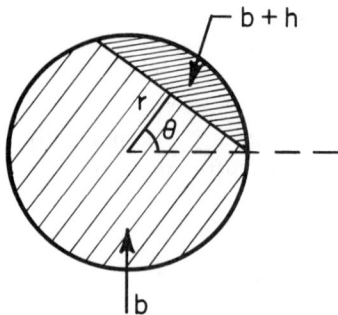

Figure 7-3: An ideal edge in a circular neighborhood

where a_i and s_i are the coefficients of expansion in the above series:

$$a_i = \sum_{\mathbf{x} \in R} H_i(\mathbf{x}) \cdot A(\mathbf{x}) \tag{7-7}$$

$$s_i = \sum_{\mathbf{x} \in R} H_i(\mathbf{x}) \cdot S(\mathbf{x}) \tag{7-8}$$

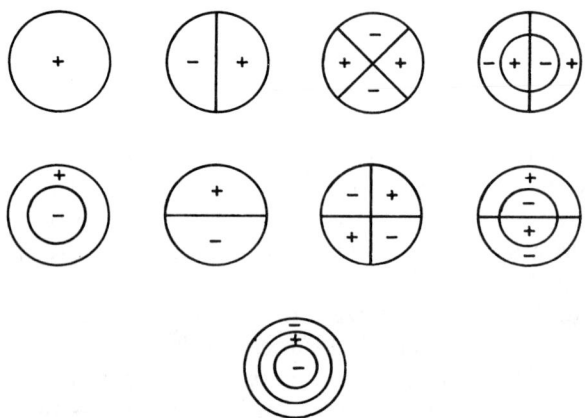

Figure 7-4: Basis functions for approximation in the Hueckel operator

Hueckel was successful in obtaining an analytical solution to determine ξ. The algebraic details are involved and may be found in

EDGE AND CURVE DETECTION

[5] and [6].

Once ξ and N' are determined, the presence of an edge is determined by requiring step height, h, to be large and N' to be small. Actually, the required step height is allowed to be a function of N', a larger step being required if the fit is poor.

A generalized Hueckel operator uses an edge model with intensity profiles as shown in Fig. 7-5. This allows the operator to detect step as well as "line" edges (defined to be edges where $b_1 \ulcorner b_3$). Vector ξ now contains two additional parameters, one for an additional intensity value and another for edge width.

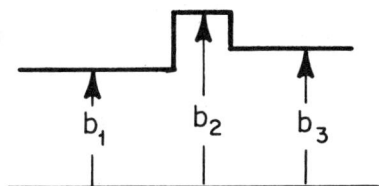

Figure 7-5: Intensity profile of a generalized edge

Mero and Vassy [7] and Nevatia [8] have described attempts to simplify this operator by using fewer terms for approximation of a step. However, such simplifications result in marked loss of performance in the presence of noise.

Hueckel's operator is claimed to be optimal under certain assumptions. However, further analysis has indicated some deficiencies in his optimization process. One is that the optimal analysis was done for continuous domain and does not necessarily apply to the digital approximations [9]. Abdou [9] and Shaw [10] have described techniques of direct edge fitting in the digital image domain without resorting to any approximations.

7.1.3 Edge Detection by Template Matching

A straightforward approach is to detect edges by matching with templates of desired ideal edges, also called *edge masks*. Two 3-by-3 edge masks, corresponding to vertical and diagonal edges, are shown in Fig. 7-6. Eight such masks were used in an edge detector described by Prewitt [4]. At each pixel in the image, a match with each of the eight masks is computed; the mask with the highest output determines the edge magnitude at that pixel, and the orientation of this mask gives the orientation of the edge. Kirsch [11] has used an edge detector with slightly different masks, as shown in Fig. 7-7. Again, eight masks are used. (This is a slightly modified description of the Kirsch operator from that given in [11].)

```
  1      1    -1
  1     -2    -1
  1      1    -1
     (a) Vertical

  1     -1    -1
  1     -2    -1
  1      1     1
     (b) Diagonal
```

Figure 7-6: Prewitt edge masks in two directions:
(a) vertical, (b) diagonal

```
  3      3    -5
  3      0    -5
  3      3    -5
          (a)

  3     -5    -5
  3      0    -5
  3      3     3
          (b)
```

Figure 7-7: Masks for Kirsch operator (two directions)

The edge masks are not limited to 3-by-3 neighborhoods. A general edge mask is shown in Fig. 7-8. For arbitrary orientations, the analog mask can be approximated by using values determined by the proportion of a cell being on either side of an ideal edge. 5-by-5 masks for 30-degree increments are shown in Fig. 7-9 (from [12]).

McLeod has suggested the use of masks where the weights drop exponentially as the distance from the edge increases. The weights also drop along the edge, as the distance from the center increases [13]. Such masks de-emphasize the effects of points away from the center.

An important parameter to select is the size of the edge mask. A larger mask offers more immunity to noise, but less discrimination between nearby edges. An adaptive way to choose an optimal mask size

EDGE AND CURVE DETECTION

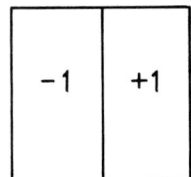

Figure 7-8: A schematic edge mask

```
-100  -100    0   100   100        -100   32   100   100   100
-100  -100    0   100   100        -100  -78    92   100   100
-100  -100    0   100   100        -100 -100     0   100   100
-100  -100    0   100   100        -100 -100   -92    78   100
-100  -100    0   100   100        -100 -100  -100   -32   100

            (a) 0°                           (b) 30°


  100   100   100   100   100        100   100   100   100   100
  -32    78   100   100   100        100   100   100   100   100
 -100   -92     0    92   100          0     0     0     0     0
 -100  -100  -100   -78    32       -100  -100  -100  -100  -100
 -100  -100  -100  -100  -100       -100  -100  -100  -100  -100

            (c) 60°                           (d) 90°


 -100   100   100   100   100        100   100   100    32  -100
 -100   100   100    78   -32        100   100    92   -78  -100
 -100    92     0   -92  -100        100   100     0  -100  -100
   32   -78  -100  -100  -100        100    78   -92  -100  -100
 -100  -100  -100  -100  -100        100   -32  -100  -100  -100

            (e) 120°                          (f) 150°
```

Figure 7-9: Edge masks in six directions: (a) 0°, (b) 30°,
(c) 60°, (d) 90°, (e) 120°, (f) 150°

is to compute the convolution outputs with masks of increasing size and choose the largest size such that the next larger size causes a significant reduction in the output value, presumably due to the introduction of a second edge. Experiments with masks of varying size have been described by Rosenfeld and Thurston [14] and by Marr [15]. The number of masks depends on the desired angular resolution and also on the mask size and shape. Long and thin masks need finer angular resolution so that the edges with orientation between two edge masks are not missed.

For large edge masks, the template match output is high not only at an edge, but also in its vicinity. The output as a function of the mask position for the mask of Fig. 7-8 is shown schematically in Fig. 7-10. A simple thresholding of the output will thus give a "thick" edge with uncertainty in position. Figure 7-11(a) shows an aerial image of an airport and Fig. 7-11(b) the magnitude of the edge output using the masks of Fig. 7-9. Simple thresholding of the edge output gives thick edges as shown in Fig. 7-11(c). The edge output can be "thinned" by selecting only the local peaks. This operation is sometimes called *nonmaxima suppression* [14]. Improved results can be obtained by thinning in a direction normal to the edge direction; a scheme to combine thinning and thresholding is described below.

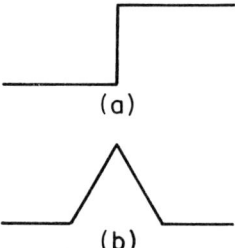

Figure 7-10: (a) Step edge, (b) output profile

Precise location and characterization of edges can be more complex than simple peak detection of the convolved output. Nevatia and Babu used step masks as shown in Fig. 7-9 and examined magnitudes and directions of pixels in a small neighborhood [12]. At each pixel, let the maximum outputs of the convolution with these masks, and the direction of the mask producing the maximum output, be known as the edge magnitude and direction, respectively, at that pixel. They required that for a pixel to be an edge pixel, its edge magnitude be higher than the edge magnitudes of the pixels on either side of it, in a direction normal to its edge direction. Further, these neighboring pixels were required to have edge orientations similar to that of the central pixel. Figure 7-11(d) shows the edges detected by this procedure in the image of Fig. 7-11(a). Note that the two sides of the vertical taxiway in the right of the image are connected in Fig. 7-11(c) and yet are separated by the described thinning process.

More complex decision procedures have used both edge and *bar* masks. A bar mask, shown schematically in Fig. 7-12, approximates second derivatives. At first, the bar masks may seem to be ideally suited for the detection of "line" like edges. However, these bar or line masks also respond strongly to bright points and to step edges.

EDGE AND CURVE DETECTION

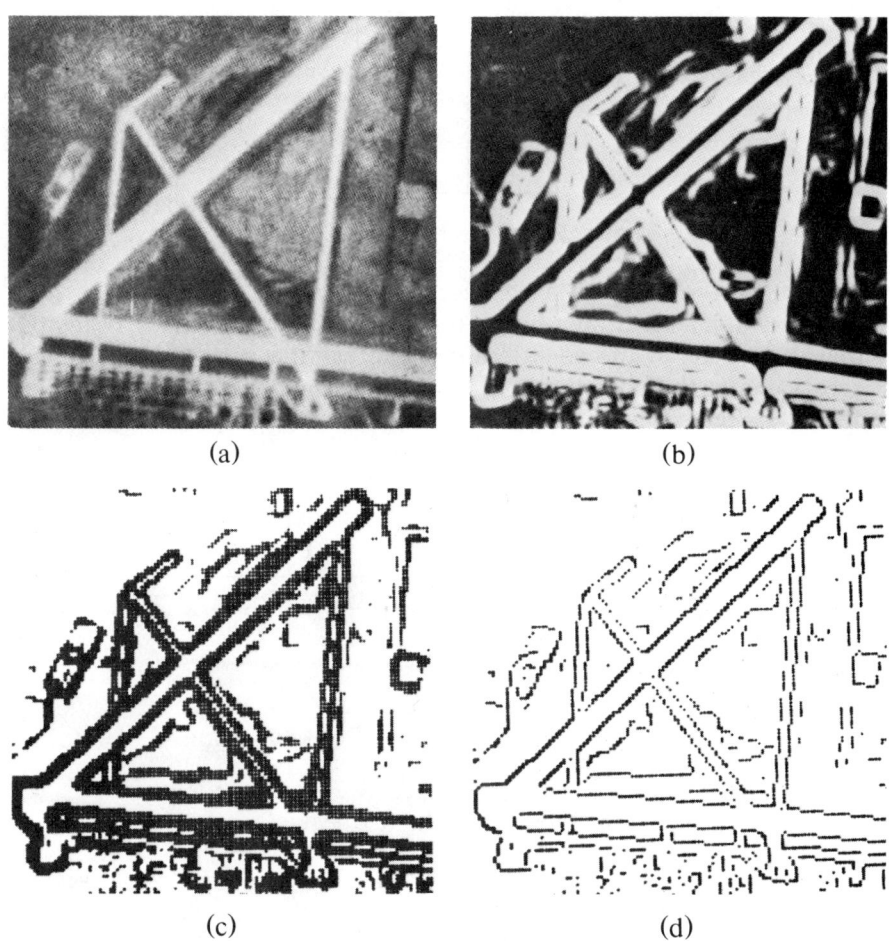

Figure 7-11: Steps in edge detection: (a) image,
(b) edge magnitude, (c) unthinned edge, (d) thinned edges

VanderBrug has suggested a "nonlinear" line detector that requires the presence of a line to be indicated not only by the total mask output being high but also by a determination along each row of the bar mask that the values in the positive part are higher (or lower) than in the neighboring negative parts [16].

Herskovits [17] and Marr [15] have used the outputs of both the edge and the bar masks for the location and description of the edges. Herskovits has defined several types of edges that occur in scenes of polyhedra, as shown in Fig. 7-13. Each edge type produces a characteristic output profile when convolved with the edge, and the bar

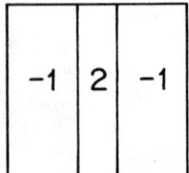

Figure 7-12: A schematic bar mask

masks and these profiles can be used to determine the edge type [15]. As an example, for a step edge, the edge mask produces a triangular output with peak at the edge location whereas the bar mask output has a zero value at the edge location, surrounded by a positive peak on one side and a negative peak on the other.

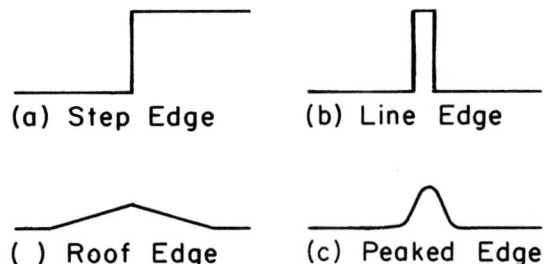

Figure 7-13: Different types of edges: (a) step, (b) line, (c) rook, (d) peaked

In later work, Marr and Hildreth used an isotropic second derivative operator, instead of the directed bar masks [18]. The simplest such operator is a Laplacian ($\partial^2/\partial x^2 + \partial^2/\partial y^2$). The operator used by Marr and Hildreth is a Laplacian of a Gaussian and has an intensity profile similar to that of a lateral inhibition operator (Section 6.2). The operator is given formally by

$$\nabla^2 G(x, y) = \frac{-1}{2\pi\sigma^4} \cdot \left(2 - \frac{x^2 + y^2}{\sigma^2}\right) e^{-\frac{x^2 + y^2}{2\sigma^2}} \qquad (7\text{-}9)$$

where $w = 2\sigma$ determines the width of the excitatory region of the operator, and $\lambda = 2\pi\sigma$ is the diameter.

As in the case of a bar mask, this operator produces a zero-crossing at the edge location for a step edge. Note that the second-derivative operators are insensitive to gradual changes in illumination. The above operator is also conjectured to have the property that zero-crossing information is sufficient to reconstruct the original image. Marr and Hildreth suggest use of four different mask sizes to correspond to observations from the human visual system.

7.1.4 Statistical Edge Detectors

Edge detection has also been viewed as a problem of statistical decision making. Griffith has described an analysis that uses the a priori probability of grey-level distributions in an image in the presence of an edge [19, 20]. For step and line edges, the optimal decision reduces to a procedure like template matching. This statistical analysis, however, requires many simplifying assumptions.

A different approach, by Yakimovsky, views edge detection as choosing between the following two hypotheses [21]:

H_0: The samples on the two sides of a line are taken from the same object.

H_1: The samples on one side are from one object and on the other side from a different object.

Under the assumptions that the object grey levels are uniform, except for added white Gaussian noise, the optimal decision reduces to a likelihood-ratio computation, depending only on the measured variances on the two sides of the hypothesized edge.

7.1.5 Choice of Thresholds

Most of the above techniques require that a certain measure of edge strength exceed a threshold for an edge presence to be declared. The choice of such thresholds should depend on the expected properties of the desired edges and the undesired variations including random noise and changes in illumination. The threshold selection should also be dependent on context; for example, it is easier for us to perceive low-contrast edges if they belong to an elongated boundary segment.

In general, however, the properties of a new scene are not known a priori, and hence the threshold must be selected by measurements on the image. Owing to an absence of adequate mathematical models for the structures in an image, the common approach is to choose an "optimal" threshold by empirical analysis of a set of typical images. These thresholds may then be changed by feedback from further analysis of the resulting edges.

For specific and restricted scenes, optimal thresholds may be determined by a mathematical analysis. Herskovits devised a technique for choosing a threshold for scenes of polyhedra viewed through a sensor with known noise characteristics to maximize the sensitivity of edge detection while minimizing the response to noise and smooth illumination gradients [17]. Abdou and Pratt have described analytical techniques with different optimality criteria using statistical decision theory methods [9, 22].

Note that the edge detectors using second-derivative masks need not use a threshold, as only a zero-crossing must be detected. The operator described by Nevatia and Babu [12] can also be used without thresholds as other tests on the output profile are used.

7.2 RESULTS OF EDGE DETECTION

How successful are the various edge detectors in providing the desired results for a given image? The answer is complicated by the dependence of the results on the particular image and the lack of a suitable model for images to use for predictions. Also, in complex images, the desired response for the edge detection process is difficult to specify, as edges are likely to occur in many positions other than the desired object boundaries because of the presence of surface texture. Mathematical analysis for even simple images is difficult owing to the complexity and the nonlinearity of the edge-detection algorithms. Some analytical results may be found in [9, 17, 22]. Abdou's results indicate that template matching is optimal, if the type of the edge is known and the noise is additive Gaussian.

Alternatives to empirical analysis are the use of a set of typical real images or synthetic images with controlled parameters. The results are easier to evaluate in the latter case, but not necessarily indicative of performance on real images. Figure 7-14(a) shows a step with Gaussian noise (the ratio of step size to signal variance is 2). The image looks noisy, but the vertical edge is distinctly visible to us. Figures 7-14(b), (c), and (d) show the outputs of the Sobel, Hueckel, and the Nevatia-Babu edge detector using six masks shown earlier in Fig. 7-9. Note that the last output is thinned, as thinning is integral with thresholding, whereas the others are not. In each case, the thresholds were adjusted for best subjective response, picking up the maximum number of desired edges without being swamped with the noise edges. For this example, the 5-by-5 mask edge detector clearly is much superior to the other two. For similar images with less noise, the differences are less pronounced, and all work nearly perfectly. A systematic and comprehensive evaluation of many edge detectors with

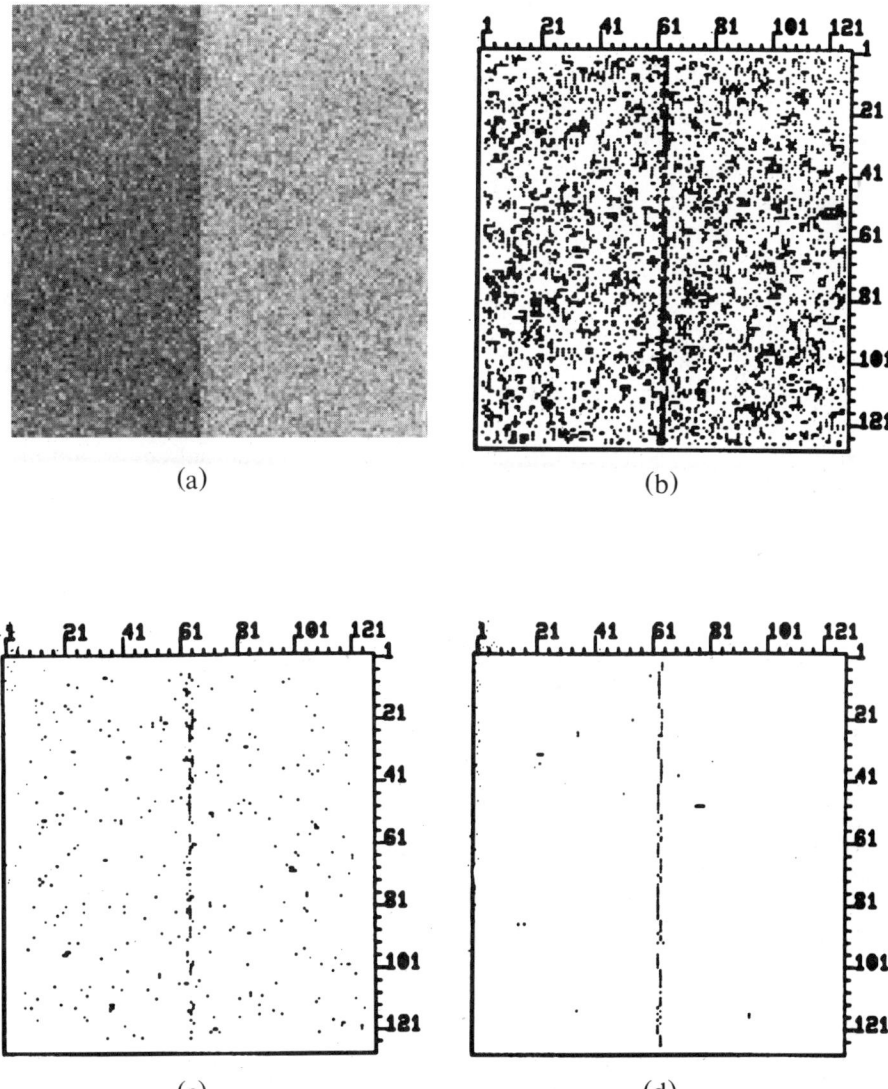

Figure 7-14: An image and the edges detected in it: (a) image, (b) Sobel output, (c) Hueckel output, (d) Nevatia-Babu output

synthetic images may be found in [9, 23, 24].

More interesting are the results of edge detection on real images. Even for simple scenes, as the polyhedral object scene of Fig. 3-4 and the slightly more complex scene of Fig. 7-11 indicate, some of the desired edges are missed and several undesired edges are present. The undesired edges are primarily due to real surface markings or texture (and may, in fact, be useful for texture analysis, as in Section 8.3.2). Two more examples are discussed below.

Figure 7-15(a) shows an image of a truck with bushes in the foreground and the background. Figure 7-15(b) shows the edges detected by the Nevatia-Babu edge detector. It is clear that some elaborate structuring of the edges is needed before the desired object boundaries can be derived. Adequacy of edge detection cannot be evaluated separately from these processes. The edge detection is far from perfect, compared to our perception. However, many of the undesired edges, such as those in the background, are real edges in the image. Many of the missing edges are due to inadequacy of the edge detector, but some, particularly those near the top of the boundary of the truck with the background, are very low-contrast edges and distinctly visible to humans only when viewed with the surrounding high-contrast edges. Such edges may be called perceptual edges and are not expected to be detected by a local edge detector.

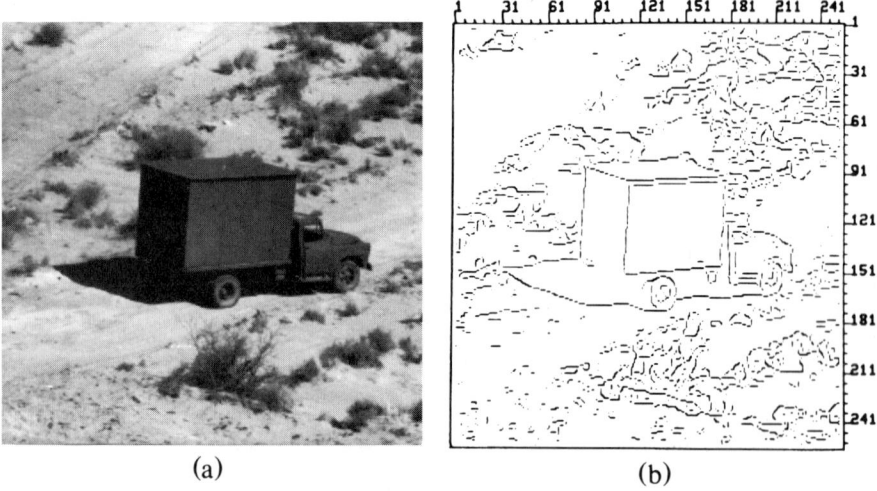

Figure 7-15: (a) A truck image and (b) edges detected in it

Figure 7-16 shows edges detected (by the algorithm described in [12]) in the aerial image of the San Francisco area shown earlier in Fig. 1-9. Here, we can recognize many important features of the image, but further analysis of this large number of edges by machine is going to be complex. However, such edge output has been used for the detection of roads, bridges, and other linear features, and along with a region segmentation technique described in Chapter 8 has also been used for matching of the image with a symbolic map; some results are given in Chapter 10. (Such processing has applications in navigation and map-updating.)

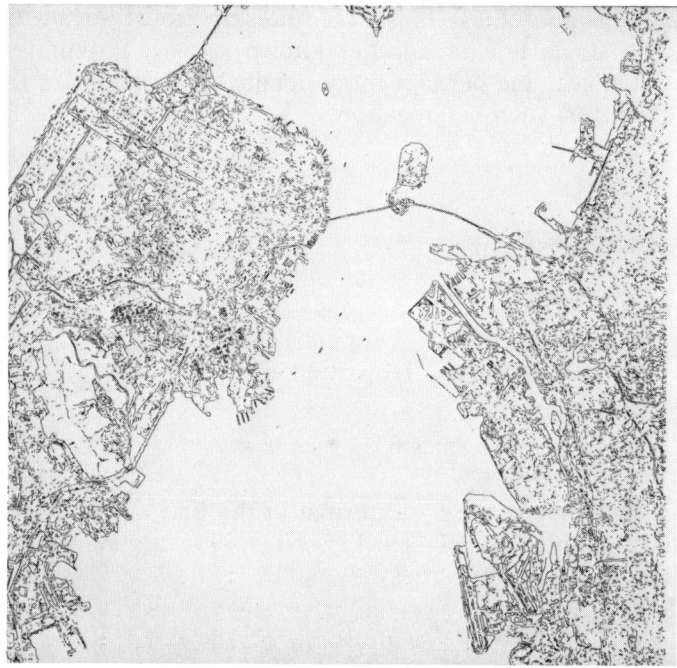

Figure 7-16: Edges detected in the aerial image of Fig. 1-9

Marr has suggested that the basic purpose of low-level processing, such as edge detection, is to provide a description of discontinuities that is adequate for higher-level processing without recourse to original intensity data [15]. In his system, the descriptions are derived by convolving the image with edge and bar masks (or Laplacian-Gaussian masks) of different sizes. In addition to the presence of a significant discontinuity, the type of the edge (for example, step or roof), its contrast and sharpness are included in the description. Such a description, termed a *primal sketch*, was conjectured by Marr to be the main result of low-level processing for humans and other primates.

7.3 LINE AND CURVE DETECTION

An important level of processing of edges detected in an image (possibly with additional descriptions as in Marr's primal sketch) is to aggregate the edge elements to form object boundaries. The shape of these boundaries may not be known a priori, but in many cases they can be approximated well by piecewise linear segments. However, it is not feasible to simply fit linear segments to all the edges in an image and discard the poor fits. It is first necessary to aggregate the edges lying along a single line or another known curve. Proximity and the directions of edges, and perhaps more detailed descriptions of the edges, can be used for such aggregation. In the following, a few such techniques are described.

7.3.1 Hough Transform

It is simpler to first describe this technique applied to the detection of a set of points lying on a straight line. The general equation of a straight line can be written as

$$x \cos \theta + y \sin \theta = r \qquad (7\text{-}10)$$

where θ is the angle made by a normal to the line with the x axis and r is the length of this normal (see Fig. 7-17). For a given point (x_i, y_i) on this line, Eq. (7-10) becomes

$$x_i \cos \theta + y_i \sin \theta = r \qquad (7\text{-}11)$$

Considering r and θ as the new variables, the above equation gives the relation between the parameters of a line constrained to go through the point (x_i, y_i). Equation (7-11) corresponds to a sinusoidal curve in the (r, θ) space (see Fig. 7-18). This relationship between the image plane and the (r, θ) plane is known as the Hough transform after the inventor [25]. For a collinear group of points in the image plane, the curves determined by Eq. (7-10) in the (r, θ) space must all intersect in one common point (corresponding to the actual parameters of the line through the image points).

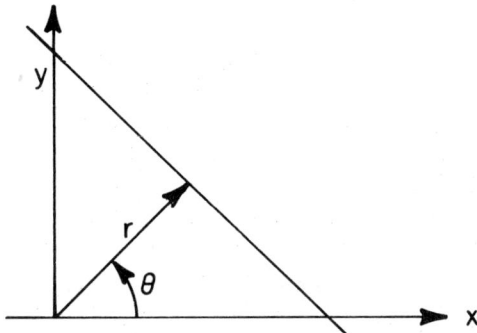

Figure 7-17: The (r, θ) representation of a straight line

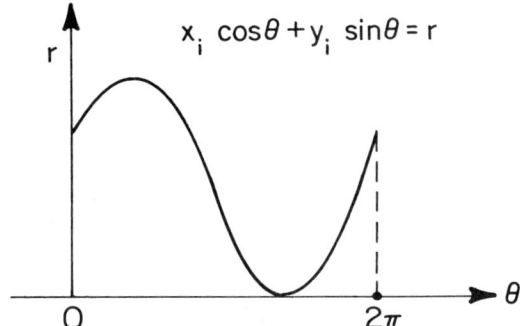

Figure 7-18: Hough transformn of a point (x_i, y_i)

Thus, to detect clusters of collinear points, we could construct the transform curves in the (r, θ) space for each point and pick the points corresponding to coincidence of three or more such curves. For implementation in a digital computer, the r and θ parameters must be quantized. θ varies between 0 and 2π, and r can be limited to the size of the image plane. Construction of a curve in (r, θ) space now requires incrementing the counters of cells along the curve. To find coincidences, we simply pick the cells with high counts. The performance is affected by the chosen quantization. A coarse digitization will fail to distinguish between nearby lines, and a very fine resolution would allow little error in collinearity.

This procedure can be made more efficient if the directions of the edges are known. Then, a single point, rather than a sinusoid, can be computed in the (r, θ) space for a given edge point. Note that the Hough transform technique does not examine the proximity of the clustered points. Groups of contiguous points must be further separated from a cluster of collinear points.

The Hough transform technique easily generalizes to detection of arbitrary curves described by a function such as

$$f(a_1, a_2, \ldots, a_n, x, y) = 0 \qquad (7\text{-}12)$$

where $a_1, a_2, \ldots, a_n$ are the parameters of the curve. For each point (x_i, y_i), we now associate a surface $f(a_1, a_2, \ldots, a_n)$ in the $(a_1, a_2, \ldots, a_n)$ space. The complexity of the computation increases with the dimensionality of this parameter space.

Hough transform techniques became widely known through work of Duda and Hart [26]. Extensions and generalizations of the basic technique, including the detection of circle and other nonlinear curves, may be found in [26-32]. An interesting generalization for nonanalytical shapes can be found in [33]. In this approach, the parameters of the Hough space are the origin of a local coordinate system for the figure and its scale and rotation.

7.3.2 Graph-Theoretic Techniques

A simple linking technique is to connect each point to one or more of its neighbors (say 8-neighbors), if they have similar orientations. This technique is feasible only if the number of branches at each step can be kept low. Nevatia and Babu have described an implementation where the number of branches is at usually one and at most two [12]. Their edge-detection method was by convolution with edge-shaped masks, followed by thinning in a direction normal to the edge. Such edge detection tends to yield edges that form lines with few gaps and few small connecting branches. If only small neighborhoods, say the 8-neighbors, are considered for possible linking, an exhaustive list of rules for allowable connections can be made.

Generally, the edge points in an image may be viewed as the nodes of a graph and a cost function associated with the connection of two edge points. The desired boundaries can then be defined as the minimal-cost (or low-cost) paths through this graph. The cost of connecting two edge points is defined to be a function of the distance between them, difference in their directions, and desired similarities in other descriptions. Various cost functions and graph search techniques have been used. Montanari, and Martelli have described dynamic programming approaches that are best suited if only a single desired curve is to be extracted [34, 35]. These techniques are efficient if starting and end points of the curve are also given. Zahn [36] has suggested the use of the longest branch of a *minimal spanning tree* for a more efficient search.

Ramer has described a graph search technique that applies to detection of one or more curves [37, 38]. His technique is a simple tree search, where at each node the number of alternatives is restricted to a few nearest neighbors only. Ramer calls the basic edge elements *strokes* and the resulting connected segments *streaks*. His program also maintains information about streak intersections and possible loops. His technique was applied to simple curved objects, such as a table lamp, in relatively clear environments.

Graph-theoretic techniques are useful when the graph search can be constrained. For special applications, specific curves have been successfully detected even in presence of large noise (for example, see [34]).

7.3.3 Method of Projections

Another approach to detection of straight-line segments is to search for these lines in a number of quantized directions over the entire range of directions. For a given direction, say vertical, the image plane is divided in strips or buckets parallel to this direction. Only the edge elements in the same bucket, and the resulting segments from neighboring buckets are linked together (see Fig. 7-19). The linking is merely in the order of increasing (or decreasing) coordinate along the direction of linking. Such a linking algorithm has been used by the author [39]. A similar algorithm is also described by Marr [15] (called the process of "theta aggregation").

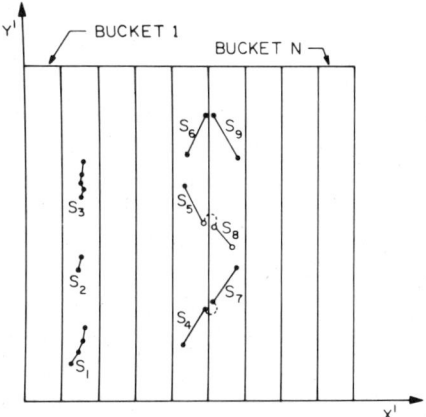

Figure 7-19: Linking by projections

7.4 CONTOUR FILLING AND FEEDBACK

The different line-detection techniques of the previous section differ in their computational costs, but the results are rather similar and largely dictated by the performance of the local edge detector itself. The detected boundaries are generally fragmented and not closed, except for some simple scenes. The gaps in the boundary further complicate the separation of object boundary segments from the "background" boundary segments. Some of the gaps are due to the failings of the local edge detector, particularly near corners and in areas of high texture. However, in real images, some of the boundaries that are perceptually continuous to us have local segments with little discontinuity in local attributes. These segments are difficult to perceive, if seen in isolation from the rest of the scene.

Small gaps in the boundaries can be filled simply by extrapolation. These extrapolations may then be "verified" by the use of a more sensitive edge detector. Many systems use such contour filling, starting from the early work of Roberts [3], but they are ad hoc and not of general applicability.

Zucker, Hummel, and Rosenfeld have described an application of stochastic relaxation labeling, described previously in Chapter 5, to improving detection of curves and lines in images [40]. Each point in the image is assigned a probability of being on a boundary or not. Initial probabilities may be computed from the output of a local edge detector. These probabilities are then modified iteratively, based on "compatibility" with neighbors. An edge point is viewed as being more compatible with other edge points of similar orientation in the neighborhood. This technique tends to cause longer lines to grow and isolated points to be removed. However, the performance is dependent on the choice of the compatibility criteria.

Shirai developed an interesting feedback mechanism for the limited domain of polyhedral objects [41]. The outer boundaries of such object assemblies are of high contrast and easily detected. The interior boundaries can have poor contrast, depending on the sources of illumination and may be hard to detect. Shirai's system detects the outer boundaries first and then proposes hypotheses for the presence of other lines, which are verified (or rejected) by a more sensitive edge detector. These rules are specifically for the domain of polyhedral objects but do not require knowledge of the particular objects present. Figure 7-20 shows the successive steps for a typical example. One rule proposes extension of any existing line at a concave vertex, such as line KJ at vertex J. Another rule suggests new lines that are parallel to other existing lines such as lines $G'M'$ and $O'P'$. A total of ten such rules is used. Verification by a sensitive edge detector is possible since a long

EDGE AND CURVE DETECTION   121

line of specific orientation and position is being evaluated. This system was successful in obtaining complete boundaries for fairly complex polyhedral scenes. The term "heterarchy" was first coined to describe this technique.

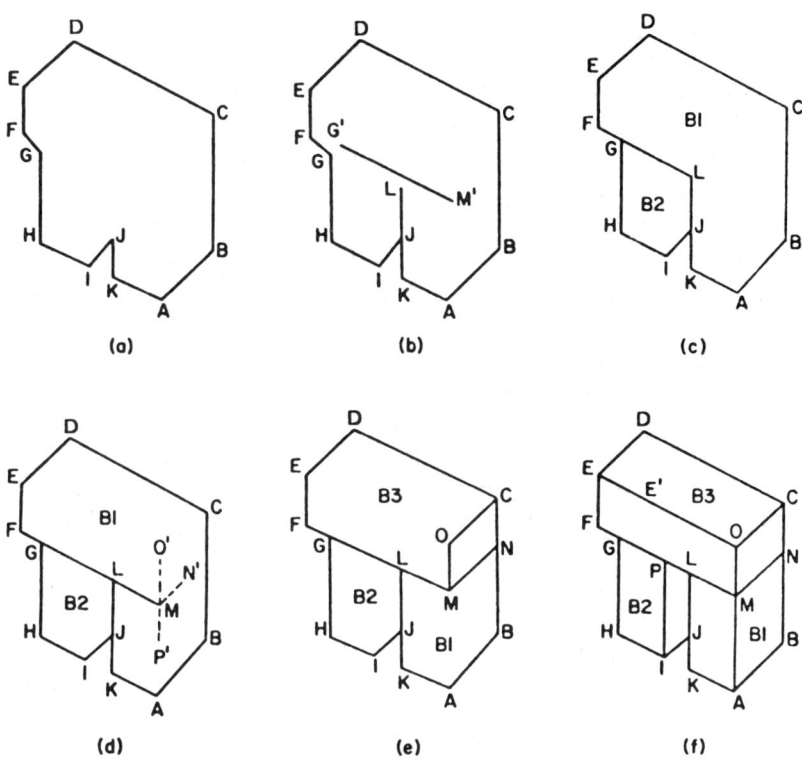

Figure 7-20: Steps in Shirai's line-detection system
(from Shirai [41])

Kelley used a *planning* approach to boundary detection [42]. A boundary is first detected in a lower-resolution image, obtained by averaging the larger image. This boundary is then expanded in scale for a higher-resolution image, and detailed analysis between the gaps can be performed. This technique can be helpful in reducing the computation time, but finer lines, such as thin roads, may be lost in the reduced image.

Several suggestions have been made to use a sequence of reduced images forming a *pyramid* structure, with processing at one level influencing the processing at higher or lower levels [43-46]. Such structures are used not only for edge and curve detection, but for all levels of processing. The levels in the pyramid defined by varying resolution should be distinguished from the levels of abstraction in processing (for one resolution level). The pyramid structures are likely to lead to efficient processing if the level with minimum adequate resolution can be isolated, without elaborate processing. Also, for certain images, the processing may be easier at certain low-resolution levels, owing to averaging of fine texture and small details.

In many instances, missing boundary segments may be obtained only by other, more difficult processing—for example, in discrimination of surfaces of different textures or of discontinuities in three-dimensional surface orientations. In some images, humans perceive contours in addition to those formed by edge discontinuities. For example, a circle connecting the end points of lines is seen in Fig. 7-21(a) and an extra triangle is perceived in Fig. 7-21(b). It has been suggested that the end points of detected boundary segments should be examined for such *subjective contours*, based on their proximity, collinearity of the segments, or the end points forming regular patterns [15].

Figure 7-21: Two instance of subjective contours

Experience with edge- and line-detection techniques indicates that complete object boundaries are difficult to obtain, and thus many of the previously described techniques of higher-level scene analysis are difficult to use directly. One point of view even contends that higher-level descriptions must be obtained from incomplete boundaries and, in turn, used to complete the boundaries. In spite of limited development of such techniques, incomplete boundaries have been used for recognition and higher-level descriptions in limited domains. Perkins, for example, has described recognition of industrial parts by matching of boundary descriptions [47]; Nevatia and Babu have described detection of roads by locating *antiparallel* lines, which are parallel lines of opposite contrast [12]. (The latter may be viewed as a very simple case of computing generalized cones, as defined in Chapter 5, from incomplete boundaries.)

7.5 COLOR EDGES

A color image is given by a triple of numbers for each pixel (in one of the many representations). To detect color edges, we can detect the edges in the three components separately and then combine the results. (In some attributes, such as hue, the range of values may be circular, or have a discontinuity. Edges can not be easily detected in these components directly.)

The simplest way to combine the edges in three color components is to form a new edge whose strength is a linear combination of the strengths of the edges in the three components. (Reconciling different edge orientations is more complicated.) However, such combination is likely to lead to results very similar to the processing of a single grey-level image, which itself is derived by a linear combination of three component images. An alternative is to accept an edge in the color image, if an edge is present in any of the components. Another alternative is to require concurrence in all components.

The author has experimented with a generalization of the Hueckel edge detector, to compute a best-fit edge in three-dimensional color space [48]. The orientation of the edge in the three components is constrained to be the same, but other edge parameters, such as brightness and the intensity profile, may vary. The three components of the resulting edge were combined in different ways, as discussed above. An analysis of many images pointed to the following conclusions (these are believed to be independent of the edge detector used):

1. Intensity and chromatic edges tend to co-occur. This may be expected as two objects of different color are unlikely to have the same intensity.

2. Chromatic edges may be useful in boundary detection in low contrast images where intensity edges are weak.

3. Requiring co-occurrence of intensity and chromatic edges may provide higher-confidence edges, useful in a multpass system.

Color has been found to be more useful in region-segmentation techniques described in the next chapter. This is consistent with the hypothesis that humans use color for distinguishing large surfaces rather than high-resolution details.

7.6 SUMMARY

This chapter has covered several techniques of edge detection, mainly distinguished by their computational definitions of local discontinuities. Various techniques for grouping local edges into boundaries have also been described. A major conclusion of experience with such techniques has been that while the local techniques can be improved, boundary detection also requires global processing, and that higher-level descriptions must be able to use incomplete boundaries.

REFERENCES

[1] L. S. Davis, "A Survey of Edge Detection Techniques," *Computer Graphics and Image Processing*, Vol. 4, No. 3, September 1975, pp. 248-270.

[2] W. K. Pratt, *Digital Image Processing*, John Wiley & Sons, New York, 1978.

[3] L. G. Roberts, "Machine Perception of Three-Dimensional Solids," in *Optical and Electro-Optical Information Processing*, J. T. Tippett, et al. (eds.), MIT Press, Cambridge, Mass., 1965, pp. 159-197.

[4] J. M. S. Prewitt, "Object Enhancement and Extraction," in *Picture Processing and Psychopictorics*, B. S. Lipkin and A. Rosenfeld (eds.), Academic Press, New York, 1970.

[5] M. H. Hueckel, "A Local Visual Edge Operator Which Recognizes Edges and Lines," *Journal of the ACM*, Vol. 20, 1973, pp. 634-647.

[6] M. H. Hueckel, "An Operator Which Locates Edges in Digitized Pictures," *Journal of the ACM*, Vol. 18, 1971, pp. 113-15.

[7] L. Mero and Z. Vassy, "A Simplified and Fast Version of the Hueckel Operator for Finding Optimal Edges in Pictures," in *Advance Papers of the Fourth International Joint Conference on Artificial Intelligence*, Tbilisi, Georgia, U.S.S.R., September 1975, pp. 650-655.

[8] R. Nevatia, "Evaluation of a Simplified Hueckel Edge-Line Detector," *Computer Graphics and Image Processing*, Vol. 6, 1977, pp. 582-588.

[9] I. Abdou, "Quantitative Methods of Edge Detection," University of Southern California, Report USCIPI 830 (Ph.D. thesis), July 1978.

[10] G. B. Shaw, "Local and Regional Edge Detectors: Some Comparisons," *Computer Graphics and Image Processing*, Vol. 9, No. 2, February 1979, pp. 135-149.

[11] R. A. Kirsch, "Computer Determination of the Constituent Structure of Biological Images," *Computers and Biomedical Research*, Vol. 4, No. 3, June 1971, pp. 315-328.

[12] R. Nevatia and K. R. Babu, "Linear Feature Extraction and Description," *Computer Graphics and Image Processing*, Vol. 13, 1980, pp. 257-269.

[13] I. D. G. Macleod, "Comments on Techniques for Edge Detection," *Proceedings of the IEEE*, Vol. 60, No. 3, March 1972, pp. 344.

[14] A. Rosenfeld and M. Thurston, "Edge and Curve Detection for Visual Scene Analysis," *IEEE Transactions on Computers*, Vol. C-20, May 1971, pp. 562-569.

[15] D. Marr, "Early Processing of Visual Information," *Philosophical Transactions of the Royal Society of London*, B275, 1976, pp. 483-524.

[16] G. J. VanderBrug, "Semilinear Line Detectors," *Computer Graphics and Image Processing*, Vol. 4, 1975, pp. 287-293.

[17] A. Herskovits, "On Boundary Detection," MIT Project MAC Memo 183, Cambridge, Mass., 1970.

[18] D. Marr and E. Hildreth, "Theory of Edge Detection," *Proceedings of the Royal Society of London*, B207, 1980, pp. 187-217.

[19] A. K. Griffith, "Mathematical Models for Automatic Line Detection," *Journal of ACM*, Vol. 120, January 1973, pp. 62-80.

[20] A. K. Griffith, "Edge Detection in Simple Scenes Using A PriorInformation," *IEEE Transactions on Computers*, Vol. 22, No. 4, April 1973, pp. 371-380.

[21] Y. Yakimovsky, "Boundary and Object Detection in Real World Images," *Journal of ACM*, Vol. 23, 1976, pp. 599-618.

[22] I. Abdou and W. K. Pratt, "Quantitative Design and Evaluation of Enhancement Edge Detector Schemes," *Proceedings of IEEE*, Vol. 67, 1979, pp. 753-763.

[23] J. R. Fram, and E. S. Deutsch, "On the Quantitative Evaluation of Edge Detection Schemes and Their Comparison with Human Performance," *IEEE Transactions on Computers*, Vol. 24, No. 6, June 1975, pp. 616-628.

[24] E. S. Deutsch and J. R. Fram, "A Quantitative Study of the Orientation Bias of Some Edge Detector Schemes," *IEEE Transactions on Computers*, Vol. 27, 1978, pp. 205-213.

[25] P. V. C. Hough, "Method and Means for Recognizing Complex Patterns," U.S. Patent 3069654, December 18, 1962.

[26] R. O. Duda and P. E. Hart, "Use of the Hough Transformation to Detect Lines and Curves in Pictures," *Communications of the ACM*, Vol. 15, January 1972, pp. 11-15.

[27] C. Kimme, D. Ballard, and J. Sklansky, "Finding Circles by an Array of Accumulators," *Communications of ACM*, Vol. 18, February 1975, pp. 120-122.

[28] S. D. Shapiro, "Transformations for the Computer Detection of Curves in Noisy Pictures," *Computer Graphics and Image Processing*, December 75, pp. 328-338.

[29] S. D. Shapiro, "Properties of Transforms for Detection of Curves in Noisy Pictures," *Computer Graphics and Image Processing*, October 1978, Vol. 8, No. 2, pp. 219-236.

[30] J. Sklansky, "On the Hough Techniques for Curve Detection," *IEEE Transactions on Computers*, Vol. 27, No. 10, October 1978, pp. 923-926.

[31] S. Tsuji and F. Matsumoto, "Detection of Ellipses by a Modified Hough Transform," *IEEE Transactions on Computers*, Vol. 27, No. 8, August 1978, pp. 777-781.

[32] F. O'Gorman and M. B. Clowes, "Finding Picture Edges Through Collinearity of Feature Points," in *Proceedings of the Third International Joint Conference on Artificial Intelligence*, August 1973, Stanford, Calif., pp. 543-555.

[33] D. H. Ballard and D. Sabbah, "On Shapes," *Proceedings of the Seventh International Joint Conference on Artificial Intelligence*, Vancouver, B.C., Canada, August 1981, pp. 607-612.

[34] U. Montanari, "On the Optimal Detection of Curves in Noisy Pictures," *Communications of ACM*, Vol. 14, May 1971, pp. 335-345.

[35] A. Martelli, "An Application of Heuristic Search Methods to Edge and Contour Detection," *Communications of ACM*, February 1976, pp. 73-83.

[36] C. T. Zahn, "Graph-theoretical Methods for Detecting and Describing Gestalt Clusters," *IEEE Transactions on Computers*, Vol. 20, pp. 68-86, January 1971.

[37] U. Ramer, "Extraction of Lines Structures from Photographs of Curved Objects," *Computer Graphics and Image Processing*, Vol. 4, pp. 81-103, June 1975.

[38] U. Ramer, "The Transformation of Photographic Images into Stock Arrays," *IEEE Transactions on Circuits and Systems*, Vol. 22, 1975, pp. 363-374.

[39] R. Nevatia, "Locating Object Boundaries in Textured Environments," *IEEE Transactions on Computers*, Vol. 25, No. 11, November 1976, pp. 1170-1175.

[40] S. W. Zucker, R. A. Hummel and A. Rosenfeld, "An Application of Relaxation Labeling to Line and Curve Enhancement," *IEEE Transactions on Computers*, Vol. 26, No. 4, April 1977, pp. 394-403.
[41] Y. Shirai, "Analyzing Intensity Arrays Using Knowledge About Scenes," in *The Psychology of Computer Vision*, P. H. Winston (ed.), McGraw-Hill, New York, 1975.
[42] M. Kelly, "Edge Detection by Computer Using Planning," in *Machine Intelligence VI*, B. Meltzer and D. Michie (eds.), Edinburgh University Press, Edinburgh, 1971, pp. 397-409.
[43] A. R. Hanson and E. M. Riseman, "VISIONS: A Computer System for Interpreting Scenes," in *Computer Vision Systems*, A. R. Hanson and E. M. Riseman (eds.), Academic Press, New York, 1978, pp. 303-333.
[44] S. Tanimoto and T. Pavlidis, "A Hierarchical Data Structure for Picture Processing," *Computer Graphics and Image Processing*, Vol. 4, No. 2, June 1975, pp. 104-119.
[45] L. Uhr, "Layered Recognition Cone Networks That Preprocess, Classify and Describe," *IEEE Transactions on Computers*, Vol. 21, July 1972, pp. 758-768.
[46] A. Klinger and C. R. Dyer, "Experiments on Picture Representation Using Regular Decomposition," *Computer Graphics and Image Processing*, Vol. 5, 1976, pp. 68-105.
[47] W. A. Perkins, "A Model-Based Vision System for Industrial Parts," *IEEE Transactions on Computers*, Vol. 27, 1978, pp. 126-143.
[48] R. Nevatia, "A Color Edge Detector and Its Use in Scene Segmentation," *IEEE Transactions on Systems, Man and Cybernetics*, Vol. 7, No. 11, November 1977, pp. 820-826.

8

REGION SEGMENTATION AND TEXTURE ANALYSIS

A complementary procedure to edge and boundary detection by locating image discontinuities is to find areas or regions such that the pixels comprising them are homogeneous in some property, and then locate the boundaries of these regions. As an example, if a desired region is known to consist solely of pixels of a certain intensity or color (hue) range, then these pixels can be picked out directly from the image and grouped into one or more connected regions.

Regions may also be defined by having uniform pixel properties computed over larger neighborhoods. The property describing the pattern of pixel attributes over a region will be known as the *texture* of the region. In this chapter, we first discuss region-segmentation techniques using single-pixel attributes, and then the various techniques of texture analysis.

8.1 REGION SEGMENTATION

Two approaches to region segmentation are the "region-growing" and the "region-splitting" techniques. In the *region-growing*, approach, the pixels are first grouped in regions based on the similarities of some attribute, say intensity, and then the resulting regions are examined for merging with the neighboring regions based on their average properties and spatial relationships. In the second approach, large regions are successively split into smaller regions based on finer distinctions between the properties of the pixels contained in them. These techniques are called *region-splitting* or *iterative (recursive)* segmentations techniques. Combination of the two techniques may be called *split-and-merge* techniques.

It should be clear that the region-segmentation techniques always give closed boundaries, by construction. For this reason, it is often easier to use their output for higher-level processing than the fragmented boundary segments obtained by edge-detection procedures. However, the fundamental difficulties of segmentation are caused by factors that are common to both techniques. A comparison of the edge and region-segmentation techniques is presented later in this chapter.

8.1.1 Thresholding and Recursive Segmentation

The simplest technique for image segmentation is that of *thresholding*. The pixels exceeding a certain threshold in some image attribute, say intensity, belong to one group and the rest to a second group. Regions are formed by collecting pixels such that each pixel in a region is a neighbor of one or more pixels in that region. A simple generalization is to form regions of pixels having attribute values within a certain range. Thresholding is well suited for scenes of objects with relatively uniform regions or surfaces against high-contrast backgrounds, such as, dark characters on a white page and a bright aircraft against a relatively dark sky, but it has also been used with more complex images (see [1] for early work with biological cell images).

Selection of proper thresholds is of prime importance. For some applications, such as segmentation of dark characters on a light paper, the fraction of pixels belonging to the desired character regions may be known from a priori statistics. For more general cases, a model of the expected image characteristics is required. A common model, usually assumed implicitly, is that the different object attributes are distributed about two different average values. The distribution functions need not be known, but the number of pixels having values much different than mean is assumed to fall off rapidly with this difference. A histogram of intensity values for such a model with two objects is expected to look characteristically like Fig. 8-1. This histogram is bimodal and a reasonable value for threshold is at the bottom of the valley between the two peaks. A better threshold selection is possible if a priori distributions of the intensity values are known. Experiments with some threshold-selection techniques are reported in [2]; Chow and Kaneko have used a statistical model for their analysis [3].

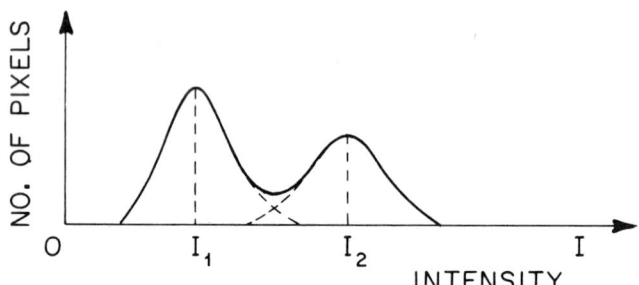

Figure 8-1: Ideal histogram for region with two objects

Ohlander-Price-Reddy Segmentor. An effective segmentor operating on complex natural images, based on some generalizations of the above ideas, has been developed at Carnegie-Mellon University by Ohlander, Reddy, and Price [4, 5]. In this segmentor, a number of attributes of the image pixels are histogrammed. For color images, hue, saturation, intensity, and other parameters derived from them (and dependent on them) are used. Additional features representing texture could be added. The histogram of the attribute having the most distinct peak, according to precedence criteria given below, is chosen for determining the segmentation attribute and range.

This process is repeated for each segmented region and the remaining image until no more new regions are found. Some distinctions between pixels of a single region become more apparent after this region has been separated from a larger region, thus permitting finer segmentation. This technique has been called *recursive segmentation* (a similar technique was independently developed by Tsujii and Tomita [6]).

As an example, consider the image shown in Fig. 8-2. (The image used for analysis is a color image, but only a grey-level equivalent is shown here.) Figure 8-3 shows the intensity histogram for this image. The dark peak in the intensity histogram is chosen for initial segmentation. Figure 8-4 shows the histograms of nine attributes after the points belong to the dark peak are excluded. The green-intensity histogram is now bimodal, and the first peak in it is chosen for further

REGION SEGMENTATION AND TEXTURE ANALYSIS

Figure 8-2: An image (Figs. 8-2 through 8-6, courtesy of Dr. K. E. Price)

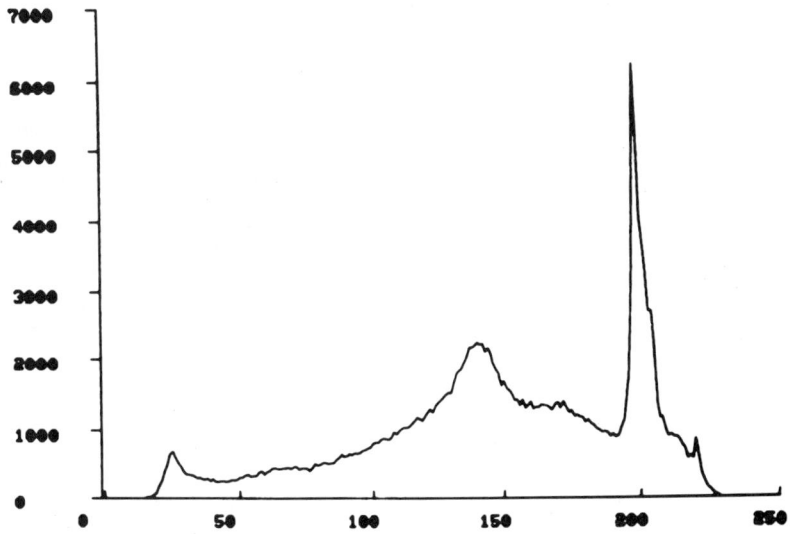

Figure 8-3: Intensity histogram of image in Fig. 8-2

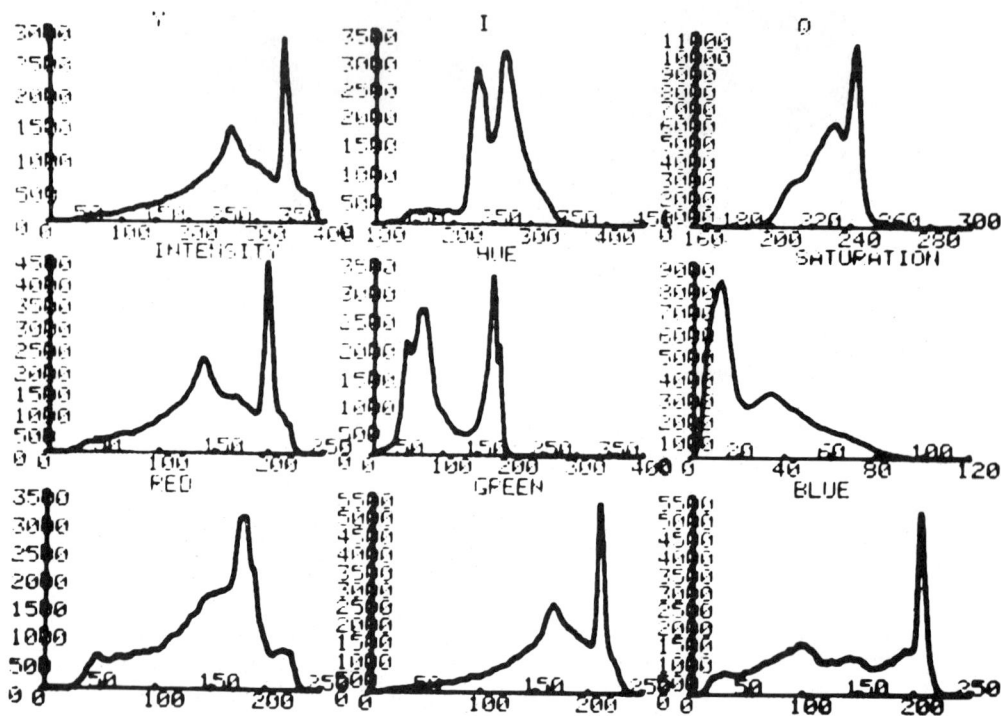

Figure 8-4: Histogram of nine attributes of image of Fig. 8-2 with dark pixels removed

Figure 8-5: Regions from Fig. 8-2: (a) pixels in one peak of green histogram, (b) remaining pixels

segmentation. Figure 8-5(a) shows the pixels in the first hue peak and Fig. 8-5(b) shows the remaining ones. Figure 8-6 shows the final segmentation.

Figure 8-6: Final segmentation for image of Fig. 8-2

Selection of peaks in the image histograms is not always obvious. In the segmentor described by Ohlander et al., peaks are chosen in the order given below:

1. An intensity peak in the low or high quarter of the range. This step removes very dark or bright regions that do not have good chromaticity information.

2. A peak with both minima < 10% of the highest value in the histogram of that attribute and the ratio of peak maximum to minimum exceeding 4. Another peak with maximum/minimum ratio exceeding 2 must also be present.

3. Same as in step 2, except that both minima < 25% of peak value.

4. Two peaks, each having maxima/minima ratio > 2. (This indicates a bimodal distribution.) If both maxima are within 10% of each other, then both peaks are used, at successive steps, else the higher peak is chosen.

5. (This measurre applies to the saturation histogram only.) Both

peak minima must be in the lower 20% of the saturation range, maximum/minimum ratio > 2, and these minima must separate another peak with maximum/minimum ratio > 1.2.

6. Peak minima are < 10% of the highest value, and 10% of all points are outside the peak. This and the following condition handle cases where only weak evidence for segmentation is available.

7. Peak minima < 70% of the highest value and maximum/minimum ratio > 1.7.

In practice, computing peak maxima and minima is complicated, as minor perturbations must be distinguished from major changes; here, however, we ignore such details, which may be found in [5].

One deficiency of histogram-based techniques is that small regions in a large image may not produce a distinct histogram peak, even if they are distinct from their surround. Some improvement can be obtained by analyzing smaller parts of an image, say the four quadrants, separately.

The Ohlander segmentor applied to a high-resolution image is computationally expensive. Considerable improvement can be obtained by using *planning*, in the sense used by Kelley for edge detection [7] and described in the previous chapter. Initial segmentation is performed on a reduced resolution image. The resulting region are used as a "plan," from which finer segmentation can be obtained by using higher resolution.

Multiple resolution images, or a pyramid of images, can also be used for region segmentation [8-11]. Improved efficiency is obtained if segmentation can be performed at the higher levels of the pyramid.

Clustering. A generalization of the region splitting technique using multiple attributes is to base the segmentation on all of the image attributes simultaneously, rather than choosing one attribute based on histogram separations. If the different attributes are viewed to span a multidimensional feature space, the pixels in one region should cluster in this space. Many clustering algorithms exist in the pattern recognition literature (for example, see [12]). Clustering is more difficult when the number of clusters is unknown, as is typical for segmentation application. Coleman and Andrews have investigated such segmentation [13]. The performance is determined largely by availability of suitable features for natural images.

8.1.2 Region Growing

In this approach, neighboring pixels whose attribute values are within a fixed predefined range are grouped together to form "atomic" regions. Neighboring atomic regions are then examined for merger based on properties and relations of these regions. Typically, the atomic regions are small and numerous if tight constraints are used on similarities of pixel attributes.

Brice and Fennema suggested a region growing procedure that first merges atomic regions with average properties (such as intensity) within a specified threshold range [14]. This threshold may be different and less stringent than the one used to form the atomic regions. Further mergers are based on relative properties of two neighboring regions. If one region largely surrounds another, the two are merged. If P_1 and P_2 are the perimeters of two neighboring regions and L is the common boundary length between them, they are merged if L/P_1 or L/P_2 exceeds a threshold. Also a merging of two regions resulting in a more "regular" new region is favored.

Performance of such region growers is strongly affected by the choice of various thresholds mentioned above. They have been successfully applied for simple scenes, but for complex textured scenes, the segmented regions tend to be small and scattered over the objects. Region-growing techniques are also described in [15, 16].

Split-and-merge procedures. One approach to reducing the dependence on choice of threshold values is to preserve a complete tree (or more generally a graph) of regions produced at various levels of region growing. The root of this tree is the complete image, and the leaf nodes are the atomic regions. The intermediate levels of the tree contain regions formed by merging of the next-level regions. The higher-level processes may now examine various alternative segmentations rather than a unique output, possibly modifying the segmentations based on possible interpretations. Such techniques are described in [17-19].

The tree describing the relations between regions at different levels is sometimes called a picture tree. The term *quad tree* is used if each pixel at one level is split into four pixels at the lower level. The quad tree is similar to pyramids mentioned earlier, but the term pyramids is more often used to represent grey-level images, where successively higher levels are obtained by averaging the grey-levels of four lower-level pixels.

Pavlidis, Horowitz, and Tanimoto have used the picture tree for a split-and-merge algorithm, where at a given stage of the processing, the regions are examined for further splitting or merging according to predefined criteria. The process switches from merging to splitting if no more regions can be merged, and vice versa. Experiments with various criteria are described in [20-22]. The split-and-merge procedure can be expected to be more tolerant than a simple region-growing procedure to the effects of initial atomic region formation.

8.1.3 Semantically Guided Region Growing

Performance of region growers can be improved if some a priori knowledge about the scenes being viewed is available. Feldman and Yakimovsky take a statistical view and assume that the a priori probabilities of the image attributes for a given region and of the boundary between two specific regions, such as sky and grass, are known [23]. The segmentation objective is to maximize the probability of correct interpretation assigned to each region; it is formulated as a Bayesian optimization problem. However, the actual solution used is a heuristic approximation of merging the regions with the "weakest" boundary between them at each step, based on some measures of the boundary, the regions surrounding it, and the assumed prior probabilities. Feldman and Yakimovsky present successful results on outdoor scenes containing cars, trees, and sky, and also on biomedical images.

In related work, Barrow and Tenenbaum attempt to combine interpretation with region growing [24]. For each region, a set of interpretations (classifications) is obtained based on its properties. Two neighboring regions with same unique interpretation are merged. If a certain interpretation of a region is incompatible with its neighbors—that is, an interpretation is not allowed to be next to any of the possible interpretations of the neighboring region—then the incompatible interpretation is removed from the list. In a variation, they also associate degrees of compatibilities for given interpretations and search for minimal-cost interpretations.

The main constraint in the use of a priori information for segmentation is the availability of such information, particularly if continuous probability distributions, and not just binary adjacency relations, are required.

8.1.4 Tracing Region Boundaries

It is useful to obtain the boundaries of a region, once the connected group of pixels forming the region have been extracted. A simple algorithm is to scan the image along a horizontal row until a pixel inside the region is found. Then a left turn of one pixel is taken. If we are still in the figure we turn left again, and if the outside of the region is reached a right turn is taken (see Fig. 8-7, where the dots are the pixels within the region). This step is repeated until the starting point is reached again. This algorithm is adequate for most cases, but the traced boundary is sensitive to the starting point. Further, parts of the region that are a single pixel wide may not be traced adequately.

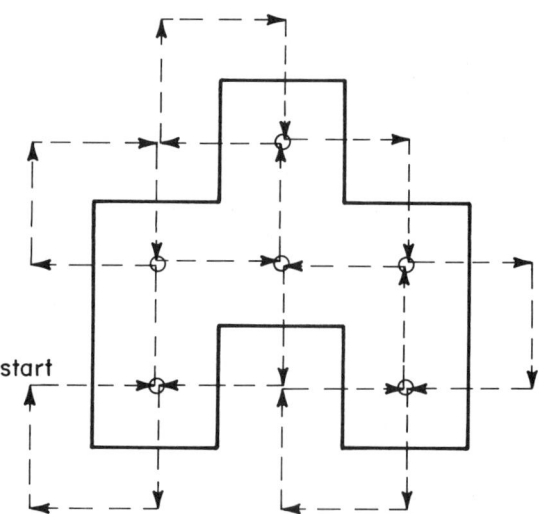

Figure 8-7: Tracing the boundary of a region

These difficulties can be avoided by a more complex algorithm, which chooses the next boundary point by examining all (8-connected) neighbors. The next point is the one with the largest counterclockwise direction from the previous path. A yet more complex algorithm, using table look-up for choosing the next boundary point, is described in [25].

Procedures are described in [26, 27] for tracing boundaries from regions represented in a quad tree, and for constructing quad-tree region representations given the boundary.

8.2 EDGE VERSUS REGION SEGMENTATION

We are now in a position to compare the edge- and region-segmentation approaches. Both techniques are aimed at finding object boundaries by finding boundaries between image attributes such as intensity and color. If useful and precise mathematical definitions of the desired discontinuities were available, we could expect the two methods to yield the same results, but perhaps with differing computational effort. However, in the absence of such models, the two methods implement similar but different intuitive notions of the desired discontinuities.

In the absence of suitable mathematical models for images and desired boundaries, it is difficult to compare the performance of the different segmentation techniques. However, the following qualitative observations can be made. These observations should hold in spite of the differences among the various edge- and region-segmentation techniques themselves.

1. Region segmentation necessarily yields closed boundaries. Edge-based approaches typically give only parts of the boundary segments. However, a tenacious "line follower" could be forced to choose a path at each point until a closed boundary is obtained.

2. Edge detection is an inherently local process. Hence, local failures may prevent complete segmentation; for example, the line-finding systems have difficulty tracing objects with irregular boundaries. On the other hand, since region segmentors are more global, they are less sensitive, and more likely to miss low-contrast boundaries, or small objects. An important case is that of long, thin objects, such as roads, which are small in area and hence have small effects on larger area statistics.

3. Improvement in performance by addition of color seems to have been much more dramatic for region segmentors than for edge-based segmentors. This is related to the observations above, as color is also believed to be used by humans as more of a global property.

4. The position of detected edges is relatively insensitive to the parameters of the procedure, such as a threshold. However, position of region boundaries can be quite sensitive to the choice of range for the segmentation attribute.

These observations imply that region segmentation may be better suited for some tasks and edge segmentation for some others, and that the two approaches are, to some extent, complementary. Homogeneous regions, with irregular boundaries. and possibly surrounded by nonhomogeneous regions, for example bodies of water, such as lakes and rivers surrounded by textured areas in aerial images, are easily detected by simple region segmentors, but present difficulties for line finders. Long, thin features, and finer details within regions, are more easily handled by edge-based approaches. Figure 8-8 shows a region segmentation of the San Francisco image of Fig. 1-9 (the region segmentation used color). It is instructive to compare this segmentation with the line segments detected in the same image and shown in Fig. 7-16. A system that uses both techniques for object location, depending on the features of the desired objects, is described in [28], and some results of this system for the San Francisco image are presented in Chapter 10.

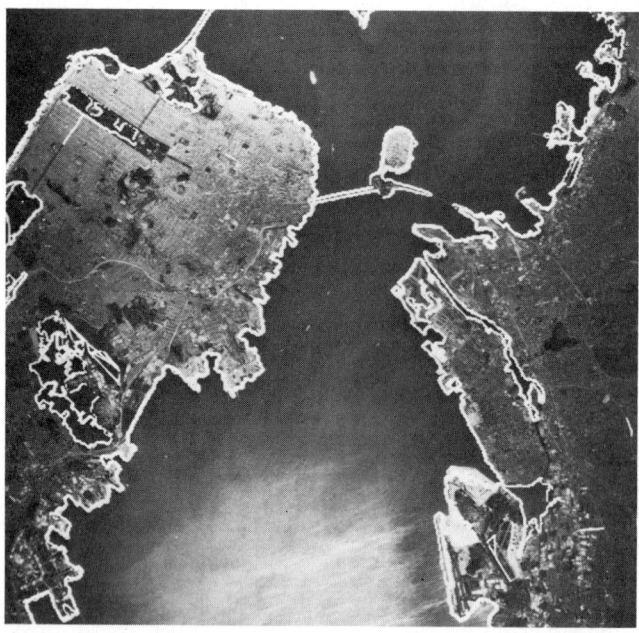

Figure 8-8: Segmented regions in the San Francisco image of Fig. 1-9

Milgram has made an interesting suggestion to combine the two approaches [29]. In this approach, different regions are computed by using a number of threshold ranges. Boundaries of these regions are compared with edges detected in the same image. The region segmentation yielding the maximum overlap of the edge and region boundary points is selected as the final segmentation. This technique has been called *segmentation by convergent evidence* and also a *superslice*

REGION SEGMENTATION AND TEXTURE ANALYSIS 141

technique. In a variation, Milgram and Herman have used clusters in a two-dimensional histogram, whose axes are the pixel grey levels and edge magnitudes [30].

It must be remembered that many of the difficulties of segmentation are due to inherent properties of images, hence are common to all segmentation methods. The desired object boundaries are essentially three-dimensional depth discontinuities and do not always correspond to image attribute discontinuities. Conversely, some discontinuities in images, such as painted patterns on a surface, do not correspond to object boundaries. Thus, "perfect" segmentation may be unachievable in general, and the higher level must deal with such imperfections.

8.3 TEXTURE ANALYSIS

Surfaces of natural objects are not always homogeneous in a local attribute, such as intensity or color, as has been implicitly assumed in the previously described segmentation techniques. Frequently the desired surfaces have a more or less uniform observed pattern, called the visual texture, possibly generated by the physical texture, as in a rough wall surface, or simply the markings on a surface, as in a wallpaper. In some cases it is natural to view a collection of objects as a single entity—for example, a grass field or a wall of bricks. In these cases, the pattern of individual objects determines the texture of the collection.

Ability to detect and describe surface textures is useful as an important clue in recognition of objects, and also for scene segmentation. However, the texture boundaries need not always correspond to physical object boundaries. Under certain assumptions, the surface texture can also be used to determine the three-dimensional surface orientations, as will be seen in Chapter 9.

For simplicity, first consider the textures contained in the synthetic image of Fig. 8-9. Two distinct regions are seen, and the textures of each can be considered to be characterized by repetition of a primitive element in a certain pattern. The textures differ in having different primitives or a different pattern, or both.

However, natural textures cannot be characterized so easily. Figure 8-10 shows examples of some common patterns. (A photo album by Brodatz contains many examples of natural textures [31].) These patterns have neither an obvious fixed primitive element nor a fixed pattern of repetition, even though each is perceived to be uniform in some sense, and different from the others. Such observations have led to study of texture as a property of the pattern that is uniform in a

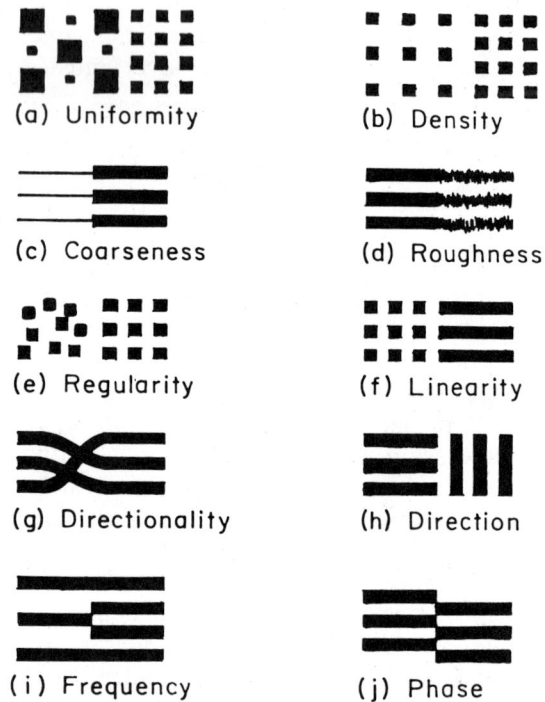

Figure 8-9: Examples of synthetic texture pairs and their distinguishing characteristics (from Laws [34])

REGION SEGMENTATION AND TEXTURE ANALYSIS

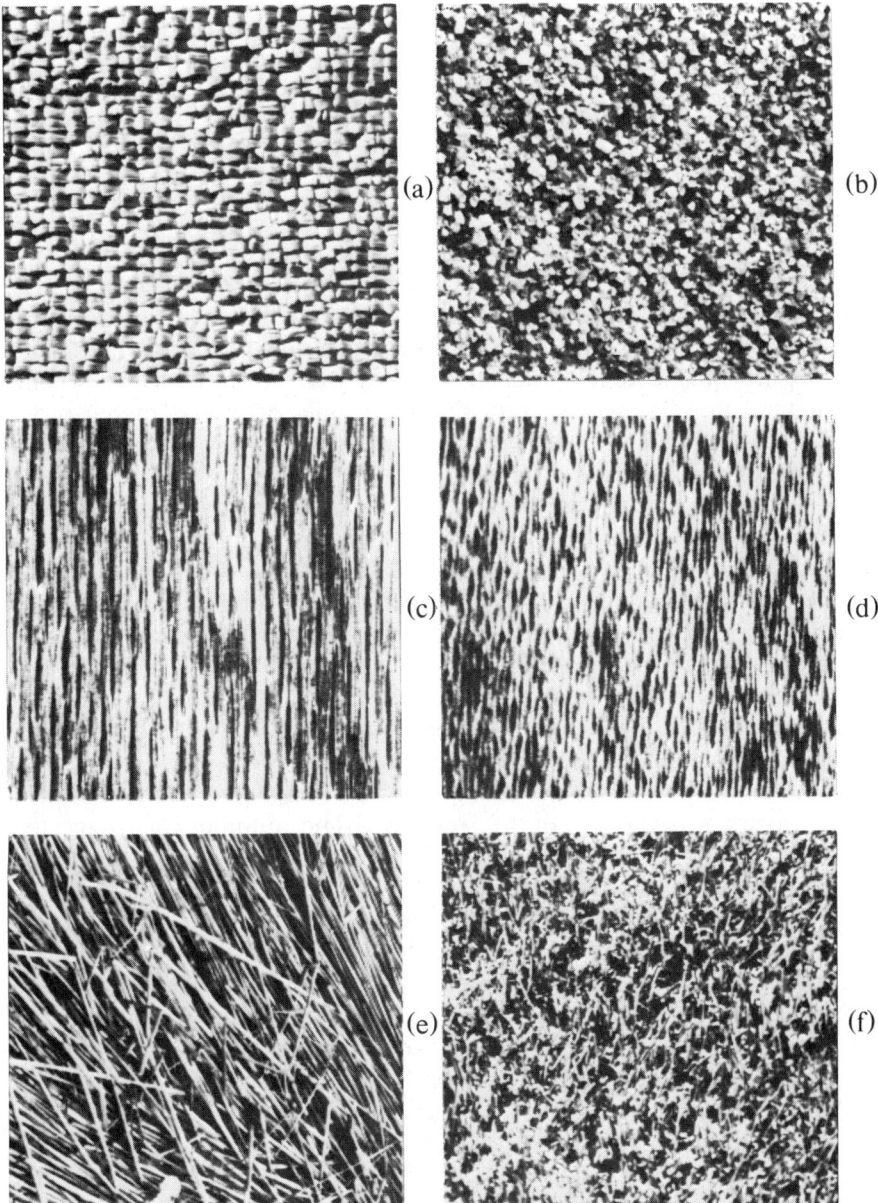

Figure 8-10: Some examples of natural textures: (a) raffia, (b) sand, (c) wood, (d) water, (e) straw, (f) grass

statistical sense, in contrast to a *structural* approach, where the texture primitives and their relationships are described explicitly. The two approaches are not mutually exclusive, as some structural properties can be inferred from statistical analysis, and some structural properties may need to be described statistically for natural textures.

8.3.1 Statistical Texture Measures

The statistical measures have been motivated by a lack of simply described patterns in natural textures. Further, these measures have been supported by an important conjecture, due to Julesz [32], that humans are unable to distinguish textures that have the same second and lower order statistics, but differ in one or more higher-order statistics. (nth-order statistics are determined by the joint probability distributions of n pixels at a time).

Figure 8-11(a) shows two easily discriminable random textures. The two textures have the same first-order but different second-order statistics. In Fig. 8-11(b), however, the top and bottom textures have the same first- and second-order statistics but differ in the third-order statistics and are not immediately distinguished. Julesz conjecture is supported by a large number of examples, however, several counterexamples have been found [33-38]. These counterexamples have patterns that have some discernible micropatterns and the local second-order statistics differ from the global ones.

Statistical measures are based on the average properties assumed to be invariant over an entire region. The number of suggested statistical measures is large, and only the commonly cited and used approaches will be described here.

First order measures. The simplest measures are based on first-order statistics—that is, probability distributions of single-pixel attributes. Some examples are mean and variance of intensity. More sophisticated first-order measures are based on histograms of the individual pixel attributes. These measures are not strictly texture measures, as they are not even dependent on the spatial distribution of the pixel attributes, but are still useful for many naturally occurring textures.

"Texture energy" measures. An improvement over the first-order measures using pixel attributes is to detect the presence of certain features in the texture and then to compute the first-order statistics of these features. The density of edges, detected by a local edge detector, is commonly used to distinguish between "coarse" and "fine" textures.

Laws [39] has generalized this concept to determining a variety of features by convolving the image with a variety of filter templates, F_1,

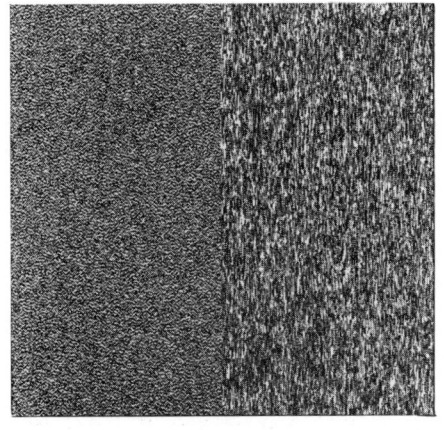

Figure 8-11: Two pairs of synthetic textures
(courtesy of Dr. D. D. Garber)

F_2, ..., F_n, as shown in Fig. 8-12 and then measuring the "energy" of the outputs (E_1, E_2, ..., E_n). The filters consist of 3-by-3 or 5-by-5 masks and detect the presence of edges and lines in various orientations, and cornerlike features. The filters were determined empirically by testing with some natural textures. The energy measures compute properties over a larger window (15-by-15). Simple measures are average and variance of the filtered outputs. As the various measures are not independent, the resulting features can be combined into a smaller set, C_1, C_2, ..., C_n.

Fourier measures. As textures are viewed to be at least semiperiodic, the Fourier transform of an image window can be expected to have distinct peaks useful for texture discrimination. Bajcsy used filters in the Fourier domain, consisting of annular rings and strips in different orientations [40]. The outputs of these filters was used to generate symbolic descriptions such as bloblike, homogeneous, random, monodirectional, and bidirectional. This technique was applied successfully to natural scenes containing textures such as grass, water, sand, and trees.

A disadvantage of the Fourier approach is that, except for perfectly periodic textures, the energy in the frequency domain is

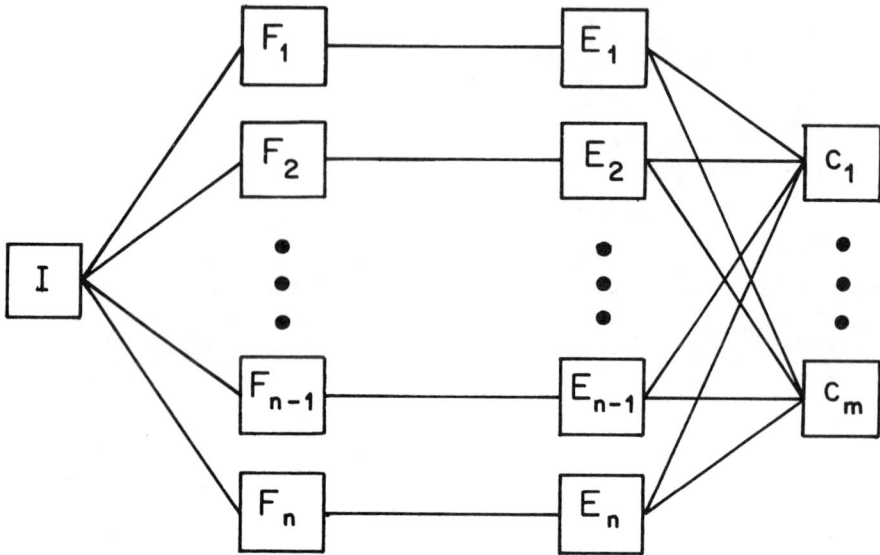

Figure 8-12: Texture energy measurement

scattered, and similar peaks may be caused by a nearly periodic texture and a single strong edge.

Second order measures. Haralick and others suggested a scheme for estimating second-order joint probability densities and devised measures based on them [41]. The second-order statistics are given by $P(i, j, d, \theta)$, the probability of a pair of pixels separated by a distance $|d|$ in direction θ having the intensity values of i and j. These statistics can be computed and stored in the form of *co-occurrence matrices*, one for each value of (d, θ). An element (i, j) of this matrix is a count of the number of pixel pairs with intensities i and j, for the given d and θ values. Note that these matrices are symmetric, as only the absolute value of d is used. Figure 8-13(a) shows a grey-level image window, with intensity values in the range of 0-3, and Fig. 8-13(b) is the corresponding co-occurrence matrix for the horizontal direction and distance of one pixel (that is, $\theta = 0$ degrees and $d = 1$ pixel). Note that computation of complete second order statistics requires co-occurrence matrices for all pairs of values of d and θ.

Haralick and others suggested various features to be computed from a co-occurrence matrix. Three of them are as follows:

$$f_1 = \sum_{i=1}^{N} \sum_{j=1}^{N} P(i, j)^2 \qquad (8\text{-}1)$$

REGION SEGMENTATION AND TEXTURE ANALYSIS

0	0	2	2
1	1	2	2
0	3	3	3
0	0	1	1

(a)

	0	1	2	3
0	4	1	1	1
1	1	4	1	0
2	1	1	4	0
3	1	0	0	4

(b)

Figure 8-13: An example of a co-occurrence matrix: (a) image grey levels, (b) co-occurrence matrix in horizontal direction ($d=1$, $\theta=0$ degrees)

$$f_2 = \sum_{n=0}^{N-1} n^2 \sum_{|i-j|=n} P(i, j) \qquad (8\text{-}2)$$

$$f_3 = \frac{\sum_{i=1}^{N} \sum_{j=1}^{N} [ijP(i, j) - \mu_x\mu_y]}{\sigma_x\sigma_y} \qquad (8\text{-}3)$$

where $P(i, j)$ are the normalized values in the co-occurrence matrix of size N-by-N, μ_x and σ_x are the average and standard deviation along the rows, and μ_y and σ_y along the columns.

f_1 is a measure of uniformity or homogeneity of a region. For a uniform region, the co-occurrence matrix contains a small number of large-valued elements, hence the sum of squares is higher than it would be if all transitions were equally likely. f_2 is a measure of "contrast" and f_3 of the correlation of the intensities. Fourteen measures including the above are given in [41].

These measures were successfully used for classification of different textures such as wood, corn, grass, and water (using four co-occurrence matrices with $d = 1$ and $\theta = 0, 45, 90,$ and 135 degrees). However, this technique has many shortcomings. First, if the number of grey levels is large, say 256, the co-occurrence matrix has 256 rows and 256 columns, and a large region is required for useful estimation of the statistics. The number of grey levels can be reduced by compressing the range, but this may introduce texture artifacts. Sometimes only the difference of grey levels is used in computing the co-occurrence matrices. It is also necessary to limit the number of values of d and θ, and methods for automatic choice of these parameters are unclear.

Other features. Faugeras and Pratt have described a different approach to estimation of texture statistics [42]. Their model assumes that underlying texture is generated as an independent, identically distributed array, say $W(j, k)$, and the observed texture, say $F(j, k)$ is obtained by a spatial operator, applied to the array $W(j, k)$. It is possible to estimate $W(j, k)$ from observed $F(j, k)$, by a so-called *whitening* transformation. The optimal linear whitening transformation can be estimated from the autocorrelation function of the observed texture. Pratt and Faugeras also demonstrated that autocorrelation alone is not sufficient for human texture discrimination and that the Julesz conjecture holds for correlated as well as uncorrelated texture fields. In their system, final texture features are derived from measurements on the decorrelated array and from the autocorrelation function.

Davis, Johns and Aggarwal have introduced a concept of *generalized co-occurrence matrices* [43]. These matrices measure the co-occurrence of some selected features in the image, and the co-occurrence is defined by satisfying a selected predicate relationship between the features. Thus, if the selected features are grey levels and the co-occurrence property is that of equality, we get the usual grey-level co-occurrence matrices. However, if the selected features are binary edges and the co-occurrence predicate requires certain angular relations between the edges (such as equality or orthogonality), other properties of texture are measured. Measures similar to those used by Haralick and others for grey-level co-occurrence matrices are used for the generalized co-occurrence matrices.

A variety of other measures have been suggested. An excellent survey can be found in [44]. Use of Markov models or time-series analysis is described in [45, 46]. Other measures using estimation theory methods and models for random placement of elements may be found in [47-50].

8.3.2 Structural Texture Descriptions

The structural approaches to texture attempt to isolate the primitives that form a texture and describe the relations between these primitives in the texture pattern. Such descriptions should distinguish between the two brick patterns shown in Fig. 8-14. However, structural descriptions may be difficult to compute for natural textures, as frequently neither the primitives nor their patterns are completely uniform and regular. Further, texture patterns may be hierarchical; that is, a particular texture pattern, may repeat to form a large texture pattern, and so on. Structural texture description techniques were suggested in early work (see, for example, [51, 52]), but not implemented until recently.

Figure 8-14: Two brick patterns

The structural view of texture is like the viewing of sentences in a language as consisting of certain primitives related by allowed rules of a grammar. Zucker has postulated that natural textures may be viewed as being generated from a two-step process [53]. In the first step, structured patterns, for example a rectangular grid, are generated according to certain rules. In the next step these patterns undergo a transformation that introduces irregularity, in either a deterministic or a random way, to yield natural textures. However, such models are only partially successful in simulating natural textures.

An important step in generating structural descriptions is to find the appropriate primitives of a given texture. These primitives can be expected to correspond to physical objects; however, choice of such primitives requires good segmentation at a detailed level. Since such capabilities do not exist in current systems for complex images, simpler primitives have been used.

Several researchers have used regions of uniform, or near uniform, intensity as primitive texture elements[54, 56]. These elements are computed by the usual region segmentation techniques described earlier. Descriptions of texture elements consist of region properties such as intensity, size, shape, and direction of elongation [54, 55]. Some textures may have random distribution of these element properties, whereas others have elements uniform in one or more of these properties. Further distinctions between textures are based on the relations between the primitives. In the work of Maleson and others [54] the relations used were the collinearity and parallelism of the axes of ellipses approximating the regions. Others have used statistics of *relative vectors* between texture elements [55, 56]. A relative vector is given by the relative coordinates of the line joining the centroids of two texture elements. Statistics of relative vectors have also also been used for synthesis of textures. Nagao and Matsuyama used them to describe artificial, regular textures in a hierarchical pattern [56].

Davis has presented a technique for describing texture pattern of dot textures. The dot patterns themselves may represent objects of interest in a real image; in the example given in this work, they are at the center of the trees in an aerial orchard image [57]. He used peaks in the histogram of the directions of line joining a point to its k nearest neighbors to detect regularity of textures; a square pattern, for example, should have to peaks separated by 90 degrees.

A technique that does not require successful segmentation first is to use line segments or more simply, the local edges. If a texture is periodic we can expect the boundaries of primitives and the local edges to occur at periodic intervals. Some simple properties of textures can be inferred by computing "edge co-occurrence" measures defined to be the number of edges that occur at a distance d in a given direction θ. The edges contributing to the matrix are required to be normal to the direction θ.

Figure 8-15 shows a simple periodic texture and the edges that may be detected in it. The elements bound by edges of opposite contrast can be viewed as comprising the texture elements. In such cases, an edge co-occurrence measure between edges of same orientations can be expected to be periodic with the distance, d, between two edge elements, and a measure between edges of opposite contrast should give the size, s, of the texture elements.

Vilnrotter, Nevatia, and Price have used such plots for analysis of

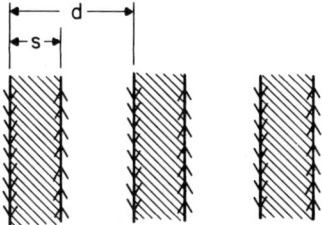

Figure 8-15: Sample texture pattern with edge directions indicated

natural scenes, and their technique seems to be useful for distinguishing between highly periodic, random, and semiperiodic textures [58, 59]. For periodic natural textures, this technique finds the period and the width of the elements, in one or more directions, using the edge co-occurrence plots described above. For non-periodic textures, a primitive element width can still be found for some textures such as grass, water, and sand. The width of the primitives is then used to actually isolate the primitives in the edge image, by searching for edges of opposite contrast separated by the known width. Other properties of primitives, such as length and area, can now be computed. Descriptions of the primitives and their arrangements are used for recognition of the textures and the recognition accuracies are claimed to be quite high, with confusion between only those textures that differ in small detail only. These descriptions have also been used for reconstruction of regular, homogeneous textures.

Measures for inferring properties of textures from edge analysis that correspond to human observations are also described in [60]. Also, Marr has suggested using elements of the primal sketch for texture description but has not specified the grouping properties to be used [61]. Some of the structural properties can also be inferred from an analysis of the grey-level co-occurrence matrices [62].

8.3.3 Comparison of Texture Features

Comparison of various texture features is complicated by the number of parameters to be considered. A large number of texture types are possible. Moreover, different samples of similar objects, such as grass and fields, may have similar but different textures. Ideally, texture features should be invariant to changes within a class, but different from other texture classes. Owing to these difficulties and the large number of suggested techniques, no authoritative comparisons have been reported.

Weszka and Rosenfeld have reported a limited study and conclude that the measures based on co-occurrence matrices are better than Fourier features [63]. Laws claims performance superior to that of co-occurrence features [39]. However, these conclusions are based on the use of a limited set of textures in testing.

Conners and Harlow give a theoretical analysis of the performance of some texture measures for certain types of textures [64]. Not surprisingly, the second order measures are concluded to be superior.

Zobrist and Thompson have studied the use of a linearly weighted combination of a number of texture features [65]. The weights were determined to agree with human judgments about the degree of dissimiliarities between given textures on a training set. Among the Haralick features, f_1, f_2, and f_3 defined in Eqs. (8-1), (8-2), and (8-3) above were determined to be most heavily weighted.

8.3.4 Texture Segmentation

One or more of the texture descriptors, constituting a feature vector, can be used to classify regions into one of the known types. These features can also be used for segmentation by edge or region techniques, analogous to other multidimensional features, such as color. Given two texture-feature vectors T_1 and T_2, we need to decide if they both belong to the same surface. However, texture is not a property of a single pixel, but of a region around it. Thus, if texture is measured by centering a window of a fixed size around each pixel, this window will encompass more than one texture near the boundary. Such techniques may lead to poorly defined boundaries, with possible uncertainty in position equal to half the window size. Another difficulty is in the choice of appropriate window size.

A model of variation in measured texture properties near the edge would be helpful in determining the appropriate window size and precise edge location (see [66]). Owing to the lack of suitable models, the common approach is to assume that the measured texture properties change smoothly from values for one texture to that of another. In this case, the edge detection corresponds to detecting a smooth ramp edge in an intensity image. Using an operator that measures gradient and choosing the gradient peak (that is, nonmaxima suppression), as described in Chapter 7, should lead to correct edge location. Some experiments are described in [66, 67].

The major application of texture analysis has been for images taken from airplanes or satellites. Such images usually have large, highly textured areas, such as forests and mountains. A common use is for classification of agricultural crops from LANDSAT satellite images.

8.4 SUMMARY

In this chapter we have surveyed region segmentation techniques using single pixel properties and analysis of the texture properties of regions. These segmentation techniques are complementary to the edge and line techniques of the previous chapter. Segmentation of an arbitrary, general scene is difficult, but useful segmentation can be achieved in limited domains, even for complex images. Texture-analysis techniques also are not adequate for all textures, but useful descriptions can be obtained for a small class of known textures. Segmentation using range information is discussed in the next chapter.

REFERENCES

[1] J. M. S. Prewitt, "Object Enhancement and Extraction," in *Picture Processing and Psychopictorics*, B. S. Lipkin and A. Rosenfeld (eds.), Academic Press, New York, 1970.

[2] J. S. Weszka, "A Survey of Threshold Selection Techniques," *Computer Graphics and Image Processing*, Vol. 7, 1978, pp. 259-265.

[3] C. K. Chow and T. Kaneko, "Boundary Detection of Radiographic Images by a Threshold Method," in *Frontiers of Pattern Recognition*, S. Watanabe (ed.), Academic Press, New York, 1972, pp. 61-82.

[4] R. Ohlander, "Analysis of Natural Scenes," Computer Science Department Report (Ph.D. thesis), Carnegie-Mellon University, Pittsburgh, 1975.

[5] R. Ohlander, K. Price, and D. Raj Reddy, "Picture Segmentation Using a Recursive Region Splitting Method," *Computer Graphics and Image Processing*, 1978, pp. 313-333.

[6] S. Tsuji and F. Tomita, "A Structural Analyzer for a Class of Textures," *Computer Graphics and Image Processing*, Vol. 2, 1973, pp. 216-231.

[7] M. Kelley, "Edge Detection by Computer Using Planning," in *Machine Intelligence VI*, B. Meltzer and D. Michie (eds.), Edinburgh University Press, Edinburgh, 1971, pp. 397-409.

[8] L. Uhr, "Layered Recognition Cone Networks That Preprocess, Classify and Describe," *IEEE Transactions on Computers*, Vol. 21, 1972, pp. 758-768.

[9] A. R. Hanson and E. M. Riseman, "VISIONS: A Computer System for Interpreting Scenes," in *Computer Vision Systems*, A. R.

Hanson and E. M. Riseman (eds.), Academic Press, New York, 1978, pp. 303-333.
[10] A. Klinger and C. R. Dyer, "Experiments on Picture Representation Using Regular Decomposition," *Computer Graphics and Image Processing*, Vol. 5, 1976, pp. 68-105.
[11] S. Tanimoto and T. Pavlidis, "A Hierarchical Data Structure for Picture Processing," *Computer Graphics and Image Processing*, Vol. 4, 1975, pp. 104-113.
[12] R. O. Duda and P. E. Hart, *Pattern Classification and Scene Analysis*, John Wiley & Sons, New York, 1973.
[13] G. Coleman and H. C. Andrews, "Image Segmentation and Clustering," *Proceedings of IEEE*, Vol. 67, No. 5, May 1979, pp. 773-785.
[14] C. R. Brice and C. L. Fennema, "Scene Analysis Using Regions," *Artificial Intelligence*, Vol. 1, Fall 1970, pp. 205-226.
[15] S. W. Zucker, "Region Growing: Childhood and Adolescence," *Computer Graphics and Image Processing*, Vol. 5, 1976, pp. 382-399.
[16] E. M. Riseman and M. A. Arbib, "Computational Techniques in the Visual Segmentation of Static Scenes," *Computer Graphics and Image Processing*, Vol. 6, No. 3, June 1977, pp. 221-276.
[17] R. A. Kirsch, "Computer Determination of the Constituent Structure of Biological Images," *Computers and Biomedical Research*, Vol. 4, No. 3, June 1971, pp. 315-328.
[18] L. J. Krakauer, "Computer Analysis of Visual Properties of Curved Objects," MIT Project MAC Report MAC-TR-82 (Ph.D. thesis), May 1971.
[19] E. Freuder, "Affinity: A Relative Approach to Region Growing," *Computer Graphics and Image Processing*, Vol. 5, 1976, pp. 254-264.
[20] L. S. Horowitz and T. Pavlidis, "Picture Segmentation by a Tree Traversal Algorithm," *Journal of ACM*, 1976, pp. 368-388.
[21] S. L. Tanimoto and T. Pavlidis, "The Editing of Picture Segmentations Using Local Analysis of Graphs," *Communications of ACM*, 1977, pp. 223-229.
[22] S. L. Horowitz and T. Pavlidis, "A Graph-Theoretic Approach to Picture Processing," *Computer Graphics and Image Processing*, Vol. 7, 1978, pp. 282-291.
[23] J. A. Feldman and Y. Yakimovsky, "Decision Theory and Artificial Intelligence: I. A Semantics Based Region Analyzer," *Artificial Intelligence*, Vol. 5, 1974, pp. 349-371.
[24] J. M. Tenenbaum and H. G. Barrow, "Experiments in Interpretation Guided Segmentation," *Artificial Intelligence*, Vol. 8, 1977, pp. 241-274.
[25] S. A. Dudani, "Region Extraction Using Boundary Following,"

Pattern Recognition and Artificial Intelligence, C. H. Chen (ed.), Academic Press, New York, 1976, pp. 216-232.
[26] C. R. Dyer, A. Rosenfeld and H. Samet, "Region Representation: Boundary Codes from Quadtrees," Communications of ACM, Vol. 23, No. 3, March 1980, pp. 171-179.
[27] H. Samet, "Region Representation: Quadtree from Boundary Codes," Communications of ACM, Vol. 23, No. 3, March 1980, pp. 163-170.
[28] R. Nevatia and K. Price, "Locating Structures in Aerial Images," Proceedings of International Conference on Pattern Recognition, Kyoto, Japan, November 1978, pp. 686-690.
[29] D. Milgram, "Region Extraction Using Convergent Evidence," Computer Graphics and Image Processing, Vol. 11, No. 1, 1979, pp. 1-12.
[30] D. Milgram and M. Herman, "Clustering Edge Values for Threshold Selection," Computer Graphics and Image Processing, Vol. 10, No. 3, June 1979, pp. 272-280.
[31] P. Brodatz, Textures: A Photograph Album for Artists and Designers, Dover, New York, 1956.
[32] B. Julesz, "Visual Pattern Discrimination," IRE Transactions on Information Theory, Vol. 8, February 1962, pp. 84-92.
[33] S. R. Purks and W. Richards, "Visual Texture Discrimination Using Random Dot Patterns," Journal of Optical Society of America, Vol. 67, June 1977, pp. 765-771.
[34] T. Caelli and B. Julesz, "On Perceptual Analyzers Underlying Visual Texture Discrimination: Part I," Biological Cybernetics, Vol. 28, 1978, pp. 167-176.
[35] T. Caelli, B. Julesz, and E. N.Gilbert, "On Perceptual Analyzers Underlying Visual Texture Discrimination: Part II," Biological Cybernetics, Vol. 29, No. 4, 1978, pp. 201-214.
[36] B. Julesz, E. N. Gilbert, and J. D. Victor, "Visual Discrimination of Textures with Identical Third-Order Statistics," Biological Cybernetics, Vol. 31, No. 3, 1978, pp. 137-140.
[37] J. D. Victor and S. Brodie, "Dircriminable Textures with Identical Buffon Needle Statistics," Biological Cybernetics, Vol. 31, No. 4, 1978, pp. 231-234.
[38] A. Gagalowicz, "Visual Discriminatio of Stochastic Texture Fields based upon their second Order Statistics," Proceedings of the Fifth International Conference on Pattern Recognition, Miami Beach, December 1980, pp.786-788.
[39] K. I. Laws, "Textured Image Segmentation," University of Southern California Report USCIPI 940 (Ph.D. thesis), January 1980.

[40] R. Bajcsy, "Computer Identification of Visual Surface," *Computer Graphics and Image Processing*, Vol. 2, 1973, pp. 118-130.
[41] R. M. Haralick, K. Shanmugam, and I. Dinstein, "Texture Features for Image Classification," *IEEE Transactions on Systems, Man and Cybernetics*, Vol. 3, No. 6, November 1973, pp. 610-621.
[42] O. D. Faugeras and W. K. Pratt, "Decorrelation Methods of Texture Feature Extraction," *IEEE Transactions on Pattern Analysis and Machine Intelligence*, Vol. 2, No. 4, July 1980, pp. 323-332.
[43] L. S Davis, S. A. Johns, and J. K. Aggarwal, "Texture Analysis Using Generalized Co-occurrence Matrices," *IEEE Transactions on Pattern Analysis and Machine Intelligence*, Vol. 1, No. 3, July 1979, pp. 251-259.
[44] R. M. Haralick, "Statistical and Structural Approaches to Texture," *Proceedings of IEEE*, Vol. 67, No. 5, May 1979, pp. 786-804.
[45] B. H. McCormick and S. N. Jayaramamurthy, "Time Series Model for Texture Synthesis," *International Journal of Computer and Information Science*, Vol. 3, No. 4, 1974, pp. 329-343.
[46] D. Garber, "Computational Models for Texture Analysis and Texture Synthesis," University of Southern California, USCIPI Report 1000, May 1981 (Ph.D. thesis).
[47] K. Deguchi and I. Morishita, "Texture Characterization and Texture-based Image Partitioning Using Two-dimensional Linear Estimation Techniques," *IEEE Transactions on Electronic Computers*, Vol. 27, No. 8, August 1978, pp. 739-745.
[48] B. H. McCormick and S. N. Jayaramamurthy, "A Decision Theory Method for the Analysis of Texture," *International Journal of Computer and Information Science*, Vol. 4, No. 1, 1975, pp. 1-37.
[49] J. W. Modestino, R. W. Fries, and A. L. Vickers, "Stochastic Image Models Generated by Random Tesselations of the Plane," *Computer Graphics and Image Processing*, Vol. 12, 1980, pp. 74-98.
[50] B. Schachter and N. Ahuja, "Random Pattern Generation Process," *Computer Graphics and Image Processing*, Vol. 10, 1979, pp. 95-114.
[51] R. M. Pickett, "Visual Analysis of Texture in the Detection and Recognition of Objects," in *Picture Processing and Psychopictorics*, B. S. Lipkin and A. Rosenfeld (eds.), Academic Press, New York, 1970, pp. 289-308.
[52] J. K. Hawkins, "Texture Properties for Pattern Recognition," in *Picture Processing and Psychopictorics*, B. S. Lipkin and A. Rosenfeld (eds.), Academic Press, New York, 1970, pp. 347-370.
[53] S. W. Zucker, "Toward a Model of Texture," *Computer Graphics and Image Processing*, Vol. 5, 1976, pp. 190-202.

[54] J. T. Maleson, C. M. Brown and J. A. Feldman, "Understanding Natural Texture," *Proceedings of ARPA Image Understanding Workshop*, Palo Alto, Calif., October 1977, pp. 19-27.

[55] F. Tomita, Y. Shirai, and S. Tsuji, "Description of Textures by a Structural Analyzer," *Proceedings of the International Joint Conference on Artificial Intelligence*, Tokyo, August 1979, pp. 884-889.

[56] M. Nagao and T. Matsuyama, *A structural Analysis of Complex Aerial Photographs*, Plenum Press, New York, 1980.

[57] L. S. Davis, "Computing the Spatial Structure of Cellular Textures," *Computer Graphics and Image Processing*, Vol. 11, No 2, October 1979, pp. 111-122.

[58] F. Vilnrotter, R. Nevatia, and K. Price, "Structural Description of Natural Textures," *Proceedings of the Fifth International Pattern Recognition Conference*, Miami, Vol. 2, December 1980, pp. 1142-1144

[59] F. Vilnrotter, "Structural Analysis of Natural Textures," University of Southern California Report USCISG100 (Ph.D. thesis), September 1981.

[60] H. Tamura, S. Mori, and T. Yamawaki, "Textural Features Corresponding to Visual Perception," *IEEE Transactions on Systems, Man and Cybernetics*, Vol. 8, No. 6, June 1978, pp. 460-473.

[61] D. Marr, "Early Processing of Visual Information," *Philosophical Transactions of Royal Society of London*, B275, 1976, pp. 483-524.

[62] R. W. Conners and C. A. Harlow, "Toward a Structural Textural Analyzer Based on Statistical Methods," *Computer Graphics and Image Processing*, March 1980, pp. 224-256.

[63] J. Weszka, C. R.Dyer, and A. Rosenfeld, "A Comparative Study of Texture Measures for Terrain Classification," *IEEE Transactions on Systems, Man and Cybernetics*, Vol. 6, No. 4, April 1976, pp. 269-285.

[64] R. W.Conners and C. A. Harlow, "A Theoretical Comparison of Texture Algorithms," *IEEE Transactions on Pattern Analysis and Machine Intelligence*, May 1980, pp. 204-222.

[65] A. Zobrist and W. Thompson, "Building a Distance Function for Gestalt Grouping," *IEEE Transactions on Computers*, Vol. 24, 1975, pp. 718-728.

[66] L. S. Davis and A. Mitiche, "Edge Detection in Textures," *Computer Graphics and Image Processing*, Vol. 12, No. 1, January 1980, pp. 25-39.

[67] W. Thompson, "Textural Boundary Analysis," *IEEE Transactions on Computers*, Vol. 26, 1977, pp. 272-276.

9

DEPTH MEASUREMENT AND ANALYSIS

Many scene analysis difficulties are caused by the loss of direct depth information in a single picture. Segmentation techniques are complicated because depth discontinuities are being implicitly inferred from intensity, color, or texture discontinuities. Shape analysis is made difficult by the changes in the projected shape caused by perspective.

Depth of visible surfaces can be measured by passive use of multiple views, as in stereo vision, or by active control of the illumination of an object. Humans are able to perceive relative depth from a single view, as in perceiving a photograph. Such inference is believed to use many complex "cues" such as occlusion, shadows, texture gradients, and size of familiar objects. Object, or viewer, motion provide another important cue for object detection and segmentation.

Only the depth of the visible surfaces can be inferred from single views or narrowly spaced stereo views. Such data is sometimes called a 2 1/2-D model of the scene. A number of views are required to obtain complete 3-D models of all surfaces. In our normal perception such complete models are, of course, not available.

9.1 STEREO AND MOTION

Each point of an opaque object's image corresponds to one point on the object. This object point must be along the ray joining the image point and the focal point for an ideal lens imaging device, but the distance to the object along this ray is unknown. However, if the object is viewed from another perspective and the same point is visible in both views, then it must be along the intersection of the rays determined from the two views, and its three-dimensional position can be computed. For example, in Fig. 9-1, the points P and Q are constrained to be along rays C_1P_1 and C_1Q_1, respectively, from the information available in the left view, and along C_2P_2 and C_2Q_2 by the second view. The two constraints together determine the positions of P and Q.

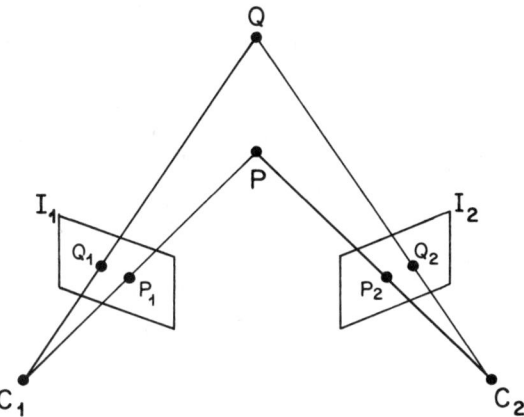

Figure 9-1: Determining position by stereo triangulation

Stereo depth measurement requires the following two operations.

1. Determination of the point pairs in the two images that correspond to the images of the same object point. This is known as the *correspondence* problem. The translation between corresponding points in two images is known as the *disparity* of the point pair. Note that the image of a small surface on the object may be different in the two images because of the changes in perspective and in surface reflectivity with the imaging angles. Moreover, some of the points in one image may not be visible in the other.

2. Determintion of the three-dimensional object point from the two image points by *triangulation*. This operation requires the relative positions and orientations of the cameras for the two views.

The triangulation problem is simple if the two cameras are calibrated with respect to each other. If enough corresponding points are obtained, the relative camera parameters can be determined by minimizing the shortest distances between the corresponding lines that should ideally intersect. The algebraic details are complex, but they can be worked out following the procedures of Chapter 3. Details may be found in [1, 2].

Correspondence between two views can be established by matching specific features, such as corners, in two views or by matching small regions by correlation without identifying any features. Matching of specific features is potentially more efficient, as their number is small. The features to be used should be distinct and also invariant to small changes in the viewing angle. Note that line segments are distinct in orientation only, and not in position. Corners are distinct in both of these parameters.

Use of features for stereo correspondence has been limited, owing partly to the difficulty of extracting reliable features. Burr and Chien [3], Arnold [4], and Baker and Binford [5] have used edges and edge segments and their associated properties such as length and contrast. Marr and Poggio [6] and Grimson [7] have described the use of "zero-crossings," of an image convolved with a Laplacian-Gaussian mask (as in Section 7.1.3). Ganapathy [8] and Underwood and Coates [9] have described matching of features using invariant properties of polyhedral scenes; Shapira and Freeman describe a technique for matching of imperfect, curved object scenes [10].

Searching for correspondence by similarity of regions in two images does not require any previous analysis of the images, but the search is more expensive. Two measures of similarity between regions are commonly used: the cross-correlation, as defined in Eq. (2-2), and the sum of the squares of the differences. The cross-correlation coefficient is independent of the contrast but requires more computation. Sum of the squares of the differences is adequate if the two views are taken under similar viewing conditions.

For a region centered around a given point in an image, the second image can be searched for a window that is most similar to the first based on one of the above measures. This operation needs to be performed for windows around each point in the first image whose depth is to be measured. Note that this is possible only for those windows that contain sufficient information for matching. Such windows should be nonhomogeneous and contain unique features. The search for a match can be quite expensive, if conducted exhaustively. Different ways to reduce this search are described in Section 9.1.1.

The correspondences found by measurement of local similarities, by region correlation, or by feature matching may occasionally be ambiguous or in error. Some of these ambiguities can be resolved by examining the disparities of several points in context, as described in Section 9.1.2.

Detection of motion has similarities with the stereo correspondence problem. However, 3-D data is more difficult to obtain from object motion. A brief survey of motion detection and analysis techniques is given in Section 9.1.3.

9.1.1 Correspondence Search

As the disparity in two images depends on the distance of the objects from the camera, if the limits of the range to the object are known, search for disparities can be limited correspondingly. More restrictions can be derived by observing that a point in one image constrains the corresponding object point to lie along a certain straight line in 3-D space and that the image of this line in a second view is also a line in that view. Thus, the search for correspondence with the image of a point need only be along a line. To account for errors in the knowledge of the relative orientations and positions of the two cameras, the search needs to be conducted in a narrow band. Again, the search distance along the line can be limited if the limits on the range to the object from the camera are known.

Barnea and Silverman used an interesting variation by not computing a similarity measure for the entire window but instead basing the decision on the rate at which the differences in the two windows accumulate [11]. A match with high error when only a few pixels have been examined is abandoned in favor of alternative matches.

Local context can be used to speed up the search, assuming that the surfaces in 3-D are smooth except at a small number of discontinuities. Disparity of the neighboring points can thus be expected to be similar, and the search can use the neighbor's disparity for a starting point.

Two search procedures using additional simplifications are described below.

Use of multiple views. The accuracy of depth measurement by stereo depends directly on the angle, hence the disparities between the two views. However, a large angle and larger disparities require a search over larger image areas. Use of multiple views between two stereo views allows high accuracy without increase in search time.

Availability of multiple views offers several alternatives for searching for correspondences. Assume that the search for disparities between the two extreme views of a series of k views can be limited to a band n pixels long and m pixels wide, as discussed above. The search for correspondences between two adjacent views can then be limited to a band n' pixels long and m' pixels wide, where $n' = (n/k-1)$ and $m' = (m/k-1)$. Let the successive views be called $view_1$, $view_2$, ..., $view_k$.

Disparities between extreme views can be determined by chaining through the intermediate views. Consider the matching of a particular, chosen region in $view_1$. Assume that a match has been found for this region between $view_1$ and $view_2$. To determine the best match for the same region in $view_i$ with a region in $view_{i+1}$, the search need be conducted only in an n'-by-m' band, centered at the center of the region of best match in the previous view ($view_i$). This process begins with matching of all regions of interest in $view_1$ with regions in $view_2$ and continues until the last view has been considered. An alternative is to match views i and $i+1$ at each step, where $1 < i \mathrel{\mathsf{K}} k-1$, and sum the disparities. For the former method, however, only crude disparities need to be found at all but the last step, and the errors of matching do not accumulate.

Assuming exhaustive searches in the specified bands, the total number of matches examined for all steps will be $(k-1)(n'm')$ which is equal to $(nm)/(k-1)$. This is a saving of a factor of $(1/k-1)$ compared to the direct search between the extreme views. If the width of the search band is assumed independent of the angle, then no savings in search results. However, use of multiple views may still be more reliable, as at each step the images differ by smaller amounts, and the search is constrained to smaller areas.

Use of multiple views, taken every 1/2 degree apart, for a total stereo angle of five to ten degrees, is described in [12]. Baumgart has used multiple views around an object to generate complete 3-D models for computer graphics applications [13].

Coarse to fine matching. A considerable saving in search time can be obtained by matching reduced-resolution images of the two views and refining the match in successively higher-resolution images. At each step of the matching, the search window can be maintained to be of the same size.

Such coarse-to-fine matching has been used by Moravec in a stereo program [14] and is similar to the use of reduced-resolution images for other purposes, as in planning procedures for edge detection and region segmentation. A possible difficulty of this approach is in loss of information in the reduced image and hence missing of some correspondences.

9.1.2 Global Correspondences

The correspondences computed by the local similarities may be ambiguous if more than one region in the same image has similar properties. Consider the left and right images in Fig. 9-2, consisting of three dark squares each, as marked. Each square in one image is similar to any of the three in the other. If we correspond L_1 and R_1, L_2 and R_2, and L_3 and R_3, the three squares will be computed to be at the same height above the background, shown by the filled circles in Fig. 9-2. If L_1 is matched with R_2, L_2 with R_3, and L_3 with R_1, then the computed heights of the squares will be as indicated by the cross marks in Fig. 9-2. Another possible interpretation is shown by the unfilled circles.

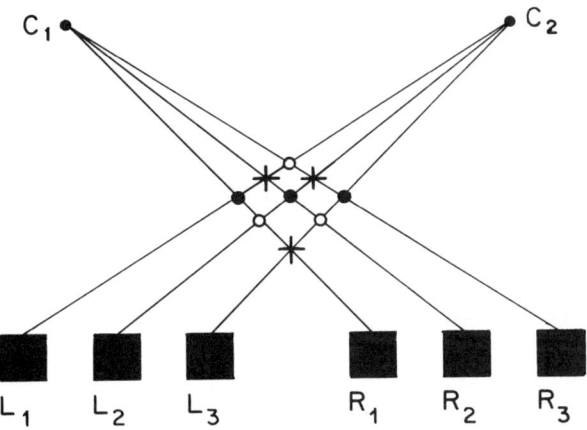

Figure 9-2: An example of ambiguous stereo correspondence

In spite of local ambiguities, our perception of stereo images is normally unambiguous. Apparently, certain correspondences are preferred as giving a total perceived surface with preferred properties. Julesz has suggested a "cooperative model" for stereopsis, where the final disparity values of each cell are influenced by disparities of neighboring pixels [15]. A dipole is associated with each pixel, pointing in the direction of the disparity. However, the direction of each dipole is also determined by its coupling by springs to neighboring dipoles. This model appears to have desirable qualitative properties but is incompletely specified and untested.

Marr and Poggio have suggested that two constraints should be satisfied in choosing global correspondences [6]:

1. *Uniqueness.* Each point in an image must be assigned at most one disparity value, as the corresponding object point has a unique

physical location. This constraint is not valid for transparent or translucent objects.

2. *Continuity*. Disparity values change smoothly, except at a limited number of depth discontinuities (since matter is cohesive).

The above two constraints lead to the choice of the simplest (most continuous) surface interpretation among the many alternatives. Marr and Poggio have described two techniques to implement these constraints.

Their first method is described by considering a three-dimensional collection of binary-valued cells, each plane corresponding to pixels with the same disparity. Let $C^t_{x,y,d}$ denote the state of a cell in this network, and its being *on* corresponds to the pixel (x, y) in the left image having a disparity d (for convenience, all disparities are considered to be in the x direction). Cells in the network either reinforce or inhibit the response of the neighboring cells. Marr and Poggio suggested the following iterative algorithm:

$$C^{t+1}_{x,y,d} = \sigma \left[\sum_{\substack{x',y',d \\ \in S(x,y,d)}} C^t - \varepsilon \sum_{\substack{x',y',d \\ \in O(x,y,d)}} C^t_{x',y',d} + C^0_{x,y,d} \right] \quad (9\text{-}1)$$

where superscript t indicates time or iteration, $S(x, y, d)$ is the excitatory neighborhood and $O(x, y, d)$ the inhibitory neighborhood of cell (x, y, d), ε is a constant parameter, and σ is a threshold function. $S(x, y, d)$ is taken to be a circular neighborhood of a certain size, (such as with a radius of five pixels) of (x, y, d) in the same disparity layer in the network, indicating a preference for the continuity of the disparity values. Cells with the same (x, y) values but with different disparities comprise the inhibitory neighborhood corresponding to the uniqueness criterion. These neighborhoods correspond to the lines of sight from the two views, if the network cells are actually located at the 3-D positions indicated by the image (x, y) coordinates and disparity d.

Marr and Poggio have described experiments with random dot stereograms and claim convergence for a wide range of parameter values in Eq. (9-1). However, these examples are characterized by relatively uniform disparities and large step discontinuities, and the performance on real images remains unclear. A similar iterative algorithm was described earlier by Dev [16].

The second algorithm of Marr and Poggio is more heuristic in nature, and a specific implementation is described by Grimson [7]. Matching between two images is between zero-crossings obtained by

Laplacian-Gaussian edge-detecting masks (as described in Chapter 7). A match for a zero-crossing in one image is centered in three locations (or three "pools") in the other image, one corresponding to the expected disparity, and the others on two sides of it. If two matches are found around the same location (or in the same pool), it is decided that no match exists. If a match is found in more than one pool, then the pool that gives a disparity value similar to disparities of other points in the neighborhood of this point is chosen. (Arnold describes a similar approach, requiring edge elements linked to a central edge to have disparities nearly equal to that of the central element [4]. Baker and Binford give additional contraints based on the connectivity of the edges [5].)

The expected disparity needed in the procedure above is obtained successively by starting from larger masks and narrowing to the smaller masks. Initially, for the largest mask, the expected disparity is assumed to be zero.

The most common use of stereo is perhaps in mapping of terrain elevation contours from aerial images. In stereo matching over natural textured areas and smoothly varying terrains, ambiguities in local correspondences are few and can be resolved by the continuity of the disparity values. Stereo correspondence is more difficult in the presence of sharp changes in range as for steep terrain or in the presence of cultural features such as buildings, and for indoor scenes with occluding objects. In such cases, no correspondences may exist for points at the boundaries or at surfaces of steep slopes. The above-described global correspondence techniques have been tested on a variety of indoor and outdoor scenes, but only those of limited complexity in the number of occluding objects. Note that for nontextured objects, stereo range information is available only at particular distinct points, such as at corners or edges.

9.1.3 Motion Detection and Analysis

Motion of an object in a dynamic scene is a very strong cue to its presence, and some animals, such as frogs, are thought to rely solely on motion in search of their prey. Motion of an object can be detected by finding corresponding points in a sequence of images. However, the same constraints cannot be used for limiting the search or establishing the global correspondences. If the object motion is small and much of the scene is static, the moving points can be detected simply by differencing the two views [17]. A spatial cluster of points with high differences may be used to distinguish the moving points from the points whose intensity changes due to noise.

Detection of motion by first segmenting objects and then matching them in a sequence of views is simple in principle, but difficulties arise owing to errors of segmentation and to possible rotation or occlusion of objects. A complete survey of such and other motion-detection techniques may be found in [18].

Some techniques have tried to use the rate of change of intensity at the pixels in an image for the estimation of the velocity of moving objects and for their segmentation from the background. Note that for objects with homogeneous surfaces, only the points at the boundaries with a component normal to the object motion have a nonzero intensity change.

For a given point, an incremental change in intensity di, due to a spatial shift $d\mathbf{s}$, is given by

$$di = -\mathbf{G} \cdot d\mathbf{s} \qquad (9\text{-}2)$$

where $\mathbf{G}$ is the spatial intensity gradient and the negative sign is due to the motion of the underlying surface (rather than the observer). Taking derivatives with respect to time, we get

$$\frac{di}{dt} = -\mathbf{G} \cdot \mathbf{U} = -(G_x U_x + G_y U_y) \qquad (9\text{-}3)$$

where $\mathbf{V}$ is the object velocity with components V_x and V_y along the x and y axes, and G_x and G_y are the components of the gradient $\mathbf{G}$.

Thus, given di/dt and $\mathbf{G}$, constraints are placed on the object velocity, but the components V_x and V_y cannot be inferred directly. Fennema and Thompson used clustering of points in the (V_x, V_y) space to infer the magnitude and the direction of the velocity [19]. Thompson also combined such velocity information with intensity information using a region-growing approach to segment objects [20]. Another important technique for segmenting objects, given points of large intensity change, is described in [21] and is based on an analysis of expected intensity changes when two surfaces move relative to each other.

Ullman has implemented a system of correspondence for motion by matching of local edges and line segments [22]. As in stereo, the local matches may be ambiguous. Ambiguities are resolved by testing whether a given set of matches could correspond to a *rigid-body* motion. Ullman shows that given three distinct orthographic views of four noncoplanar points in a rigid configuration, the structure and motion compatible with the three views are uniquely determined. Inference of nonrigid motion from moving light displays is described in [23].

DEPTH MEASUREMENT AND ANALYSIS

Apparent velocities of the points in an image, called *optical flow*, can also be useful for inferring the three-dimensional structure of the object surfaces under certain simplifying assumptions. These techniques have been tested only on very limited, simple scenes and will not be described here; the reader is referred to [24] and [25], which also contain extensive bibliographies.

9.2 ACTIVE RANGING

Range measurement by stereo requires only *passive* observation of the pointscene from multiple viewpoints. Range can be measured more easily if active control of the illumination is allowed. Two approaches are described below: triangulation of a pattern of light and measurement of time of flight of a signal to the object.

9.2.1 Triangulation Ranging

Consider viewing an object illuminated by a single ray of light of known 3-D position and orientation. The illuminated point on the object will form a single-point image on the camera screen. Given this point in the image, we can constrain the illuminated object point to be on a line through the image point and the camera center, computed from a known camera transform. As the object point must also lie on the illuminating ray, its position can be determined by the intersection of the two constraining lines. This is known as triangulation ranging, and is similar to the stereo ranging shown in Fig. 9-1, with one of the cameras replaced by a collimated source of light. To obtain positions of all points on the object, the object needs to be scanned by varying the position and the orientation of the illuminating beam.

The scanning of an object can be speeded up if it is illuminated by a plane of light rather than a single collimated beam. The object is then illuminated along a planar curve in 3-D and forms a line image on the imaging plane as shown in Fig. 9-3. For each point along this image curve, a straight line to the corresponding object point can be associated as before. The object must lie along the intersection of straight line and the known illuminating plane. To obtain other object points, the object can be scanned by a series of parallel planes.

This procedure will give poor resolution for object surfaces nearly parallel to the illuminating plane. Two mutually orthogonal series of scans may be used to overcome this difficulty. Agin and Binford [26] and Shirai [27] first described such ranging implementations independently. The plane of light is produced by illuminating a linear

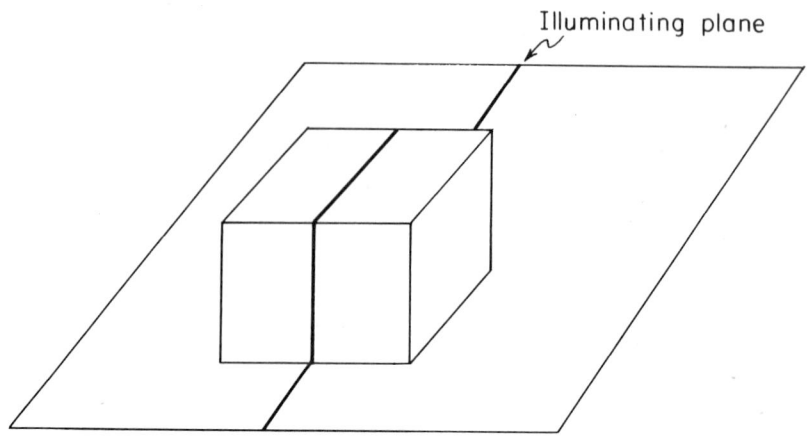

Figure 9-3: Illumination of an object by a plane of light

slit or by passing a collimated beam through a cylindrical lens. In the latter case, the desired orientations can be obtained by rotating the lens. A series of parallel scans can be obtained by a scanning mirror.

Figure 9-4 shows a TV camera image of a scene containing two objects. Figure 9-5 shows laser scans in two directions. Boundaries of objects can be derived by linking the end points of these scans, as they correspond to the depth discontinuities in the scene. A boundary may not cross any of the scans or itself. Figure 9-6 shows boundaries derived from Fig. 9-5 (from [28]). Note that the objects are well separated from the background, but the touching parts of the doll and the snake are not.

The ranging process can be further speeded by illuminating the objects with a grid of a predetermined pattern, say a light square grid on a dark background. If such a grid were to illuminate polyhedral objects, the images of parallel lines on a face would be parallel, ignoring perspective distortions, but the angles of these lines would depend on the orientation of the surface. Thus, discontinuities in surface depth and slope would result in discontinuities in the image lines and their slopes, respectively. Will and Pennington have described a *grid coding* technique that uses a square grid illumination, and different faces of polyhedral objects are separated by providing separate peaks in a Fourier transform of the image [29]. They suggest that other grid patterns may be suited for other specific objects. Unfortunately, precise 3-D positions of object points cannot be determined by grid illumination, unless the individual grid lines can be identified, say, by color.

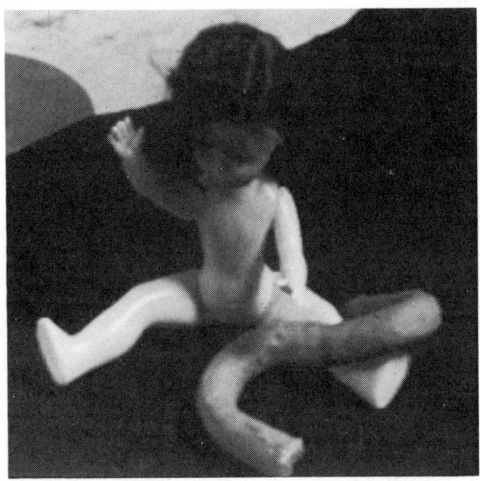

Figure 9-4: A TV picture of a scene

Figure 9-5: Laser scans for the scene of Fig. 9-4

Figure 9-6: Boundary derived from the scans of Fig. 9-5

9.2.2 LIDAR Ranging

Distance of an object from the observer can be determined by transmitting an electromagnetic signal and measuring the time interval for the reflected signal to come back, as in the use of RADAR for aircraft range measurement. For objects only a few meters away, signals need to be of shorter wavelength than are commonly used in RADAR. The visible light spectrum is suitable, and such systems have been called LIDAR (Light Detecting and Ranging) systems.

Range can be measured by transmitting a short pulse of light and measuring the time interval for the return path, or by transmitting a continuous wave signal and measuring the phase shift. A pulsed system is described in [30] and a continuous wave system in [31]. The latter system is shown schematically in Fig. 9-7. Discussion of details of electronics for time or phase measurements is beyond the scope of this book.

9.3 SEGMENTATION USING RANGE

Use of range data enables us to segment objects in a scene by the property that different objects are separated in 3-D space, rather than by discontinuities in their surface properties. Of course, objects that touch each other or rest on top of another cannot be segmented so easily. Segmentation using range data basically requires isolating the discontinuities in range. Analogous to the processing of intensity data,

DEPTH MEASUREMENT AND ANALYSIS

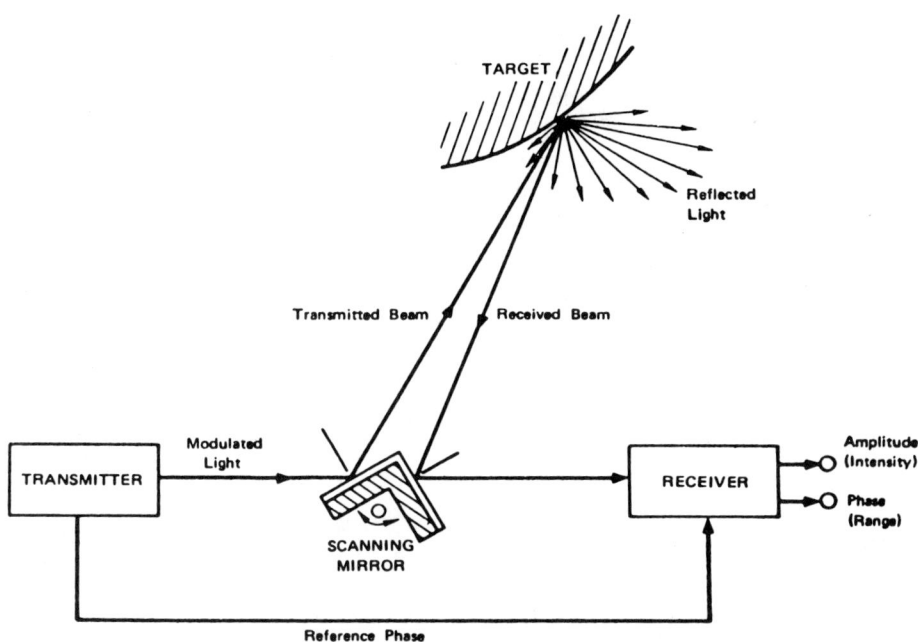

Figure 9-7: Block diagram of a laser ranging system
(from Nitzan et al. [31])
(© 1977 IEEE)

either edge or region types of methods may be used.

9.3.1 Boundary Detection

Discontinuities in range can often be found simply by a large jump in the range values, as different objects are separated by distances that are large compared to the range resolution. Connecting such discontinuities gives the "jump boundaries." Certain boundaries, such as the intersection of two planar surfaces, will not be detected as jump boundaries. Use of first-derivative discontinuities, as is common for intensity edge detection, is also not useful, as any slanting surface has a high range derivative. Such boundaries can be detected by using the second derivative, but with increased probability of errors due to noise in the range data.

Boundaries obtained by detecting range edges can usually be expected to be more robust than those using the intensity data.

However, these boundaries may still not be complete and contain gaps and spurious edges. In some cases, these gaps can be filled by using the additional information available in range data (see [32]). Duda and Nitzan have also suggested the use of registered intensity data, as certain boundaries may be more apparent in intensity data [33]. Sugihara has used constraints on edges at vertices of polyhedral objects (given by the Huffman-Clowes theory described in Chapter 4), to hypothesize and verify the missing lines, and has also described extensions for curved objects [34].

9.3.2 Detection of Planes and Surfaces

Surfaces of known shape, such as planes, can be detected directly in the range data. However, detection of such surfaces is more complicated than testing if a given set of points lies on such a surface.

The easiest surfaces to detect are horizontal planes, since the only unknown is the height, z. As the points on the same horizontal surface should have the same height, a histogram of the z values can be expected to have peaks corresponding to such surfaces. Another method is to take slices of the points in various ranges of height and find the points belonging to a single surface (see [31, 33]).

Detection of vertical surfaces involves an extra degree of freedom. One approach is to project the points on a horizontal plane $(x-y)$. The vertical planes should project into straight lines, which can be detected by a Hough transform or other methods described in Chapter 7.

Detection of planes of arbitrary orientation is more difficult. In principle, these planes can be detected by the use of a Hough transform, but the dimensionality of the transform space is likely to cause computational difficulties. Duda, Nitzan, and Barrett use peaks in intensity histograms, after the horizontal and vertical surfaces have been removed, to identify potential candidates for other planar surface, and they verify the hypothesized regions using range data [33].

Presence of planes could also be detected by computing normals to the local surfaces around each point and by clustering the orientations of these normals. This method may be sensitive to noise, as a derivative operation is required, and the directions may be in error near the boundary of two intersecting planes.

Curved surfaces of a given type could also be detected by a Hough transform approach, but the computational requirements are further increased because of the larger number of parameters. Oshima and Shirai have used an alternative approach [35]. They first group points into small surface elements and fit a plane to them. These elements are then merged into larger approximately planar regions, which are classified into plane, curved, or undefined classes. The curved regions are further merged if the larger regions fit a quadratic surface. This approach is akin to the region-growing approach for intensity-image segmentation.

9.4 SHAPE FROM SHADING

Humans are able to extract depth information, at least in a relative and qualitative sense, from single images. Among the many cues believed to be used are occlusion, texture gradients, size of familiar objects, and smooth changes in shading. Our understanding of these processes is very preliminary, and most of the machine implementations apply in very restricted cases only. We first consider shape from shading.

In normal segmentation using edge or uniform region analysis, smooth variations in surface intensity are viewed as a source of difficulty. However, these variations can provide clues to the 3-D shape of the surface. To perform such computation, we need a better understanding of the image-formation process.

For most surfaces, the proportion of incident light reaching the viewer is a function of the surface orientation. For a single light source the ratio can be represented as a function $\Phi(i, e, g)$ of the three angles $i, e,$ and g, known as the incident, emittance (or view), and phase angles, respectively (see Fig. 9-8). The incident angle is between the local surface normal and the incident ray, the emittance angle between the surface normal and the ray to the viewer, and the phase angle between the incident and the emitted ray.

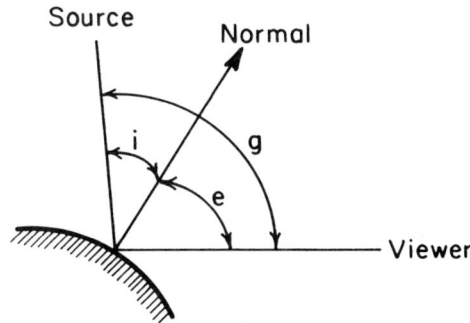

Figure 9-8: The incidence, emittance, and phase angles for determining reflectivity

For a given object point, illuminated by incident light intensity $A(\mathbf{r})$, the intensity of the corresponding image point $B(\mathbf{r}')$ is given by

$$B(\mathbf{r}') = A(\mathbf{r}) \cdot \phi(i, e, g) \qquad (9\text{-}4)$$

To compute shape from shading, we assume that $A(\mathbf{r})$ and $\Phi(i, e, g)$ are known and $B(\mathbf{r}')$ is obtained from the image. We wish to recover the surface orientation using (94). Horn has shown that this equation is a nonlinear partial differential equation, and has given a numerical technique for its solution under some simplifying conditions regarding the source and the camera locations [36]. The solution procedure starts from an initial contour and traces other contours satisfying the equation. The initial contours are derived from the brightest and the darkest points in the image. Horn was able to recover shape of smooth objects from a monocular view. (This technique is a generalization of an earlier technique to estimate shape of the lunar surface from a single view, where the reflectivity function has a simple, known form [37].)

Note that this technique requires complete knowledge of the light source and the reflectivity function $\Phi(i, e, g)$ for all combinations of the parameters. The reflectivity function may be known for some simple surfaces but must be measured carefully for others; mathematical models using surface properties are not very advanced. Also, in general, the surface materials of the of objects in a scene are not known a priori.

If an orthogonal, rather than a perspective, projection is used, a simpler and more elegant formulation using *reflectance maps*, also developed by Horn [38], is possible and is discussed below.

9.4.1 Reflectance Maps

Reflectance maps are based on the concept of gradient spaces, introduced in Chapter 4. The local surface normal of a surface $z = f(x, y)$, can be described by two parameters, $p = \partial z / \partial x$ and $q = \partial z / \partial y$. Parameters (p, q) constitute the gradient space. The shape-from-shading problem is essentially to estimate the (p, q) values for the points in an image.

In an orthographic projection, the viewing direction and hence the phase angle, g, is constant for all object points. Thus, for a fixed light source and viewing geometry, the reflected light and hence the image intensity depend only on the surface normal—that is, the gradient coordinates p and q. The reflectance map, $R(p, q)$ determines the image intensity as a function of p and q.

DEPTH MEASUREMENT AND ANALYSIS

Let us consider a perfect Lambertian, or matte surface, which appears equally bright from any viewing angle. Here the reflectivity R is simply proportional to $\cos(i)$, where i is the incident angle. Also, if the source is near the viewer,

$$\cos(i) = \frac{1}{\sqrt{1 + p^2 + q^2}} \quad (9\text{-}5)$$

For this case, the reflectance map, plotted as a function of p and q, consists of concentric circles (see Fig. 9-9). A somewhat more complex relationship applies if the light source is positioned away from the viewer. For a source whose direction is given by the vector $(P_s, q_s, -1)$ it can be shown that

$$\cos(i) = \frac{1 + p_s p + q_s q}{\sqrt{1 + p^2 + q^2}\sqrt{1 + p_s^2 + q_s^2}} \quad (9\text{-}6)$$

The corresponding contours in the reflectance map for a particular source location are shown in Fig. 9-10. (The reflectance map is fixed for a given source position.)

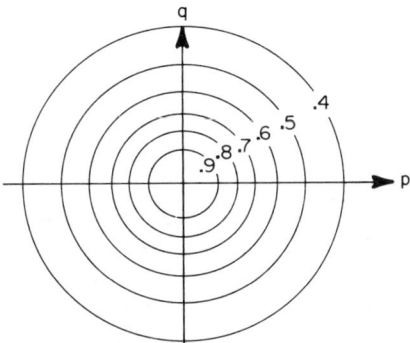

Figure 9-9: Contours in gradient space for a matte surface; source is at the viewer (adapted from Horn [38])

For a perfect mirrorlike reflector, the reflectance map is simply an impulse for one point in the (p, q) space. Reflectivity of most surfaces has both a mirrorlike specular component and a matte component.

The material in the maria (seas) of the moon also has a particularly simple reflectance function. Here, $\Phi(i, e, g) = \cos(i)/\cos$

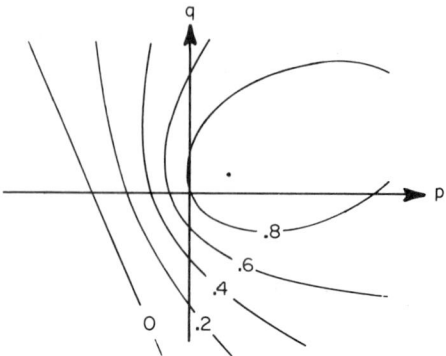

Figure 9-10: Another reflectance map for a matte surface; direction to the source is (0.7, 0.3) (adapted from Horn [38])

(e) and the corresponding reflectance map consists of parallel lines in the (p, q) plane.

The reflectance map representation is a convenient form for storing the reflectance properties and is useful for synthesizing images, given the surface of the shape. For the inverse process of shape from shading, a given intensity constrains the surface normal to be along a particular contour in the reflectance map. Assuming continuity of neighboring points on the surface, local shape can be determined as before. The basic process consists of tracing *base characteristics* in the image and computing corresponding *characteristics* in the reflectance map. The paths in the two spaces are related in the following manner. A step in the image space is perpendicular to the contour in the gradient space, and a step in the gradient space is perpendicular to the corresponding intensity contour in the image plane. (Further details are given in [38].) A parallel relaxation approach is described in [39].

Note that such processing requires an estimate of the initial conditions. It has been suggested that such an estimate may be derived from the surface boundaries. For smooth surfaces, at the external boundaries, the surface must be tangential, and the surface normal orthogonal to the line of sight [40]. Woodham gives some interesting constraints on the surface shape computation, if general properties of the surface, such as convexity, are known [41].

Woodham also suggests a novel approach to depth measurement, called *photometric stereo*, that uses two or more views of a scene by moving the light source rather than the camera [41]. For a given position of the light source, for each point in the image, a contour constraining the orientation of the surface at the point is given in the gradient space. Another position of the light source gives another such contour, and the surface must be at one or more of the points of their intersection. More views can be used to improve accuracy and reduce any remaining ambiguities. Photometric stereo has not been tested extensively but is of potential use where illumination can be controlled, as for industrial applications. The advantage of photometric stereo over conventional stereo is that no correspondence solution is needed, as the images are in perfect registration. However, photometric properties of the surface—that is, its complete reflectance function must be known in advance and the surface must be uniform. Practical advantages of this scheme over the conventional stereo are unclear.

Another application of reflectance maps, described by Horn and Bachman, is for registration of satellite images taken with different sun angles [42]. One image is first converted to a reflectance or *albedo* image by conversion of image intensity into surface reflectance. This, however, requires knowledge of surface orientation, which is obtained by terrain data of the region, and of the reflectance function. A new synthetic image can now be obtained for any desired sun angle and used for registration.

The reflectance-map representation is also useful in explaining the occurrence of certain types of edges in polyhedral scenes, such as steps, roofs, and peak (as in Chapter 7). The peak edges are likely to be due to convex edges, the roof edges due to convex edges, and the step edges due to obscuring edges. Reflectance-map properties can also be used to extend the gradient space analysis of Mackworth (Section 4.3). (In the example of a trihedral vertex shown in Fig. 4-16, the size of the triangle in the dual space can be fixed by requiring the points A', B' and C' to lie on reflectance contours in the gradient space given by the intensities of the three faces A, B and C).

9.5 TEXTURE GRADIENTS

Smooth variations in texture, or *texture gradients*, can give clues to local surface shape. Figure 9-11 shows a picture of a brick wall. The bricks in the distant parts of the wall are smaller, in the image, and more closely spaced. The picture gives us a strong sense of the orientation of the wall, and the appropriate cue seems to be the gradient of the texture pattern. Figure 9-12 shows a synthetic image where a surface is suggested, again presumably by the changes in the elements of the perceived texture. The importance of texture gradients was suggested by Gibson as early as in 1950 [43].

Stevens has defined three causes of texture gradients [44]. The gradient may be caused by the variations in distance, called a *scaling gradient*, or by the variations in surface orientation, called a

Figure 9-11: Texture gradient in a brick wall

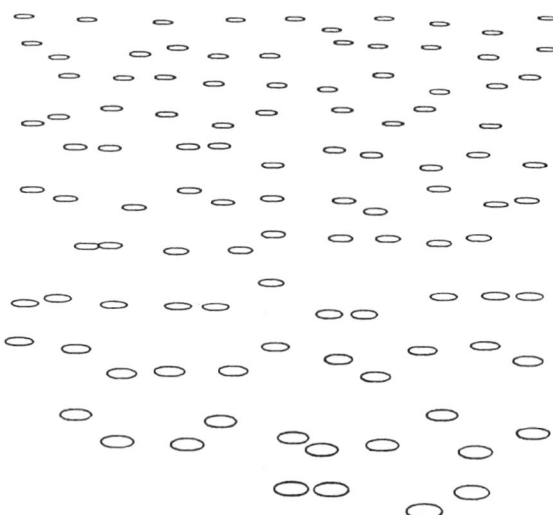

Figure 9-12: Perception of a surface from synthetic texture gradient (from Stevens [44])

foreshortening gradient, or by the variations in the physical texture itself. Normally, the physical texture is assumed to be constant.

Stevens has also suggested a modified gradient space representation for the normal to a surface that decomposes the effects of the scaling and the foreshortening gradients. He suggests the use of

DEPTH MEASUREMENT AND ANALYSIS

polar coordinates τ and $\tan \sigma$, of a point (p, q), in the gradient space as shown in Fig. 9-13. τ and σ are called the *tilt* and the *slant* of the surface. Tilt may be considered to specify "which way" the surface normal is oriented and slant to specify "how much." Consider a vertical image plane. A surface parallel to the image plane has zero tilt and slant. If the surface is rotated about a vertical axis, the tilt remains zero and the slant depends on the degree of rotation. Similarly, for all rotations about the horizontal axis, the tilt is 90 degrees and the slant gives the amount of rotation.

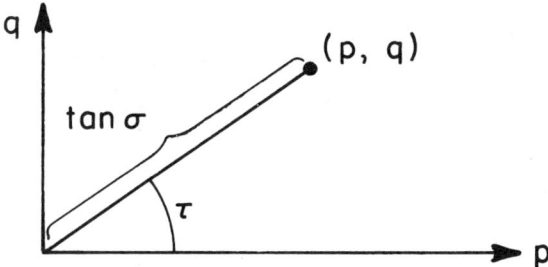

Figure 9-13: Tilt-slant representation of surface orientation

The scaling gradient of a texture can be computed from *characteristic dimensions* that are not foreshortened, and hence must be parallel to the image plane. In the image, these are in a direction normal to the direction of the most rapid change in any measure of texture regularity that is sensitive to scaling. This direction of most rapid change also gives the tilt angle τ. Alternately, the characteristic dimensions are locally aligned with the orientation of the greatest regularity. One or the other definition may be easier to apply for a particular texture. In Fig. 9-12 the direction of the major axes of the ellipses is along the characteristic dimension, and in Fig. 9-11 it is along the vertical dimensions of the bricks.

Once the characteristic dimensions and the tilt have been obtained, distances of the various texture elements can be determined simply by the magnitudes of the characteristic dimensions, since they are inversely proportional to the distance. The slant component of the surface orientation can be computed from these distances. An alternate expression for slant in terms of the gradient of the characteristic dimension δ is given by

$$\tan \sigma = \frac{\nabla \delta}{\delta} \qquad (9\text{-}7)$$

Bajcsy and Liebermann, used the period of a regular texture as the dimension σ, computed from a Fourier analysis of the texture, to compute surface orientation [45, 46]. (Their analysis is, however, not in terms of the use of a characteristic dimension.)

The above method is ineffective if the projection is orthographic—that is, the surface is far from the viewer. In this case a measure based on the foreshortening gradient may be useful. A measure with this property is the *height/width* ratio or the *aspect ratio* of a texture element—for example, the ratio of the major to the minor axes dimensions for the ellipses of Fig. 9-12. The "width" and the "height" of an element are measured along and normal to the characteristic dimension. If the aspect ratio is ϵ, slant is given, as before, by

$$\tan \sigma = \frac{\nabla \epsilon}{\epsilon} \tag{9-8}$$

The above measure assumes uniformity of the texture elements but not their spacing. It may not apply to natural textures, as the sizes of the elements (such as pebbles and grass blades) may change and, further, some elements may be occluded by others. A related technique, using the distribution of the directions of the tangents to the texture element boundaries as a function of the surface slant, is described in [47] and has been applied to simple natural textures.

Kender has explored the constraints imposed on the local surface shape, if certain assumptions are made about the texture property [48]. These constraints are expressed in terms of a *normalized texture property* that must be present in the 3-D scene for an assumed orientation of the surface, and they are expressed as contours in the gradient space, analogous to the reflectance maps of the previous section. The texture properties may be length, slope, density, and so on. Use of the gradient space implies that the projection is orthographic. Also, the texture elements are assumed to be "painted" on the surface, rather than "pointed" away from the surface (for example, trees in a forest texture).

For example, consider a vertical line texture primitive of a given length in an image. The "deprojected" length of this line in the 3-D scene depends on the local orientation of the surface; that is, the deprojected length is fixed for each point (p, q) in the gradient space. The constraints can be expressed as equal-length contours; in this case they consist of vertical parallel lines in the (p, q) plane. Note that this information alone is not sufficient to specify the surface orientation.

Now, if another texture primitive consists of a line of another orientation, a corresponding map can be constructed for this line. If it is further assumed that the two lines have the same length in the scene, then the surface must lie at the intersection of the contours in the two maps. A third texture property such as a known angle between the two lines (in the scene) is needed to constrain the surface to be one of the two orientations, one being the reflection of the other in the gradient space. Such a relation may come, for example, by assuming that orthogonal lines in the scene are orthogonal on the 3-D surface.

Note that the above analysis only specifies constraints under certain assumptions and is consistent with the analysis of shape from shading of the previous section if intensity is considered as a primitive texture property. The texture properties to use must still be found by the use of *heuristic* rules.

9.6 CONTOUR ANALYSIS

The boundaries of objects themselves convey some 3-D shape information; for example, see Fig. 9-14, where the two figures have similar line configurations but are perceived to be of different shape (a cube and a truncated pyramid). We are also able to infer 3-D shape from 2-D contour lines that are projections of 3-D curves; such representations are common for graphic display of 3-D functions. Techniques for inferring shape from contours basically assume that the observed regularities or near regularities, such as parallelism and symmetry, are not accidental and correspond to similar regularities on the 3-D surface.

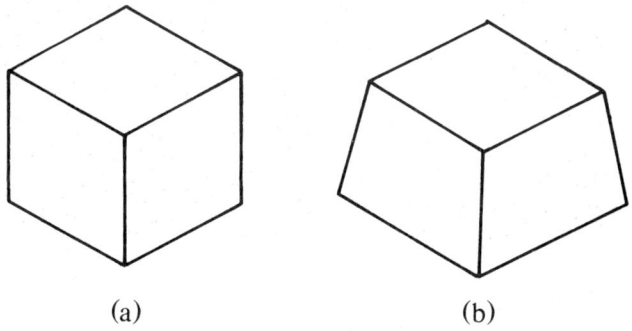

(a)   (b)

Figure 9-14: Two polyhedral objects of different shape
(after Kanade [49])

Kanade has described a method suitable for planar surfaces [49]. His process assumes that parallel lines in the image are also parallel in the scene and that a *skewed symmetry* is the projection of a real symmetry. A symmetry in 2-D has an axis for which the opposite sides are reflective. In skewed symmetry, the corresponding points need not be perpendicular to the axis but may be at some fixed angle to it. Figure 9-15 shows a figure with skew symmetry and the axes of symmetry. Constraints on the orientation of the plane of this surface can be determined if it is assumed that the axes of the skew symmetry are projections of the orthogonal axes of real symmetry. (The constraints are in fact a hyperbola in the gradient space. A particular pair of orientations may be chosen by picking the points closest to the origin. Details are given in [49]. Stevens has described experiments on human observer's ability to estimate surface orientations from skew symmetry using images as in Fig. 9-15 [44].) The two assumptions used by Kanade's method are also sufficient to explain the perceived shapes of the two objects in Fig. 9-14. A promising start has been made by Lowe and Binford in interpretation of three-dimensional structure from image curves for much more general scenes [50, 51]. These techniques also make use of shadow information to infer heights of objects above ground.

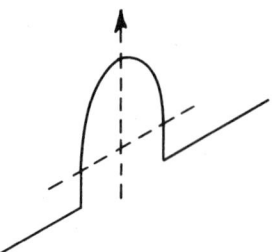

Figure 9-15: A skew-symmetric figure and axes of symmetry

Barrow and Tenenbaum have suggested integrating various analyses, yielding *intrinsic scene characteristics* [40]. These characteristics, for each point in the image, are the distance from the viewer, surface orientation, reflectance, and illumination. Partial object contours can provide local characteristics, which are then propagated inward, and consistency of the intrinsic values is established. This processing should, in turn, lead to the completion of the initial partial contours. The described processing is, again, directly applicable to simple scenes only.

9.7 SUMMARY

In this chapter we have studied techniques for measuring or estimating the three-dimensional positions of the visible surfaces of objects in a scene. Such information is helpful in scene segmentation. Depth measurement by use of stereo views is passive, but the problems of global correspondence need to be solved. Active ranging requires use of special equipment and may not be suitable under all conditions.

Range can also be estimated from monocular images, using variations in intensity, texture gradients, and the contours in the image. Such estimates require assumptions about the scene being viewed. Current techniques are applicable only under special conditions and for simple scenes only.

REFERENCES

[1] M. J. Hannah, *Computer Matching of Areas in Stereo Images*, Stanford Artificial Intelligence Laboratory Memo AIM-239, July 1974 (Ph.D. thesis).

[2] D. B. Gennery, "Modelling the Environment of an Exploring Vehicle by Means of Stereo Vision," Stanford Artificial Intelligence Laboratory Memo AIM-339, June 1980.

[3] D. J. Burr and R. T. Chien, "A System for Stereo Computer Vision with Geometric Models," *Proceedings of the Fifth International Joint Conference on Artificial Intelligence*, Boston, 1977, p. 583.

[4] R. D. Arnold, "Local Context in Matching Edges for Stereo Vision," *Proceedings of Image Understanding Workshop*, Cambridge, Mass., May 1978, pp. 65-72.

[5] H. H. Baker and T. O. Binford, "Depth from Edge and Intensity Based Stereo," *Proceedings of the Seventh International Joint Conference on Artificial Intelligence*, Vancouver, Canada, August 1981, pp. 631-636.

[6] D. Marr and T. Poggio, "A Computational Theory of Human Stereo Vision," *Proceedings of Royal Society of London*, B204, 1979, pp. 301-328.

[7] W. E. L. Grimson, "Aspects of a Computational Theory of Human Stereo Vision," *Proceedings of Image Understanding Workshop*, University of Maryland, April 1980, pp. 128-149.

[8] S. Ganapathy, "Reconstruction of Scenes Containing Polyhedra from Stereo Pair of Views," Stanford Artificial Intelligence Laboratory Memo AIM-272, December 1975.

[9] S. A. Underwood and C. L. Coates, Jr., "Visual Learning from

Multiple Views," *IEEE Transactions on Computers*, Vol. 24, No. 6, June 1975, pp. 651-661.

[10] R. Shapira and H. Freeman, "Reconstruction of Curved Surface Bodies from a Set of Imperfect *Projections*," *Proceedings of Fifth International Joint Conference on Artificial Intelligence*, Cambridge, Mass., August 1977, pp. 628-634.

[11] D. I. Barnea and H. F. Silverman, "A Class of Algorithms for Fast Digital Image Registration," *IEEE Transactions on Computers*, C-21, 1972, 179-186.

[12] R. Nevatia, "Depth Measurement by Motion Stereo," *Computer Graphics and Image Processing*, Vol. 5, 1976, pp. 203-214.

[13] B. G. Baumgart, "Geometric Modelling for Computer Vision," Stanford Artificial Intelligence Laboratory Memo AIM-249, October 1974.

[14] H. P. Moravec, "Obstacle Avoidance and Navigation in the Real World by a Seeing Robot Rover," Stanford Artificial Intelligence Laboratory Memo AIM-340, September 1980.

[15] B. Julesz, *Foundations of Cyclopean Perception*, University of Chicago Press, Chicago, 1971.

[16] P. Dev, "Perception of Depth Surfaces in Random-Dot Stereograms A Neutral Model," *International Journal of Man-Machine Studies*, Vol. 7, 1975, pp. 511-528.

[17] R. L. Lillestrand, "Techniques for Change Detection," *IEEE Transactions on Computers*, Vol. 21, July 1972, pp. 654-659.

[18] H. H. Nagel, "Analysis Techniques for Image Sequences," *Proceedings of the Fourth International Joint Conference on Pattern Recognition*, Kyoto, Japan, November 1979, pp. 186-211.

[19] C. L. Fennema and W.B. Thompson, "Velocity Determination in Scenes Containing Several Moving Objects," *Computer Graphics and Image Processing*, Vol. 9, April 1979, pp. 301-315.

[20] W. B. Thompson, "Combining Motion and Contrast for Segmentation," *IEEE Transactions on Pattern Analysis and Machine Intelligence*, Vol. 2, No. 6, November 1980, pp. 543-549.

[21] R. Jain, W. N. Martin and J. K. Aggarwal, "Segmentation Through the Detection of Changes Due to Motion," *Computer Graphics and Image Processing*, Vol. 11, September 1979, pp. 13-34.

[22] S. Ullman, *The Interpretation of Visual Motion*, MIT Press, Cambridge, Mass., 1979.

[23] R. F. Rashid, "Towards a System for the Interpretation of Moving Light Displays," *IEEE Transactions on Pattern Analysis and Machine Intelligence*, Vol. 2, No. 6, November 1980, pp. 524-581.

[24] B. K. P. Horn and B. G. Schunk, "Determining Optical Flow," MIT Artificial Intelligence Laboratory Memo No. 572, Cambridge,

Mass., 1980.
[25] K. Prazdny, "Determining the Instantaneous Direction of Motion from Optical Flow Generated by a Curvilinearly Moving Observer," *Proceedings of Image Understanding Workshop*, Washington, D.C., April 1981, pp. 14-21.
[26] G. J. Agin and T. O. Binford, "Computer Description of Curved Objects," *Proceedings of the Third International Joint Conference on Artificial Intelligence*, Stanford, Calif., 1973, pp. 629-640.
[27] Y. Shirai, "Recognition of Polyhedra with a Range Finder," *Pattern Recognition*, Vol. 4, 1972, pp. 243-250.
[28] R. Nevatia, *Computer Analysis of Scenes of 3-Dimensional Curved Objects*, Birkhauser-Verlag, Basel, Switzerland, 1976.
[29] P. M. Will and K. S. Pennington, "Grid Coding: A Preprocessing Technique for Robot and Machine Vision," *Artificial Intelligence*, Vol. 2, 1971, pp. 319-329.
[30] R. A. Lewis and A. R. Johnson, "A Scanning Laser Rangefinder for a Robotic Vehicle," *Proceedings of the Fifth International Joint Conference on Artificial Intelligence*, Cambridge, Mass., August 1977, pp. 762-768.
[31] D. Nitzan, A. E. Brain, and R. O. Duda, "The Measurement and Use of Registered Reflectance and Range Data in Analysis," *Proceedings of IEEE*, Vol. 65, February 1977, pp. 206-220.
[32] S. Inokuchi and R. Nevatia, "Boundary Detection in Range Pictures," *Proceedings of Fifth International Conference on Pattern Recognition*, Miami, November 1980, pp. 1301-1303.
[33] R.O. Duda, D. Nitzan, and P. Barrett, "Use of Range and Reflectance Data to Find Planar Surface Regions," *IEEE Transactions on Pattern Analysis and Machine Intelligence*, Vol. 1, No. 3, July 1979, pp. 259-271.
[34] K. Sugihara, "Range-Data Analysis Guided by a Junction Dictionary," *Artificial Intelligence*, Vol. 12, 1979, pp. 41-69.
[35] M. Oshima and Y. Shirai, "A Scene Description Method Using Three-dimensional Information," *Pattern Recognition*, 1979, pp. 9-17.
[36] B. Horn, "Obtaining Shape from Shading Information," in *The Psychology of Computer Vision*, P. H. Winston (ed.), McGraw-Hill, New York, 1975.
[37] T. Rindfleisch, "Photometric Method for Lunar Topography," *Photogrammetric Engineering*, Vol. 32, 1966, pp. 262-276.
[38] B. Horn, "Understanding Image Intensities," *Artificial Intelligence*, Vol. 8, 1977, pp. 201-231.
[39] R. J. Woodham, "A Cooperative Algorithm for Determining Surface Orientation from a Single View," *Proceedings of the Fifth*

International Joint Conference on Artificial Intelligence, Cambridge, Mass., 1977, pp. 635-641.

[40] H. Barrow and J.M. Tenenbaum, "Recovery of Intrinsic Scene Characteristics from Images," in *Computer Vision Systems*, A. Hanson and E. Riseman, (eds.), Academic Press, New York, 1978, pp. 3-26.

[41] R. J. Woodham, "Reflectance Map Techniques for Analyzing Surface Defects in Metal Castings" MIT Artificial Intelligence Laboratory Memo AI-TR-457, June 1978.

[42] B. K.P. Horn and B. L. Bachman, "Using Synthetic Images to Register Real Images with Surface Models," *Communications of ACM*, Vol. 21, No. 11, November 1978, pp. 914-924.

[43] J. J. Gibson, *The Perception of the Visual World*, Houghton Mifflin, Boston, Mass., 1950.

[44] K. Stevens, "Surface Perception from Local Analysis of Texture and Contour," MIT Artificial Intelligence Laboratory Memo AI-TR-512, February 1980.

[45] R. Bajcsy, "Computer Identification of Visual Surface," *Computer Graphics and Image Processing*, Vol. 2, No. 2, 1973, pp. 118-130.

[46] R. Bajcsy and L. Liebermann, "Texture Gradient as a Depth Cue," *Computer Graphics and Image Processing*, Vol. 5, No. 1, March 1976, pp. 52-67.

[47] A. P. Witkin, "A Statistical Technique for Recovering Surface Orientation from Texture in Natural Imagery," *Proceedings of the First Annual National Conference on Artificial Intelligence*, Stanford, Calif., August 1980, pp. 1-3.

[48] J. R. Kender, "Shape from Texture," Carnegie-Mellon University, Computer Science Technical Report CMU-CS-81-102, Pittsburgh, November 1980.

[49] T. Kanade, "Recovery of the Three-Dimensional Shape of an Object from a Single View," Carnegie-Mellon University, Computer Science Report CMU-CS-79-153, Pittsburgh, October 1979.

[50] D. G. Lowe and T. O. Binford, "The Interprettion of Three-Dimensional Structure from Images," *Proceedings of the Seventh International Joint Conference on Artificial Intelligence*, Vancouver, Canada, August 1981, pp. 613-618.

[51] T. O. Binford, "Inferring Surfaces from Images," *Artificial Intelligence*, Vol. 17, 1981, pp. 205-244.

10

SYSTEMS AND APPLICATIONS

Visual perception systems may be "general purpose" or tailored for special tasks. A general-purpose system is expected to have capabilities similar to the human visual system and handle a wide variety of scenes under a variety of viewing conditions. Under normal viewing conditions, humans may expect of certain objects to be present in the scene, but our ability to perceive seems to be almost as good when we are presented with a randomly chosen photograph. We are able to generate high-quality descriptions of unfamiliar objects, such as pictures of new planets, or photomicrographs of molecules. General-purpose vision may be defined to have capabilities similar to human perception; a more fundamental definition is difficult, owing to the inherent ambiguity of the images.

Our understanding of the perceptual processes needed to achieve general vision is poor, and the performance of the techniques discussed in the previous chapters is low in comparison to human performance. Fortunately, a great many applications of practical importance do not require this generality, as the domain of objects is often small, and significant knowledge of the scene is available a priori. Special-purpose *knowledge-based systems* aim to maximize the utilization of such knowledge.

In this chapter we examine some requirements for a general-purpose system and describe some knowledge-based systems with applications.

10.1 GENERAL SYSTEMS

As visual information is inherently ambiguous, some knowledge and assumptions are required for its interpretation. These assumptions may occasionally lead to incorrect conclusions, but the human system's perfomance is amazingly accurate in almost all instances in our daily experience. General-purpose and knowledge-based systems differ not only in the range of objects they encounter, but also in the type of knowledge they use. The systems attempting to be general tend to use *generic* rather than *specific* knowledge. Generic knowledge includes restrictions due to physical phenomena, such as surface reflectivity, continuity, object coherence, and support requirements. Specific knowledge refers to the knowledge of particular objects likely to be present in the scene, their properties, and the specific viewing conditions. Also, the general systems tend to defer use of specific knowledge, whereas the knowledge-based systems tend to utilize such knowledge early in the processing hierarchy. A general-purpose system needs at least the following abilities:

1. To perceive lightness and color of surfaces under a variety of illumination conditions;

2. To detect significant changes in intensity and perform 2-D segmentation into useful regions, even in the presence of texture;

3. To infer 3-D structure of the surfaces of a scene from a variety of monocular cues and also from a sequence of stereo or motion images;

4. To organize the surfaces and regions into objects of interest;

5. To generate descriptions of objects and recognize them among a potentially large class of objects; and,

6. To make nonvisual intelligent inferences about the scene based on the visual processing.

The above processes may be considered to form a hierarchy of abstraction levels. Two methods of data flow among these levels are *bottom-up* and *top-down*. In bottom-up processing, the information flows from one level to the next higher level without any influence from the expectations of this higher level. In top-down control, the processing at a lower level is specifically directed to satisfy an expectation or goal of a higher level. At the highest level, the goal may be to verify if a certain object is present in the scene. It seems that our ability to perceive unexpected or unfamiliar scenes requires capabilities of bottom-up processing, to the level of meaningful object descriptions. However, extensive communication between the various levels is needed, hence the processing is not strictly bottom-up. Humans are capable of top-down processing also, as indicated by our ability to see a suggested object in an otherwise confusing scene (for example, a suggested pattern in the clouds in the sky).

There are currently no systems even approaching the level of general-purpose performance of the human system. However, the desire for future generality leads to very different design strategies than those for knowledge-based systems for specific tasks, as discussed below.

10.2 KNOWLEDGE BASED SYSTEMS

Consider the typical office scene as shown in Fig. 10-1. A general system might proceed by attempting to segment the image using edge and/or region methods, possibly aided by range information to describe the objects and surfaces by the chosen representations. It is likely that the scene is too complex for resulting descriptions to be directly in terms of the objects that we perceive. However, specific tasks can be performed if scene knowledge is utilized judiciously. Consider the sample task of locating the telephone on the table. We could search the image for a region of known properties (known color and approximate size). However, it may be more efficient to locate the table top first, which is easily located if range data is available, and constrain the search for the telephone to the table top.

Tenenbaum has described a system to perform such tasks [1]. The knowledge in his system consists of the properties of the objects, such as color, size, and shape, and their relationships to other objects in the scene, such as the table having to be on the floor and the telephone on the table. The program operates in two phases, an acquisition and a validation phase. Acquisition is based on attributes that are easy to compute and are distinct. Other attributes and relations are used to validate the initial hypotheses.

Garvey extended this approach to automatic generation of a plan to locate objects, given the properties and the relations of the objects [2]. These systems may be viewed since following top-down processing, since each step of low-level processing is to satisfy a specific high-level goal. Such processing is likely to be useful if the scene has small variations and if the properties of the objects and even their locations are known approximately.

Bajcsy and Tavakoli have described a system to locate objects, such as roads, rivers, and bridges, in aerial images using models of

Figure 10-1: A typical office scene (from Tenenbaum [1])

these objects in a scene [3, 4]. Road models at the scene level are inferred from more abstract properties (by the designers and not by the program). A functional definition of a road is a path to allow for the passage of certain vehicles, persons, or animals. From this follow physical and geometrical properties requiring a road to be relatively smooth and firm and to have bounded steepness, width, and curvature. These requirements in turn define image properties such as roads being narrow strips of bounded width and curvature and spectral properties of materials such as concrete, asphalt, and rocks. Also, roads must be connected to other roads or other cultural features. Similarly, a bridge is defined to be over water, but connected to land masses on either side. Note that such models are generic and not for a particular scene.

Nevatia and Price have described a system to locate specific objects, such as airports in aerial images, by first locating larger and easier to locate objects [5]. In the image of the San Francisco area, shown in Fig. 1-9, the San Francisco International Airport can be recognized more easily if it is known to be along the edge of the bay, and south of the city of San Francisco. The city may in turn be located by the bridges, which are distinct. This system uses an approximate model of the scene, in the form of a rough map without precise distance

SYSTEMS AND APPLICATIONS

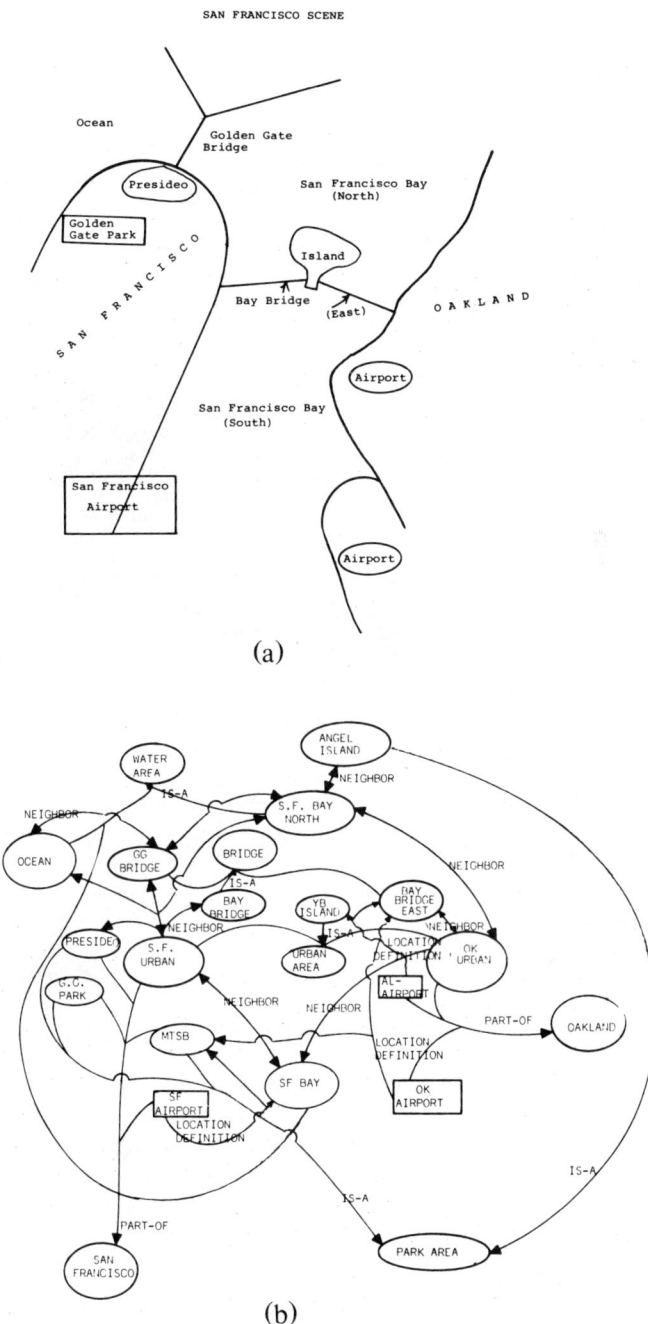

Figure 10-2: (a) A map of the San Francisco area and (b) its graph representation

information as shown in Fig. 10-2(a). Figure 10-2(b) shows the corresponding graph model used in the analysis. Segmentation of the scene uses both region and edge segmentation and is basically bottom-up, but it also employs some model information, such as the maximum width of the roads and bridges, and the features to use for segmentation of water areas. Figure 10-3 shows the segmented regions and roadlike and bridgelike features, with labels associated by matching with the map. Expected locations of the airports can now be estimated from the known features and these locations examined in more detail for verification.

Figure 10-3: Segmented scene with recognized elements

Freuder has proposed that vision systems should utilize knowledge at the earliest levels of processing, even when a specific goal is not specified [6]. Thus, if a region of constant intensity can be identified to be a part of one or a few objects, this knowledge should be used to guide further processing. The main difficulty here is that of *indexing*—that is, of retrieving the set of likely objects based on their low-level descriptions. Without contextual information, indexing requires good high-level descriptions.

A system called ACRONYM having many modules of general utility has been developed at Stanford University [7]. This system has

SYSTEMS AND APPLICATIONS

abilities for top-down predictive processing and also for bottom-up descriptions. At the top level, object models are described as 3-D volumes in an *object graph*. The modeling system is quite general and allows generic as well as specific objects to be described. For a given model geometric reasoning techniques are used to predict feature which will be invariantly observable; that is, features which are visible over a range of viewing conditions. A *prediction graph* is generated whose nodes are predictions of image features and the arcs specify relations which must hold between them. A *picture graph* is generated from the image which describes the features in that image. Generation of picture graph may be guided by inputs from the prediction graph. Interpretation of the scene and recognition of objects takes place by matching between the prediction and the picture graphs. Much of this system is implemented in form of rules and is extensible. ACRONYM has been applied to tasks of complex object recognition; a typical example is recognition of a commercial aircraft parked at an airport terminal, in an aerial image. For this application, the prediction and picture graphs are essentially in terms of "ribbons" which are two-dimensional projections of three-dimensional generalized cones. The major performance limitations of the system are because of the weaknesses of the lower level description modules.

Another system intended for a broad range of scenes, called VISIONS, is described in [8]. The systems referred to here are not the only knowledge-based systems that have been designed, but they suggest the range of tasks that have been approached.

10.3 APPLICATIONS

Potential application areas of a general purpose machine vision system are vast. However, current application tasks must be carefully chosen to match with the current capabilities of machine techniques. The successful applications tend to be for specific and well defined tasks, within a limited domain of objects, and with adequate a priori knowledge. Because of the large and increasing number of application tasks, only the major areas of applications and some typical tasks are described below.

10.3.1 Industrial Applications

A major area of industrial applications is the visual inspection of manufactured parts. The inspection tasks can range from detection of major flaws such as missing parts to detection of small defects, misalignments, size measurement, subtle color changes, and so on. For humans, these tasks tend to be dull, and their repetitiveness leads to decreased performance.

Successful practical applications require fast processing, inexpensive hardware, and high reliability. To simplify the image-analysis problems, lighting may be controlled to give high-contrast images. Back lighting or fluorescent conveyor belts may enable thresholding to provide satisfactory segmentation. Special lighting may also be required to make visible some defects, such as cracks in a glass seal [9].

Major successes have been achieved in the inspection of electronic printed circuit boards (PCBs) and integrated circuits (ICs). A direct approach is to compare the images of the patterns to stored images of defect-free patterns on a pixel by pixel basis. However, difficulties are caused by the variability of the images, alignment errors, changes in size, and so on. Another approach is to examine small neighborhoods, such as 5-by-5 or 7-by-7 binary windows, and classify the patterns as defective or not [9]. Ejiri and others developed an interesting system to detect small defects, defined to be patterns with widths less than the board conductors. These defects appear as thin blobs of extra or missing metal [10]. A region of the image is first expanded and then shrunk by the same amount. This removes convex blobs of a certain size. The processed pattern is then compared with the original to detect the convex defects. Concave defects are detected by first shrinking and then expanding.

Baird describes a system developed at General Motors for orienting IC chips correctly before they are bonded [11]. The orientation is basically determined by a histogram of edges detected in the image. Other systems for orienting IC chips are described in [12, 13]. Some of these systems are reported to be in large scale production use.

Agin has described laboratory experiments at detection of flaws in castings such as missing or incorrectly dimensioned holes, and inspection of other industrial objects [14]. The orientation of the parts is constrained so that the perspective variations are avoided.

Another important area of applications is in materials handling. Here, the parts are usually in a heap or a bin with other similar or different parts. A part needs to be identified and grasped by a mechanical manipulator at the appropriate points. Partial success has been obtained, if the possible orientation of the parts can be restricted, and they are unoccluded or else occluded in small areas only [15] (a typical scene is shown in Fig. 1-7).

Visual feedback for automated assembly is made difficult by the complexity and cluttered nature of the scenes. Some simplification can be obtained by marking objects by patches of specific shape or color (for example, see [12, 16]). Use of more elaborate markings is limited by visibility and space requirements. We can also take advantage of the slow and predictable variations in the scene for incremental analysis (see [17]).

More examples of industrial applications may be found in [18, 19].

10.3.2 Photo Interpretation and Change Detection

Images taken from airplanes or orbiting satellites provide a rich source of information for monitoring changes on the surface of the earth. The applications include surveying crops, forests, pollution, and other natural resources, military surveillance and monitoring of new construction of roads and other man-made structures, and automatic mapping from the images. Manual analysis of aerial images is not only tedious and labor intensive, but also the large volume of data transmitted to earth causes a major communications bottleneck that could be eliminated by on-board processing.

Image analysis of aerial scenes is more complex than analysis of industrial scenes, owing to the presence of fine texture and a variety of objects in a single scene, and the requirements of high resolution for observing the fine details. However, the scenes are largely two-dimensional with little occlusion, even though the effects of shadows and presence of mountainous terrain can be significant. Generally, unguided segmentation of aerial images is error prone. Some regions—for example, uniform water areas such as lakes— can be extracted easily and reliably.

A simple processing approach, commonly used for crop identification, is classification of each pixel by its multispectral properties (the sensors may include infrared, radar, and so on in addition to the visual sensors). This approach suffers from its ignoring of the context that helps in distinguishing between ambiguous cases. Other applications have concentrated on the development of specific techniques for the extraction of specific features, such as roads and railroads [20].

Some photo interpretation tasks are extremely labor intensive and tedious; for example, making maps from aerial images involves manual tracing of small features with high accuracy. For such applications, partial automation with interactive human control would still result in large savings. Some instances of interaction are: correcting machine errors, pointing to certain examples (such as, a central area of a region is to be extracted and its properties used to extract the larger region), and following a road if its intensity profile is initially traced interactively. Descriptions of some implementations are given in [20-22].

Change detection requires comparison of two regions, taken at two different times, and possibly with different sun angles and weather conditions, different viewing angles, and maybe even different sensors. Changes can be detected by simple grey-level correlation of the two images if the changes caused by these factors are small [23]. For larger changes, matching at the symbolic level, by first extracting features such as uniform regions and roads, has been more successful [24]. Again, the main limitation is in computing adequate symbolic descriptions for complex scenes. Change detection may also be aided by the use of a previous map of the scene.

10.3.3 Guidance, Navigation, and Scene Registration

A major use of vision by humans and animals is for navigating in the surrounding environment, avoiding obstacles, and reaching desired locations. Much of the current automatic navigation of machines, such as commercial aircraft, is by the use of special navigation sensors, such as radar, located along the desired route. Some applications—for example, exploration of distant planets—require navigation without modification of the environment and with little or no human intervention, and without a priori knowledge of the terrain.

For surface vehicles, a major concern is to avoid obstacles and hazards in the path of a moving vehicle. For space applications, the obstacles are rocks, craters, loose surface materials, and the like. Experimental studies for a lunar rover have been conducted at the Jet Propulsion Laboratories. Moravec constructed a vehicle that navigated in simple indoor and outdoor scenes and avoided obstacles perceived by a stereo vision system [25]. Roving vehicles in urban environments have a more complex task, owing to the large variety of the objects in the scene and other moving objects. Specially prepared roadways may be of help here.

Following a chosen trajectory is of major concern for airborne vehicles. Here, a "map" of the trajectory and surrounds is available, either in symbolic form or as a sequence of images along the path. Because of the variability in the images under different flight conditions, simple grey level correlation is unlikely to be effective. More success has been obtained by correlating the terrain elevation profiles.

Processes using matching of features extracted from a perceived image with features extracted from stored images are likely to be more tolerant to changes in images. One implementation for matching scenes having different scale and some perspective changes, taken from possibly different sensors, with different seasonal and viewing conditions, using lines extracted from the two scenes is described in [26]. Surveys of various approaches may be found in [27].

A human pilot, flying under visual guidance, navigates by locating specific, distinguished features on the earth and relating them to the map symbols. Some of the above mentioned techniques can also be used for such *image-to-map correspondence* (for example, see [5, 24, 26]). Another interesting iterative technique is described in [28]. Here, selected features in a map, with 3-D data, are projected onto the image, using an estimate of the camera position. These projected points are matched to the closest similar points in boundaries extracted from the image. The new matches now define a new camera transform, and the process is repeated until the projected points and the matched points are within an acceptable range.

10.3.4 Medical Applications

Many medical diagnostic procedures use images—for example, chest and other x-rays, microscope photographs of blood cells, acoustic images of various organs, and three-dimensional "images" of organs obtained by computer tomography. Highly trained medical personnel are required for interpretation of such images, and shortage of such people is a deterrent to a more widespread use of these techniques.

Medical images have some significant characteristics. These images frequently use illumination that penetrates the objects; that is, the object surfaces are not opaque. The defects to be detected may be small and subtle, sometimes characterized by smooth changes in the grey levels only (as for bone structures). Also, the allowed margin of error is small, owing to the potentially serious consequences of an incorrect diagnosis. However, significant a priori information is available in many cases from human anatomy, and viewing conditions can be controlled.

Analysis of chest x-rays has received considerable attention. A method for the diagnosis of pneumoconiosis (coal miner's disease) by an analysis of the texture of dark blobs in the x-rays is described in [29]. Other x-ray analysis techniques are described in [30-31]. For chest x-rays, it is useful to be able to first isolate ribs and other bone structures, as certain types of tumors do not occur there. However, the ribs are typically of low contrast and only partially visible (see Fig. 1-8).

Knowledge of the approximate shape and relative locations of the ribs has been used for their detection [32-34].

Analysis of blood-cell images and human chromosomes for genetic defects has also been popular. In some cases, as for chromosome analysis, new biochemical techniques can simplify or replace visual techniques.

Use of computers to obtain three-dimensional data of brain and other organs, by use of multiple two-dimensional views, has been hailed as a major advance in the diagnostic procedures. Much of this work has concentrated on rapid and accurate reconstruction of the three-dimensional data from the two-dimensional views, rather than the automatic analysis of the resulting 3-D data.

The area of medical applications has grown so that several symposia are entirely devoted to them. A good source of current progress is the proceedings of these symposia (for example, see [35]).

10.3.5 Hardware Requirements

The large computational requirements of visual processing are a constraint on the range of practical applications. The resolution of the images is limited to far less than that of human vision or the optical resolution of an average camera. The complexity of the processing algorithms must be limited to meet response time requirements. The more sophisticated algorithms take several minutes (or hours) to run on modern large computers (executing 1 to 5 million operations per second). The continuing increase in the speed of generrral-purpose computers, with simultaneous reduction in cost and size, will be helpful in the future. However, it is unlikely that complex high-resolution visual processing will be feasible by using sequential, general-purpose machines alone.

Fortunately, the structure of visual processing is suited to *parallel* implementation. Much of the processing time is taken for simple, low-level processes, such as convolution for edge detection and histograms for region threshold selection. Usually at the higher levels of processing the amount of data to be processed decreases dramatically, hence the processing time decreases even though the operations on each data are more complex. The lower-level processing is usually simple, uses information from small neighborhoods only, and hence can be easily implemented using parallel processors. Some efforts at developing parallel machines for visual processing are described in [36, 37].

Simplicity of the lower-level processes also allows for their implementation in special-purpose hardware. Algorithms such as edge detection, histogramming, and thresholding have been implemented on single chips using CCD (charge coupled devices) technology and operate at or near TV frame rates [38-40]. The deployment of the VLSI (very large scale integrated circuits) technology should have a major impact on the complexity of algorithms that can be implemented in a few IC chips [38, 41-42].

10.4 SUMMARY AND FUTURE

This chapter has outlined the state of the art in applications of machine perception techniques and the range of the tasks to which they are applied. Successful applications have been where the tasks are well defined and the domain is restricted. The simplicity of the algorithms currently used, in comparison to the known techniques, and the rapid advances in the hardware technology of general-purpose computers and special-purpose devices assures evolutionary progress in the use of machines to perform more and more complex tasks. The science fiction fantasy (or fears) of "super-human" robots replacing and outperforming humans in complex perceptual tasks remains far from reality.

REFERENCES

[1] J. M. Tenenbaum, "On Locating Objects by Their Distinguishing Features," *Computer Graphics and Image Processing*, Vol. 2, 1973, pp. 308-320.

[2] T. Garvey and J. M. Tenenbaum, "On the Automatic Generation of Programs for Locating Objects in Office Scenes," in *Proceedings of the Second International Joint Conference on Pattern Recognition*, Copenhagen, August 1974, pp. 162-168.

[3] R. Bajcsy and M. Tavakoli, "Computer Recognition of Roads from Satellite Imgaes," *IEEE Transactions on Systems, Man and Cybernetics*, Vol. 6, No. 9, September 1976, pp. 623-637.

[4] R. Bajcsy and M. Tavakoli, "Image Filtering—A Context Dependence Process," *IEEE Transactions on Circuits and Systems*, May 1975, pp. 463-474.

[5] R. Nevatia and K. Price, "Locating Objects in Aerial Images," *Proceedings of the Fourth International Conference on Pattern Recognition*, Kyoto, Japan, November 1978, pp. 686-690.

[6] E. Freuder, "A Computer System for Visual Recognition Using Active Knowledge," MIT Artificial Intelligence Laboratory Memo AI-TR-345, June 1976.

[7] R. A. Brooks, "Symbolic Reasoning Among 3-D Models and 2-D

Images," Stanford Artificial Intelligence Laboratory Memo AIM-343, June 1981.
[8] A. R. Hanson and E. M. Riseman, "VISIONS: A Computer System for Interpreting Scenes," in *Computer Vision Systems*, A. R. Hanson and E. M. Riseman (eds.), Academic Press, New York, 1978, pp. 303-333.
[9] J. F. Jarvis, "Visual Inspection Automation," *IEEE Computer*, May 1980, pp. 32-39.
[10] M. Ejiri, T. Uno, M. Mese and S. Ikeda, "A Process for Detecting Defects in Complicated Patterns," *Computer Graphics and Image Processing*, Vol. 2, 1973, pp. 326-339.
[11] M. L. Baird, "SIGHT-1: A Computer Vision System for Automated IC Chip Manufacture," *IEEE Transactions on Systems, Man and Cybernetics*, Vol. 8, February 1978, pp. 133-139.
[12] M. Yachida and S. Tsuji, "Industrial Computer Vision in Japan," *IEEE Computer*, May 1980, pp. 50-64.
[13] B. K.P. Horn, "A Problem in Computer Vision: Orienting Silicon Integrated Circuit Chips for Lead Bonding," *Computer Graphics and Image Processing*, Vol. 4, No. 3, September 1975., pp. 294-303.
[14] G. J. Agin, "Computer Vision Systems for Industrial Inspection and Assembly," *IEEE Computer*, May 1980, pp. 11-20.
[15] W. A. Perkins, "A Model-Based Vision System for Industrial Parts," *IEEE Transactions on Computers*, Vol. 27, 1978, pp. 126-143.
[16] A. Gill, "Visual Feedback and Related Problems in Computer Controlled Hand Eye Coordination," Stanford Artificial Intelligence Laboratory Memo AIM-178, October 1972 (Ph.D. thesis).
[17] R. Bolles, "Verification Vision for Programmable Assembly," *Proceedings of the Fifth International Joint Conference on Artificial Intelligence*, Cambridge, Mass., August 1977, pp. 569-575.
[18] W. Thompson (ed.), Special Issue on Machine Perception, *IEEE Computer*, Vol. 13, No. 5, May 1980.
[19] G. G. Dodd and L. Rossol (eds.), *Computer Vision and Sensor-Based Robots*, Plenum Press, New York, 1979.
[20] H. G. Barrow, "Interactive Aids for Cartography and Photo Interpretation," SRI Technical Report 5300, Menlo Park, Calif., November 1976.
[21] L. H. Quam, "Road Tracking and Anomaly Detection in Aerial Imagery," *Proceedings of Image Understanding Workshop*, Cambridge, Mass., May 1978, pp. 51-55.
[22] J. M. Tenenbaum and H. G. Barrow, "Interpretation Guided Segmentation," *Artificial Intelligence*, Vol. 8, 1977, pp. 241-274.
[23] R. L. Lillestrand, "Techniques for Change Detection," *IEEE*

Transactions on Computers, Vol. 21, July 172, pp. 654-659.
[24] K. Price and D. R. Reddy, "Matching Segments of Images," *IEEE Pattern Analysis and Machine Intelligence*, Vol. 1, No. 1, January 1979, pp. 110-116.
[25] H. P. Moravec, "Obctacle Avoidance and Navigation in the Real World by a Seeing Robot Rover," Stanford Artificial Intelligence Laboratory Memo AIM-340, September 1980.
[26] C. S. Clark, W. O. Eckhardt, C. A. McNary, R. Nevatia, K. E. Olin, and E. M. Van Orden, "High-accuracy Model Matching for Scenes Containing Man-made Structures," in [27], pp. 54-62.
[27] *Proceedings of Symposium on Digital Processing of Aerial Images*, SPIE, Vol. 186, 1979.
[28] H. G. Barrow, J. M. Tenenbaum, R. C. Bolles, and H. C. Wolf, "Parametric Correspondence and Chamfer Matching: Two New Techniques for Image Matching," *Proceedings of the Fifth International Joint Conference on Artificial Intelligence*, Cambridge, Mass., August 1977, pp. 659-663.
[29] R. P. Kruger, W. B. Thompson, and A. F. Turner, "Computer Diagnosis of Pneumoconiosis," *IEEE Transactions on Systems, Man and Cybernetics*, Vol. 4, 1974, pp. 40-49.
[30] H. Ballard and J. Sklansky, "A Ladder Structured Decision Tree for Recognizing Tumors in Chest Radiographs," *IEEE Transactions on Computers*, Vol. 25, 1976, pp. 503-513.
[31] C. A. Harlow and S. A. Eisenbeis, "The Analysis of Radiographic Images," *IEEE Transactions on Computers*, Vol. 22, July 1973, pp. 678-689.
[32] H. Wechsler and J. Slansky, "Finding the Rib Cage in Chest Radiographs," *Pattern Recognition*, Vol. 9, 1977, pp. 21-30.
[33] D. H. Ballard, "Model-directed Detection of Ribs in Chest Radiographs," *Proceedings of the Fourth International Joint Conference on Pattern Recognition*, Kyoto, Japan, November 1978, pp. 907-910.
[34] J. Toriwaki, Y. Suenaga, T. Negoro, and R. Fukumura, "Pattern Recognition of Chest X-ray Picture Patterns," *Computer Graphics and Image Processing*, Vol. 2, December 1973, pp. 252-271.
[35] *Proceedings of Symposium on Computer-Aided Diagnosis of Medical Images*, Coronado, Calif., November 1976 (IEEE Computer Society Publication 76CH1170-0C).
[36] G. R. Allen and P. G. Juelten, "SPARC-Symbolic Processing Algorithm Research Computer," *Proceedings of Image Understanding Workshop*, Palo Alto, Calif., April 1979, pp. 171-174.
[37] C. Rieger, "ZMOB: A Mob of 256 Cooperative 280-A Based Microcomputers," *Proceedings of Image Understanding Workshop*,

Los Angeles, Calif., November 1979, pp. 25-30.
[38] G. Nudd, "Image Understanding Architectures," *Proceedings of the National Computer Conference*, Anaheim, Calif., 1980, pp. 377-390.
[39] G. R. Nudd, G. D. Thurmond, and S. D. Fouse, "A Charge Coupled Device Image Processor for Smart Sensor Applications," *Proceedings of the SPIE Symposium*, San Diego, August 1978, pp. 15-22.
[40] T. J. Willett and G. E. Tisdale, "Hardware Implementation of a Smart Sensor: A Review," *Proceedings of Image Understanding Workshop*, Cambridge, Mass., May 1978, pp. 1-8.
[41] T. J. Willett, A. R. Helland, and G. E. Tisdale, "Higher Level Algorithms: Evaluation and Implementation," *Proceedings of Image Understanding Workshop*, Los Angeles, Calif., November 1979, pp. 15-24.
[42] W. L. Eversole and D. J. Mayer, "Investigation of VLSI Technologies for Image Processing," *Proceedings of the Image Understanding Workshop*, College Park, Md., April 1980, pp. 182-189.

INDEX

ACRONYM, 191,193
Adjacency, 4- or 8-, 13
Albedo image, 177
Anti-parallel lines, 123
Applications, 193-199
    aerial images, 195-196
    change detection, 196
    guidance and navigation, 196-197
    industrial, 194-195
    medical, 197-198
    photo-interpretation, 195-196
    scene registration, 195-197
Arc consistency, 82
Area shape measures, 67-72
    analytical measures, 69-70
    medial axis transform, 70-72
    moment measures, 69-70
    simple measures, 67-68
Area-to-perimeter ratio, 67
Artificial intelligence, relation to, 2

Assembly of objects, polyhedral, 55-58
Aspect ratio, 180

Bar mask, 108-109
Blum transform, 70-72
Border following (*see* Contour following)
Bottom-up processing, 188
Boundary detection (*see* Line detection)
Boundary following (*see* Contour following)
Brightness (*see also* Lightness):
    constancy, 91, 96-98
    local measurements, 92
    simultaneous contrast, 91, 96-97

Camera calibration, 39-40
Camera model, 39
Camera transform, 39

CCD chips, 199
Chain code, 63-65
Change detection, 196
Characteristic dimension, 179
Character representation, 2-3
Charge coupled devices, 199
Chromaticity components, 94
Classifiers, 16-17
Clowes labels (*see* Huffman-
    Clowes labels)
Clustering for segmentation, 135
Color:
    constancy, 91, 97-98
    edges, 123-124
    perceived attributes, 93-95
    primaries, 93
    triangle, 94-95
Complex objects:
    polyhedral, 41-60
    general, shape representation,
        62-63
Concave deficiency, 68
Concave edge, 46
Cones:
    generalized, 73-79
    in human vision, 92
Connectivity, in digital
    geometry, 13
Contour:
    analysis for shape, 181-182
    filling, 120-123
    following, 138
    subjective, 122
    tracing, 138
Convex edge, 46
Convex hull, 68
Co-occurrence matrices, 146-148,
    150
    edge, 150
    generalized, 148
    grey-level, 146-148
Coordinates, transformation of,
    34-37
Correlation coefficient, 15

Correspondence for stereo, 159-165
    coarse-to-fine, 162
    feature-based, 160
    global, 163-165
    multiple views, 161-162
    search techniques, 161-162
Crack edge, 49
Cross-correlation:
    for stereo matching, 161-162
    in template matching, 15-16
Curve detection (*see*
    Line detection)
Curve fitting (*see* Line
    fitting)

Depth measurement:
    active ranging, 167-170
    monocular, 173-182
    stereo, 159-165
Differentiation for edge
    detection, 101-103
Digital picture, 12
Dual graphs, 51-54

Edge co-occurrence, 150
Edge detection, 100-116, 123-124
    color, 123-124
    by edge fiting, 103-105
    by enhancement and
        differencing, 101-103
    examples, 112-116
    statistical method, 111
    by template matching, 105-111
    threshold selection, 111-112
Edge detectors:
    Hueckel, 103-105
    Kirsch, 105-106
    Laplacian-Gaussian, 110-111
    Marr-Hildreth, 110-111
    McLeod, 106
    Nevatia-Babu, 106-108
    Prewitt, 102, 105-106

INDEX

Roberts, 26-27
Sobel, 102-103
Edge masks, 105-111
Eye (*see* Human visual system)

False contours (*see* Subjective contours)
Feature space in pattern classification, 16-17
Feedback, for boundary detection, 120-122
Fourier texture measures, 145-146
Fovea, in human eye, 92

Generalized cones, 73-79
    computation, 75-79
    definition, 73
Generalized co-occurrence matrices, 148
General position, definition, 45
Geometric transformations, 34-37
Goal-directed systems (*see* Knowledge-based systems)
Gradient space:
    definition, 52
    use for polyhedral scenes, 52-54
    use in shape-from-shading, 174-176
Grammars, formal, 21
Grammatical pattern classification, 21-22
Graph matching, 80-82
Graph-theoretic methods, for line detection, 118-119
Grey-level dependency matrix (*see* Co-occurrence matrices, grey-level)
Grid coding, 168
Grouping regions, of polyhedra (*see* Guzman's method)
Guidance for autonomous vehicles, 196-197
Guzman's method, 41-45

Hardware requirements, 198-199
Heterarchical systems,
    for boundary detection, 120-121
Hexagonal grid, 14-15
Homogeneous coordinates, 32-34
Hough transform, 116-118
Hue, 93
Hueckel edge detector, 103-105
Huffman-Clowes labels, 45-48
Human visual system, 92

Illusions (*see* Visual phenomena)
Image analysis, definition, 8
Image processing, 10
Image segmentation (*see* Segmentation of images)
Image-to-map correspondence, 197
Image understanding, 10
Impossible objects:
    conditions for, 48, 51-53
    examples of, 45-46
Indexing into model database, 85-86
Industrial applications, 194-195
Integrated circuit inspection, 194
Intrinsic scene characteristics, 182
Isomorphism, of graphs, 80
Iterative endpoint fitting, 65

Kirsch edge detector, 105-106
Knowledge-based systems, 187, 189-193

Labeling (*see* Relaxation, Line labels)
Laplacian-Gaussian edge masks, 110-111
Lateral inhibition, 95-97
Learning:
    perceptron parameters, 19
    structural descriptions, 58-59

Lightness:
    computation, 95-98
    definition, 91
Line approximation, 65-66
Line classification, 45-50
Line detection, 116-123
        (*see also* Edge detection)
    graph-theoretic methods,
            118-119
    heterarchy, 120-121
    Hough transform, 116-118
    planning, 121
    projections, 119
    subjective contours, 122
Line fitting, 116
Line following, 138
Line labels, 45-46
Line shape measures, 63-67
    analytical measures, 66-67
    by approximation, 65-66
    chain coding, 63-65
Line types, 45-46
Linking of edges, 118-119

Mach bands, 95-96
Map making, 195-196
Marr-Hildreth edge detetor,
        110-111
Matching (*see* Model matching,
        Template matching)
Maximal cliques, 81-82
McLeod edge detector, 106
Medial axis transform, 70-72
Medical applications, 197-198
Minimal spanning tree, 118
Mobile robots, 196-197
Model fitting, 37-39
Model matching:
    general:
        graph, 80-82
        multi-level, 85-86
        relaxation labeling, 82-84
    for polyhedra:
        geometrical, 29, 37-39
        topological, 28

Model transformations, 30-37
    geometric, 34-37
    use of homogeneous
        coordinates, 32-34
    perspective, 31
Moments as shape descriptors,
        69-70
Mondrian surfaces, 97
Monitoring of resources, 2
Monocular determination of three-
        dimensional surfaces,
        173-182
    contour analysis, 181-182
    shading, 173-177
    texture gradients, 177-181
Motion, 165-167
    correspondence for, 166
    detection of, 165-166
    optical flow, 167
Multiple size masks for edge
        detection, 106-108

Navigation for autonomous
        vehicles, 196-197
Nearest-neighbor classifier, 17
Near-miss in learning, 58-59
Nevatia-Babu edge detector,
        106-108
Non-linear line detector, 109
Non-maxima suppression, 108

Object recognition (*see*
        Model matching, Pattern
        classification methods)
Obscuring edge, 46
Ohlander segmentor, 130-135
Optical axis, 31
Optical character reader, 16
Optical flow, 167

Parallel implementations, 198

INDEX

Path consistency, 83
Pattern classification:
   feature space methods, 16-17
   perceptrons, 18-21
   syntactical methods, 21-22
   template matching, 15-16
Pattern recognition (see
     Pattern classification)
Perceptrons, 18-21
   capabilities of, 20
   diameter-limited, 19
   learning, 19
   limitations of, 20
   order-limited, 19
Perspective transformation, 31-34
Photometric stereo, 176-177
Photo-interpretation, 195-196
Picture tree, 136
Pixel, definition of, 12
Planning:
   for edge detection, 121
   for object location, 189
   for region segmentation, 135
Polygons, approved 28-29
Polyhedra, analysis of, 24-60
Primal sketch, 116
Primary colors, 93
Printed circuit board inspection, 194
Prewitt edge detector, 102, 105-106
Projection for line detection, 119
Psychology, relation to, 9
Pyramids, 121-122, 136

Quad-trees, 136-137
Quench function, 71

Range measurement, active,
     167-170
   LIDAR, 170
   by triangulation, 167-168
Range segmentation, 170-173
   detection of surfaces, 172-173
   jump boundaries, 171

Receptors, in human retina, 92
Recognition (see Model matching,
     Pattern classifiction)
Recursive segmentation, 130-135
Reflectance maps, 174-177
Reflectivity function, 173
Region growing, 136-137
Region segmentation
   (see Segmentation of images)
Region tracing, 138
Registration of scenes, 195-197
Relational descriptions,
     definition of, 63
Relaxation:
   for curve detection, 120
   discrete labeling, 50, 82-83
   probabilistic labeling, 83-84
Retina, human, 92
Retinex theory, 97
Road detection, 123, 189-190
Road following, 196
Roberts' method, 24-39
   edge and line detection, 26-28
   model matching, 28-30, 37-39
Rods in human retina, 92

Sampling of images, 12
Saturation, 93
Segmentaion comparison, edges
     versus regions, 139-141
Segmentation of images, 129-138,
     152-153
   by clustering, 135
   using range, 170-173
   region growing, 136-137
   region splitting, 129-135
   semantically guided, 137
   split-and-merge, 136-137
   using texture, 152-153
Segmentation of polyhedral
     scenes, 41-51
   Guzman method, 41-45
   Huffman-Clowes labels, 45-48

Waltz method, 49-51
Self-guided vehicles, 2
Shading, shape from, 173-177
Shadow edge, 49
Shadows, in polyhedral scenes, 49-51
Shape descriptions of:
   areas, 69-72
   complex objects, 62-63
   lines, 63-67
   three-dimensional objects, 72-79
Shape from shading, 173-177
Simultaneous contrast, 91, 96-97
Skeleton of a figure (see Medial axis transform, Generalized cones)
Skew symmetry, 181-182
Slant of a surface, 179
Sobel edge detector, 102-103
Spanning tree, minimal, 118
Split-and-merge method, 136-137
Statistical edge detection, 111
Statistical texture analysis, 144-148
   energy measures, 144-145
   first-order measures, 144
   Fourier measures, 145-146
   second-order measures, 146-148
   time-series analysis, 148
   whitening transform, 148
Stereo, 159-165, 176-177
   correspondence search, 161-162
   global correspondence, 163-165
   photometric, 176-177
Stick figure, 74
Structural descriptions, concepts, 21, 63
Structural texture descriptions, 149-151
   edge co-occurrence, 150
   relative vectors, 150
Subjective contours, 122
Superslice, 140-141
Syntactical pattern classification, 21-22
Systems, 187-193
   general, 188-189
   knowledge-based, 187, 189-193

Tele-operator systems, 2
Template matching:
   for edge detection, 105-111
   for object recognition, 15-16
Texture analysis, 141-153
   comparison of features, 151-152
   segmentation, 152-153
   statistical measures, 144-148
   structural descriptions, 149-151
Texture, definition of, 90
Texture energy measure, 144-145
Texture gradients, 177-181
   characteristic dimension, 179
   foreshortening, 178
   scaling, 177
Texture property, normalized, 180
Texture segmentation, 152-153
Thinning, 108
Three-dimensional shape descriptions, 72-79
Thresholding:
   for edge detection, 111-112
   for region segmentation, 129-130
Tilt of a surface, 179
Top-down processing, 188-189
Topological property, 28-29, 68
Triangulation:
   in stereo, 159
   ranging, 167-168
Two-and-a-half dimensions, definition of, 62

Vertices, types of, 42-43
Visual inspection, 194
Visual phenomena:
   Mach bands, 95-96
   perceived lengths, 4-5
   simultaneous contrast, 91, 96-97

Volume descriptions (*see* Three-
 dimensional shape
 descriptions)

Waltz labeling algorithm, 49-51
Whitening transform, 148

X-ray analysis, 5, 197-198

TK7882.P3 N48 1982
Nevatia / Machine perception